ZONES OF PEACE

ZONES OF PEACE

Edited by

Landon E. Hancock and Christopher Mitchell

Kumarian
Press, Inc.

Zones of Peace
Published in 2007 in the United States of America by Kumarian Press, Inc.,
1294 Blue Hills Avenue, Bloomfield, CT 06002 USA

The text of this book is set in 10/12 Palatino.

Production and design by Joan Weber Laflamme, jml ediset
Proofread by Beth Richards.
Index by Robert Swanson.

Printed in the United States of America by Thomson-Shore. Text printed with
vegetable oil-based ink.

∞The paper used in this publication meets the minimum requirements of
the American National Standard for Information Sciences—Permanence
of Paper for printed Library Materials, ANSI Z39.48–1984

Library of Congress Cataloging-in-Publication Data

Zones of peace / edited by Landon E. Hancock and Christopher R. Mitchell.
  p. cm.
  Includes bibliographical references and index.
    ISBN 978–1–56549–233–2 (pbk. : alk. paper) — ISBN 978–1–56549–234–9
(cloth : alk. paper)
1. Peace-building—Developing countries—Case studies. 2. Conflict management—Developing countries—Case studies. 3. Developing countries—Social conditions—Case studies. I. Hancock, Landon E., 1964– II. Mitchell, C.
R. (Christopher Roger), 1934–
    JZ5538.Z66 2007
    303.6'9—dc22

                                                                    2006036555

---

16 15 14 13 12 11 10 09 08 07   10 9 8 7 6 5 4 3 2 1   First Printing 2007

We dedicate this work to all of those who have worked to create peace in their communities and in their countries, many of whom have sacrificed their lives, and to those who continue in the struggle to create islands of sanctuary in the midst of civil violence.

Dedicamos este trabajo a todas las personas que han trabajado para crear la paz en sus comunidades y en sus paises, muchos de ellos quienes han sacrificado sus vidas, y a los que continúan luchando para crear pequenos sanctuarios en medio de la violencia.

CONTENTS

ACKNOWLEDGMENTS

The editors and authors would like to acknowledge the many members of ICAR's Zones of Peace working group whose contributions helped make this work possible, including Dr. Wallace Warfield, Pablo Carvajal, Al Fuertes, Dr. Edmundo Garcia, Giselle Huamani Ober, Maneesha Pasqual, María Dolores Rodríguez, Daniel Stillwagon, Laura Villaneuva, and Zheng Wang. In addition we would like to thank Sara Ramirez, who served as the working group's eyes and ears in Colombia, often at considerable risk. We would also like to extend our thanks to ICAR and its director, Dr. Sara Cobb, for their generous moral and financial support and to the United States Institute of Peace, which provided a grant to support the working group's investigation of zones of peace in Colombia. Naturally, the viewpoints expressed in this work are those of the authors and editors and do not represent those of USIP.

ACRONYMS AND ABBREVIATIONS

AFP	Armed Forces of the Philippines
ARENA	Alianza Republicana Nacional party (El Salvador)
AUC	United Authorities of Colombia
BEC	basic ecclesiastical community (the Philippines)
BRIMOB	Police Mobile Brigade (Indonesia)
CfP	Coalition for Peace (the Philippines)
CODHES	Consultancy for Human Rights and Displacement (Colombia)
COHA	Cessation of Hostilities Agreement (Indonesia)
COHA/FAIM	Cessation of Hostilities Agreement/Framework Agreement with Interim Measures (Indonesia)
CPP	Culture of Peace Program (El Salvador)
CWIN	Child Workers in Nepal
DAZ	designated assembly zone (El Salvador)
DDR	disarmament, demobilization, and reintegration
ELN	National Liberation Army (Colombia)
FARC	Fuerzas Armadas Revolucionarias de Colombia
FMLN	Farabundo Martí de Liberación Nacional (El Salvador)
FSSCA	The Foundation for Self-Sufficiency in Central America
GAM	Gerakan Aceh Merdeka (Indonesia)
HDC	Henri Dunant Centre (Switzerland)
ICAR	Institute for Conflict Analysis and Resolution (George Mason University)
IDP	internally displaced person
IEP	Instituto de Estudios Peruanso (Peru)

JUSTAPAZ	Christian Center for Justice, Peace, and Nonviolent Action (Colombia)
KMT	Kuomintang (China)
LTTE	Liberation Tamil Tigers of Elam (Sri Lanka)
LZP	Local Zone of Peace (El Salvador)
MILF	Moro Islamic Liberation Front (the Philippines)
MNLF	Moro National Liberation Front (the Philippines)
NATO	North Atlantic Treaty Organization
NIC	National Islamic Congress (Sudan)
NPA	New Peoples Army (the Philippines)
OLS	Operation Lifeline Sudan
REDEPAZ	Network of Initiatives for Peace and against War (Colombia)
REDPRODPAZ	National Network of Development and Peace Programs (Colombia)
SDA	special development area
SPLA	Sudan People's Liberation Army
SPLM	Sudan People's Liberation Movement
TNI	Tentara Nasional Indonesia (Indonesian army)
UNHCR	(Office of the) UN High Commissioner for Refugees
UNPA	UN Protected Areas
UNPROFOR	UN protection force (initially in Croatia; expanded later)
UNSZ	UN safe zone (Croatia and Bosnia)
USAID	United States Agency for International Development
USIP	United States Institute of Peace
ZANLA	Zimbabwe African National Liberation Army
ZoP	zone of peace
ZOPFAN	Zone of Peace, Freedom, and Neutrality (the Philippines)
ZOPIF	Zones of Peace International Foundation

PREFACE

The *Human Security Report* would have us believe that the world is a safer place than it was forty years ago.[1] There are fewer conflicts globally (just under forty), and they are less deadly (fewer people die). This sounds, generally, like good news, until you read the part of the report that details not just the deaths from political violence but the rapid and significant increase in displaced and refugee populations. There has been roughly a seven- to eightfold increase in displaced persons, over the last forty years. While refugee populations have doubled in that time, the number of internally displaced persons (IDPs)[2] has increased even more: in 1964 there were approximately one million IDPs; in 2006 there were almost twenty-four million in fifty countries across the globe, including Sudan, Indonesia, Uganda, Lebanon, Colombia, Congo, Afghanistan, Eastern Europe, Iraq, and Central America.[3] Millions all over the world live without adequate shelter, without adequate food, without work, without extended networks, without education for their children, without the protection of their community leaders. The young and healthy struggle to help the old and the infirm, leaving behind their homes, their livelihoods, and many times their extended family members in order to escape the violence. While it may take generations to develop a thriving community in which adequate nutrition and education support the growth of the next generation, it takes only a day to destroy it all.

People do not leave everything behind unless they fear for their lives and for the lives of their loved ones. Once instilled, fear takes root—even if they eventually return to their homes, they often can never really "go home" again. Reinsertion or reintegration is often difficult, as those who come back have to be accepted by those who remained; there are often strong political, social, and/or ethnic differences between those that remained and those that left. Return can be also be complicated by the fact that those that stayed often "squat" in their neighbors' abandoned homes and appropriate their fields.

How to intervene? Peacekeeping helps. Forces deployed within and between countries, often from regional or international forces, reduce violence and can allow IDPs and refugees to return to their homes. However, funding and jurisdictional issues reduce the viability of peacekeeping in many contexts. Sometimes nations deploy their own police and security forces to provide security to a region, but one need only look at the current conditions in Iraq to see that there are serious limitations to the effectiveness of these forces. As the country hovers on the edge of civil war, the people of Iraq suffer horribly. And while the rest of the world watches (and/or pays billions), there seems no clear way to reduce the threat and to promote safety and security— and all that comes with them, such as economic, political, and social development. No, neither peacekeeping nor even outright occupation can necessarily provide long-term security for people living in conflict zones; even further, these external controls on violence often backfire, cementing divisions between groups and fanning the flames of resistance.

There is, however, a new and emerging strategy, one that enables the victims of local and regional violence to protect their own communities and promote their own security. A zone of peace (ZoP) is a place that declares itself a refuge from those who would seek to harm or threaten those within the zone. Such zones emerge as an expression of collective will and are a function of the negotiated relationships within the zone as well as those outside the zone; these negotiations form the basis of a set of rules or norms that maintain the ZoP as a place that is off-limits to violence. Recognizing that no governmental or international agency or international NGO is going to be able to promote local and regional security, these zones emerge as self-organized sanctuaries where those within the zone take responsibility for setting up the policies and practices that keep them safe from both the outsiders who want to occupy or control the zone and from insiders who want to destabilize it.

This book provides a much needed description of the complexity of ZoPs. Drawing on cases from around the world, the authors reveal and discuss the constellation of issues that surrounds the formation and evolution of ZoPs. Their case-study research demonstrates that there is no "one size fits all" theory as to how these zones emerge and become sustainable. Some of these zones are situated within the regions from which the threats to that region emanate. In other cases the zone is located at a distance, geographically or jurisdictionally, from the location of the threat. In some cases the zone has emerged locally but is positioned or framed as part of a national peacebuilding effort, while in other cases the ZoP struggles to remain neutral with regard to national efforts. In fact, as some of these case studies suggest, governments may actually begin to target ZoPs that refuse to adopt or legitimize the government's designation of who is a "guerilla" and who is a "freedom fighter." In some ZoPs international humanitarian aid saves lives, but it also seems to contribute to the externalization of responsibility; authors in this book address the relative benefits of aid for the viability of a ZoP. Some of these ZoPs seem to create a negative peace, or the absence of violence, whereas others focus on also creating a positive peace, building toward collaborative relationships that, in turn, can develop the resources to meet human needs, reduce inequality, and promote human rights within the zone.

ZoPs represent a paradigm shift in how we understand security. At a time when governments are often either unable to protect people or are themselves the perpetrators of the violence against people, the people themselves must make their own security a priority, an organizing principle for the negotiations with all those who may want to harm them. The case studies in this book disclose the variety of contexts in which ZoPs occur and provide some very important "lessons learned" about how these zones function. For this reason this book makes a significant contribution to the field of conflict resolution, using empirical case studies to ground emerging "wisdom."

As these authors discuss the complexities with regard to ZoPs, this wisdom is as much about what we do not know as what we do know. The questions they raise help us to recognize the boundaries of our ignorance; for indeed, we must know that we do not know in order to learn. These case studies emerged from a learning environment at the Institute for Conflict Analysis and Resolution (ICAR) at George Mason University. Over the past six years, a group of faculty that included Chris Mitchell, Wallace Warfield, and Kevin Avruch developed research on ZoPs in Colombia and around the world. They formed a working group with students who included both masters and doctoral candidates from a wide variety of national backgrounds, many of whom are authors of the case studies in this book. The group worked systemically, supported in part with funding from the United States Institute of Peace, and developed theory from data collected in Colombia, presenting its research to the community at ICAR as well as to outside conferences. The "Zones of Peace" initiative at ICAR has captured the imagination and interest of a generation of graduate students. This speaks not only to the importance of the topic, but also to the learning environment that the ICAR faculty has provided. The questioning style of this book has been part of the learning environment of this working group at ICAR over the past several years. Students and faculty, side by side, learned by asking questions, and now, we, in the broader field of conflict resolution, are able to witness the nature of the questions with which they have struggled. As we, in turn, grapple with the questions they raise, we can gain some satisfaction in the knowledge that the development of the theory of ZoPs may give us all some hope that we can develop theory and practices that may effectively reduce suffering from death and displacement in all regions of the world.

SARA COBB
Director
Institute for Conflict Analysis and Resolution

Notes

[1] For the statistical details contained in this report, see *Human Security Report 2005*, available online.

[2] Internally displaced persons are uprooted individuals who remain within their country of residence. See UN Economic and Social Council, "Specific Group and Individuals: Mass Exoduses and Displaced Persons," E/CN.4/2006/71 (January 12, 2006), 4. Available on the http://www.brooks.edu website.

[3] See the Internal Displacement Monitoring Centre report on the http://www.internal-displacement.org website.

1

THE THEORY AND PRACTICE OF SANCTUARY

From Asylia *to Local Zones of Peace*

CHRISTOPHER MITCHELL

Introduction

Efforts by people to find security and safe spaces for themselves have a long history, and the writings about sanctuary are almost as extensive as are actual attempts to find safe refuge. Very many societies—if not a majority—have developed some arrangements for refuge. These either involve *rules of conduct* about the safety and security of "others" that are—at least in theory—to be followed by all members of the society, or they involve *places* where norms about "acceptable" uses of violence are suspended or amended in a search for some form of nonviolence and *conflict mitigation*.

Historically, there have been two different means by which protection from violence has been afforded to individuals, groups, and categories of people. The first has been the gradual establishment of some widely accepted norm about persons who were generally inviolable—immune from attack—although there are also many examples of such security from violence being established by specific—and possibly temporary—agreements between communities and their leaders. Envoys and diplomats have most frequently been afforded such inviolability, and other common examples of (at least notionally) protected categories have included priests or other "holy" individuals, merchants and traders, doctors and other medical personnel, peasants, women, and children. This particular mitigating practice is best termed *personal inviolability*.

1

The second means involved the establishment of an inviolable location or territory. Those living there were safe from violence and other forms of unpleasantness simply because they were physically *on* that territory—and hence under some form of guaranteed protection—or because they had individually and voluntarily moved there and sought protection by becoming *supplicants* to the protection provider. This kind of security and safety could be termed *locational* or *spatial protection* and is usually what people mean when they talk about sanctuaries. Hence a working definition of *sanctuary* usually focuses on this geographical aspect of a search for protection; that is, a sanctuary is a place where certain individuals, communities or categories of people can go to be safe from those who would otherwise harm them, usually through the use of violence.

One widely understood method of achieving security has been to establish particular locations within one's country or society in which protection could legitimately be sought. An equally familiar method has been to seek safety by physically leaving one's own society and entering the sanctuary provided by another's territory as an exile or a refugee, an option sometimes forced upon whole communities who find themselves threatened with death, destruction, and (sometimes) annihilation. Sanctuary is usually sought wherever one can best find it.

Any overview of the general practice of sanctuary and protection seeking therefore starts with a typology of these various forms of inviolability or protection from violence, distinguishing between *locational* protection either within or outside the threatening society—"This place is a sanctuary and therefore inviolable"—and *personal* protection—"This person is a member of X category/community and hence is inviolable." As far as personal protection is concerned, this could be offered to a threatened individual (Demosthenes, the Athenian leader in fifth-century Greece, or the Manchu mayor of Peking in twentieth-century China); to categories of persons under threat (for example, escaping slaves or Christian converts in nineteenth-century China); or to communities in the path of some generalized violence that flee to some secure location (such as a village in the Philippines regularly being fought over by government troops and insurgents from the New Peoples Army). As far as locational protection is concerned, security and safety are usually offered to everyone within a given space regardless of who or what they are.

In many situations the two types of protection—locational and personal—overlap and can work to reinforce each other. Medical personnel often enjoy personal inviolability when carrying out their work, while the institutions in which they work—hospitals, clinics, aid posts—are simultaneously viewed as inviolable locations. Both types of protection from attack become of increasing importance in times of war or civil war, when the practical maintenance of the inviolability of neutral persons or neutral space becomes more and more problematic, especially with the protraction of such conflicts and the increased tendency for more and more people to seek security through some form of sanctuary. However, even in relatively peaceful times, the effectiveness of sanctuaries has never been absolute, especially in cases when individual criminals, wrongdoers, or political refugees fleeing threats have sought the protection afforded by locational sanctuaries. This uncertainty gives rise to the continuing question of what circumstances historically have made some forms of sanctuary more effective than others, a question that this chapter takes up with particular but not exclusive regard to locational sanctuaries established within the boundaries of the society providing the threat.

Indeed, the focus of this present book is on one of the most recent examples of a search for sanctuary, one that occurred in the last two decades of the twentieth century. This is the practice of local communities caught in the midst of protracted and violent intrastate conflicts to declare themselves peace communities or their home territory as a local zone of peace (ZoP). Examples of this type of search for sanctuary can be found amid the civil wars in Central America, the Philippines, Colombia, Sri Lanka, and many other societies where local people suffer the extreme effects of unlimited violence, often themselves becoming the direct targets of violence, destruction, and displacement by the warring adversaries. Being "fought over" in recent decades has been reason enough for local people to seek some form of protection from violence by trying to construct a sanctuary. Being the targets of threats, unwilling recruitment, ejection, and killing is a major spur to finding or creating a place where whole communities are safe—even if only temporarily.

In trying to understand this latest, security-seeking practice, this chapter takes up two themes in the study of sanctuary. One involves a brief analysis of a number of historical efforts to create safety and security for individuals and communities under some type of existential threat but lacking reliable protection. From this emerges a second theme, namely, the search for common factors that help to increase the chances of sanctuaries being effective in offering protection to those within the spatial and other boundaries of some protected and (hopefully) inviolable zone. In other words, the chapter attempts to examine the practice of establishing sanctuaries in order to move in the direction of a theory of effectiveness, and thus determine what factors contribute to increasing the likely inviolability and durability of sanctuaries, by what means, and in what circumstances.

Origins of the Concept of Sanctuary

Tracing the ideas underlying sanctuary back to their original roots is probably impossible, yet the widespread nature of the practice among both pre-modern and modern societies forces any analysis back toward phrases like "from time immemorial." This seems to be the case, even if one concentrates on the practice of establishing locational sanctuaries, the main focus of the chapter. Certainly, ethnographic studies provide numerous examples of efforts to establish safe spaces where violence was forbidden or to which people could repair for security and protection. Francisco Benet (1957) in his early studies of segmented and feuding societies among the Berbers of Morocco has described how even temporary, outdoor markets *(suqs)* could develop aspects akin to locational sanctuaries in order to allow peaceful trading and the exchange of surplus goods. Similarly, William Lewis (1961) has noted the inviolability of women in places of prayer in Morocco as an example of local norms about nonviolence involving both places and persons.

Frequent examples of locational sanctuary, as well as personal inviolability, occur in many other societies. An early work by Edward Westermarck (1909, 161–64) provides numerous and varied examples of places that provided safety and protection to those fleeing threats of retaliation, revenge, or punishment for previous wrongdoing. In many cases, of course, protection was limited and only provided to those who had committed an offense accidentally; or temporary, until tempers had time to cool or investigations, trials, or other accepted procedures for settlement could take place. Communities ranging from the Barotse in southern Africa, the Acagchemen Indians in California, the Aruntas in central Australia, the Ashanti in Ghana, the Samoans in the Pacific, and many more are all reported by Westermarck as having places that provided refuge and protection for individuals and, in some cases, a safe retreat for noncombatants. The practice of providing some form of sanctuary appears continuous and nearly universal.

Cities of Refuge

One of the earliest recorded examples of a society systematically providing some form of locational sanctuary for a category of its "wrongdoing" citizens was the establishment of sanctuary cities in ancient Israel. Even from the very earliest times, some form of protection for homicides, and even for political offenders, seems to have been provided by all altars and temples (particularly the shrine in Jerusalem) dedicated to Yahweh, offering sanctuary for offenders from the socially accepted retaliation of avengers of blood. (A distinction seems to have been made between those who killed accidentally, who could legitimately claim the sanctuary offered by Yahweh's protection, and those who killed deliberately, who could be taken, even from the altar, and put to death.) Later the right of sanctuary was withdrawn from most local shrines and three sanctuary cities west of the Jordan were established to which offenders could flee and live in safety until the elders of their city decided the case. If the decision supported an alleged offender's innocence, that person could remain under the protection of the city of refuge and would be safe there. After the Exile three more cities were added to the list of recognized sanctuaries and, in Joshua's time, the refugee, once declared innocent, was allowed to return home, safe from retaliation, after the death of the high priest within whose reign the original offense had been committed (Singer and Adler 1925).

Examples of cities formally set aside to act as sanctuaries can be found in other parts of the world, although the rules about who could be afforded protection there, for how long, under what circumstances, and for what infringement of laws or social norms varied a great deal. The Barotse possessed one such location, and there were several in the Hindu Kush, one of which was reported to be inhabited mainly by descendants of those who had slain a fellow tribesman. Two cities of refuge—*puhonuas*—on nineteenth-century Hawaii not only provided sanctuary to fugitives of all descriptions but also offered a safe retreat to neighboring noncombatants in time of war (Westermarck 1909). In England, at the height of the Reformation, Henry VIII established seven cities of permanent refuge for offenders who would otherwise have sought temporary refuge in a church and then had to leave the realm. At the same time the king removed the privilege of sanctuary from those committing "heinous" crimes—murderers, rapists, burglars, highway robbers, and arsonists.[1]

The institution of sanctuary cities in Israel and elsewhere demonstrates a number of characteristics that can be found in many other versions of locational sanctuary. First, the space providing sanctuary was usually sacred and hence those in it were ultimately under divine protection, quite apart from any secular protection provided by custom, by law, or by the ruler. Second, protection normally existed only within the boundaries of that location until some process had taken place that changed the person seeking sanctuary from one category—accused—to another—innocent. Last, the basic protection offered was against retaliatory violence but not against legal process, judgment, and an end to protection if the judgment was negative. In other words, the provision of sanctuary and security was limited and conditional, never absolute.

Sanctuary in Classical Greece and the Hellenistic World

The first sanctuary system of which we have any extensive records is that which developed in classical Greece from approximately the sixth century BC onward. Starting with the assumption that certain places in nature were sacred and under the protection of specific deities, there developed both the idea that such supernatural protection could be afforded those seeking it within that place and the practice of establishing numerous, specific sites where sanctuary was available, recognized, and effective. It should be emphasized that the offering of a god's protection to those seeking safety and security was not the primary purpose of Greek sanctuaries; the setting aside of sacred space in the form of an altar, a temple, or a larger territory was mainly intended to honor and placate a particular god.[2] As one historian has written about the main functions of religious sanctuaries:

> The Greeks ... were in awe of the universal power exerted on the fortunes of mankind by the supernatural. ... One gains the impression that the whole destiny of man is controlled by the gods, who manipulate him like a puppet. ... It is possible ... for a man to take action to win the support and favour of the gods. This is done largely by offerings to them; if the gods are pleased, they look favourably on the men who make the offerings. Similarly, their anger may be turned aside by a suitably imposing sacrifice. (Tomlinson 1976, 11–13)

However, it seems that, as sacred spaces moved from groves, mountaintops, grottoes, and other natural sites to elaborate temples and arenas, the function of such spaces in affording refuge and protection to those facing threatening or violent situations changed. How common—and how successful—was this practice is a matter for some debate among scholars of the Greek world, although there is agreement that respect for the inviolability of such sanctuaries was in decline by the middle of the fourth century BC, when many were invaded and plundered for their valuable collections of offerings. Ulrich Sinn (1993, 88–89), for example, argues that the protection offered by Greek sanctuaries was used frequently by a wide variety of individuals and not just by the famous fleeing political retribution from their enemies, such as Demosthenes at Poseidon's sanctuary on the island of Kalaureia, or by deposed kings and their families, such as the Spartan Kleombrotos II in 241 BC (Schumacher 1993, 72). Sinn mentions refuge being afforded to fleeing slaves, orphans, girls seeking to avoid a forced marriage, and runaway wives, as well as political exiles. He notes in addition that victims of wars and civil wars frequently made use of the protection afforded by the sanctuaries. According to Sinn, offering refuge was both a right and an obligation that was possessed by all sacred sites in Greece and, moreover, that it was not "an occasional obligation" (Sinn 1993, 88).

Whatever the truth about the frequency of use, it is clearly the case that the Greeks had a sophisticated intellectual understanding of the nature of sanctuary, both as a concept and as a practice. The inviolability of the particular territory of a sanctuary arose from the Greek concept of *asylia*. This was a widely recognized social institution, originally guaranteeing safe conduct for those traveling abroad whose business legitimately took them across city boundaries, outside the jurisdiction of their own state—envoys, artists, and athletes, for example. Usually, this kind of protection was guaranteed by prior agreements (or sometimes granted to individuals as an honor), and occasionally this specific status was granted to particular sanctuaries. However, it was also the case that the inviolability of all sanctuaries—and those physically on their premises, such as priests, pilgrims, festival participants, and supplicants—was guaranteed by a more general form of *asylia*, arising from the fact that everything within the sanctuary was the possession of the god, rendering it taboo for human beings to be attacked there. Hence, all sanctuaries were themselves protected by *asylia*.

However, simply being within a sanctuary was not enough to protect an individual—or, presumably, a community—seeking refuge and protection from some threat. A person seeking protection had to undergo the ceremony of appearing openly, setting forth the reasons for coming to request protection, and asking to become a supplicant or *hiketes*. Once that status had been granted, the sanctuary—usually in the person of one of the priests—had an obligation to work toward the solution of the problem, acting both as adviser to the supplicant as well as a mediator. This could often be a tricky and sometimes a dangerous role, especially if the supplicant had committed some misdeed engendering a process of revenge seeking or was a political refugee seeking to avoid retaliation from successful political rivals.[3]

Given the widespread need to placate the gods and the general acceptance of the social need for places of refuge and protection (although even among the Greeks there seems to have been some confusion about the distinction between *asylia* and *hiketeia*), it is not surprising that classical Greece saw the widespread establishment of various types of sacred space and sanctuary. At the risk of oversimplifying, Greek locations that were sacred and inviolable seem to have been of three types (Marinatos and Hèagg 1993, 229–30). First and probably most famous were urban sanctuaries placed in the center of the *polis*, often on a hill within the city limits. The temples on the Acropolis in Athens and the temple of Apollo in Corinth are prime examples of such locations. Second were intra-urban or pan-Hellenic sanctuaries, which were situated in a kind of "no man's land" away from the actual territory of particular city-states, although possibly under the administrative control of a nearby *polis*. Olympia and Delphi were the best known examples of such sanctuaries, whose general aura of neutrality also made them appropriate sites for contacts, competitions, and conferences. Last were extra-urban sanctuaries, which lay within the territorial boundaries of particular city-states but which were frequently somewhat remote from the city itself. The relative isolation of many sanctuaries from their urban centers has raised an interesting debate about why this should have been the case. On the one hand, it is possible that some sanctuaries were sited where they were because of their association with the god who was being honored. Sanctuaries dedicated to Poseidon were frequently located on peninsulas and promontories, while some dedicated to Zeus were on or near mountaintops. An alternative view is that an isolated and not easily approachable location increased the protection available to those seeking safety and security, at least at a psychological level. Against this idea Sinn makes the point that if a political rival or personal revenge seeker was not deterred from violating a sanctuary by religious awe, then topographical remoteness—or even the fortifications that existed at some sacred sites—would not be much of a deterrent (Sinn 1993, 103).

Sinn offers a third reason for the siting of many sanctuaries in marginal areas, remote from an urban center: the existence of a sanctuary containing possibly large numbers of political supplicants (or even a single important one) in the very center of the *polis* could pose a major danger of disruption and instability. This could come about simply through the supplicants' being there and attracting political supporters and activity or by the supplicants' behavior (or suspected or anticipated behavior) while within the sanctuary (Sinn 1993, 106). This suggestion raises the crucial issue of what those seeking refuge in a sanctuary were allowed to do while maintaining their protected position and what sorts of behavior within a sanctuary would make it more or less likely that the sanctuary would remain inviolable. What were the obligations of sanctuary seekers within the sacred precinct, and how did their behavior increase—or decrease—the likelihood that inviolability would be maintained?

This issue of proper and acceptable behavior of those within protection will be taken up again later in the chapter, for it forms part of the far broader question of the reasons for sanctuary being observed rather than broken. Historians from Herodotus onward have recorded many cases of sanctuary being broken, of the law of sacred immunity being disregarded, of the whole conception of sanctuary, safety, and security breaking down. However, both Ulrich Sinn (1993) and Rob Schumacher (1993, 68–70) have argued that this picture of the failure of sanctuary is one-sided and inaccurate, simply because examples of the ineffectiveness of sanctuary were the ones that were unusual enough to be recorded, while normal situations in which sanctuary was observed, however unwillingly, were so normal as to pass relatively unremarked.

Whatever the actual balance of success and failure, two reasons have been advanced for whatever successes Greek sanctuaries achieved in affording safety to individuals or to communities. The first and lesser of these is the self-interest argument. Sanctuary was observed because everybody had to reckon with the possibility that at some point in the future it might be necessary to seek the protection afforded by a sanctuary. This was especially the case given the volatility of factional politics within Greek city-states and the constant wars and defeats that occurred among those states. The list of Spartan kings driven to take sanctuary is long enough to make the point that scrupulous observation of sanctuary might be the best course of action for any prominent political figure wishing to ensure against an uncertain future.

Far more prominent among arguments regarding factors that preserved the inviolability of sanctuaries were those involving inevitable sanctions for breaking sanctuary. Arguments about divine sanctions play a major role in accounting for success in the struggle to provide effective security within sanctuaries. The wrath and retaliation of the gods for breaking sanctuary would rarely be risked, even by the most intrepid, even when other, secular rewards might be considerable. The deterrent effects of such sanctions seem to have been considerable and to have been backed up in Greek culture by numerous stories of disasters—illnesses, military defeats, or natural catastrophes such as earthquakes or tidal waves—attributed directly to the gods' reaction to some ruler's or community's violation of divine protection. To quote Ulrich Sinn, "The harshness of the divine retribution is a measure of how highly the institution of sacred protection was valued by the people" (Sinn 1993, 93).

As with the Jewish sanctuary cities, Greek sanctuaries offer a number of features that recur in later efforts to provide protection for individuals or communities under some forms of threat, especially of violence. The first of these is that Greek sanctuaries offered protection both for those that were themselves the specific targets of violence or other unpleasantness—offenders, criminals, political rivals, runaway slaves—and for those that were simply threatened by dangers concomitant on being caught up in wars, civil wars, intercity feuds, or other forms of protracted conflicts while not themselves being deliberately singled out as specific targets for mayhem and violence.

The second feature is that, as in the sanctuary cities in Israel, basic protection was afforded by supernatural sanctions as well as a set of social norms that condemned sanction violators even while it was recognized that sanctuary could be abused by supplicants. Third, those within a sanctuary had limitations imposed upon their conduct while they remained within sanctuary. The need to remain "inoffensive" arose for both religious and pragmatic reasons. One did not offend a god while enjoying his or her protection on his or her sacred territory. Neither did one act in such a manner as to bring danger and instability into the host community in which the sanctuary was situated. Last, it seems that in many cases geographical remoteness played an important part in the selection and delineation of sites for Greek sanctuaries, and while scholars disagree somewhat on the overall effectiveness of this factor, most do seem agreed on another factor—the importance of clear and well marked boundaries in helping to maintain the inviolability of the sanctuary.

If divine sanctions contributed to the success of locational inviolability and protection, then this account might seem to have arrived at the point where it is possible to begin raising the question about the effectiveness of various forms of sanctuary. To some degree, however, answers to the question of effectiveness will vary depending on how one answers preliminary questions about who the sanctuaries were for and what threats they were intended to ward off. Sanctuaries for whom and from what?

Clearly, Greek sanctuaries could offer inviolability to a wide range of persons: envoys and diplomats, individuals who had harmed others, individual political refugees or refugee groups, runaway slaves, women seeking to avoid a forced marriage or an abusive spouse, and communities threatened by involvement in war or civil war. They could and did provide protection from a variety of threats, the most obvious being the threat of violence, either personal or communal. In other cases it was possible to seek protection from threats involving seizure of self and property. Sanctuary could be provided for slaves seeking security from being returned to their owners and, presumably, to a situation of punishment and retribution. (The sanctuary at Tainaron in Lakonia was particularly renowned for providing protection for runaway Spartan *helots*.) In this case there seem to be clear similarities to sanctuary seeking in the early part of the nineteenth century by African American slaves in the United States, who sought

safety and protection in free states in the North, or the political refugees from El Salvador, Guatemala, and Nicaragua who sought a refuge from the combatants in the civil wars in those countries at the
end of the twentieth century.

The discussion will return to important characteristics of Greek
sanctuaries later, taking up again the theme of what might affect the
success of these and other sanctuaries. For the moment, however, we
return to other examples of protection through the establishment of
various types of religious sanctuary in medieval Europe.

The Tradition of Church Sanctuary

The Greek tradition of divinely sanctioned, inviolable spaces where
refuge could be afforded to miscreants and security to noncombatants continued throughout the Hellenistic and Roman eras and onward into medieval Europe, when both the idea and the practice were
taken up and extended by the Catholic Church. The right of sanctuary became recognized and widespread in the Roman Empire, when
an increasing number of imperial temples and even some imperial
statues gained that right. When the empire became Christianized a
similar claim was made for all churches, although it was not until the
fourth century that formal laws were enacted regulating what was
then described as "a privilege already recognised and well established" (Cox 1911, 3). Originally enacted by Theodosius the Great in
AD 392,[4] the right of sanctuary at first applied only to the altar in the
church but a later, more practical law of Theodosius the Younger extended the limits of immunity to the walls and precincts of the church-
yard (Cox 1911).

It is clear that the practice of churches providing sanctuary survived the collapse of the Western Empire and was carried into the
earliest centuries of the European Middle Ages.[5] Acceptance of the
right and practice of sanctuary was probably helped by similar traditions that seem to have been developed by both Germanic and Slavic
peoples. Such traditions were reinforced by the church's belief that
there was no crime that could not be pardoned through fear of and
reverence for God, although limitations on an absolute right of sanctuary were always accepted for practical and political reasons. Such
limitations tended to take the form of (1) denying that certain categories of offender—arsonists, highway robbers, those who had committed sacrilege—had any right of sanctuary; (2) limiting the time
that sanctuary could be afforded the fugitive by establishing dead-
lines; or (3) setting out clearly actions that had to be undertaken or
conditions that had to be fulfilled for protection to be continued. In
Anglo-Norman England, for example, common law allowed anyone

accused of a felony to take refuge in a sanctuary, but the local community then had the duty of preventing the fugitive from escaping. The local coroner negotiated with the offender, who had the choice of submitting to trial or confessing and then leaving the kingdom. In the latter case, where the offender "abjured the kingdom," he was assigned a port of departure and given forty days immune from attack to leave. He could return only with the king's permission. If the fugitive refused both options, he would be starved into submission while remaining within the sanctuary.

The development of the centralized, dynastic state throughout Europe in the sixteenth and seventeenth centuries saw the right of sanctuary for wrongdoers and locations where they would be safe from civil power—where "the king's writ did not run"—much diminished. The right of sanctuary had virtually vanished in Western Europe by the start of the eighteenth century.[6] The idea survived, however, in the setting of "international anarchy" and through the concepts of national sovereignty, territorial inviolability, the "extraterritoriality" that granted immunity to the persons of diplomats, and the "extraterritorial" space occupied by diplomatic missions in foreign capitals. Thus, from early modern times the idea of sanctuary and safety became focused on protection that could be gained through escape to a location beyond the boundaries of one's own society. The dominant concept of sanctuary became one in which protection could best be gained "outside" one's own country, in a place from which the person or persons seeking refuge could not be brought back. Sanctuary could best be sought across some border, which would act as a barrier to the threat either for individuals or sometimes even for whole communities seeking refuge.

Safe from Return:
Extra-societal Sanctuary through Distance

The major alternative to seeking protection within intra-societal (or domestic) sanctuaries traditionally has been to seek sanctuary by leaving and finding protection outside the boundaries of one's own society. Throughout history, rather than seek the uncertain protection of sanctuaries located physically within their own societies, many who could—as well as many who had little choice—have looked for safety in extra-societal sanctuaries located geographically and (more important) jurisdictionally outside the limits of their own country. Those seeking protection escape physically and seek the protection of neighboring rulers and governments. Individuals and communities have thus sought safety by putting miles between themselves and their persecutors, thus becoming asylum seekers, political exiles, or refugees. Expressed slightly differently, this strategy involves putting geographical distance and jurisdictional barriers between threatened and threateners, as opposed to the strategy of staying put and setting up thresholds, signposts, and sanctions as means of reducing insecurity.

In the modern era the most familiar examples of this strategy of sanctuary abroad have involved individuals who have left their own countries to live in exile as political refugees. They have thus become (relatively) safe from the violence that threatened them in their own society and from return through a process of extradition.[7] An elaborate network of rules governing the granting and withholding of asylum and the rights and obligations of asylum seekers and granters has grown up in international law.[8] One of the more contentious issues often concerns the abilities of political refugees to continue activities aimed at harming, undermining, or even overthrowing the leadership in their country of origin from a safe base in another country.[9] Once again, this raises the issue of what sorts of things the denizens of sanctuaries are permitted to do; how their actions from inside the sanctuary affect the tolerance both of those outside, who are the targets of such actions, and those who are providing the sanctuary; and the long-term durability of the sanctuary itself.

As with all sanctuaries, a central question is always what level of security is afforded by these "sanctuaries at a distance," given that they are often a long way from the source of the original threats and outside the formal jurisdiction of the rulers of the home society. Clearly, as with any sanctuary, the answer has to be that security is neither absolute nor permanent. The fate of Leon Trotsky in Mexico is one of the most widely known instances where sanctuary failed to provide security for prominent individual exiles. More recently, the activities of Israeli agents in kidnapping or killing Palestinian militants irrespective of their geographical location; the seizing in Caracas of the Colombian Ricardo Gonzalez (Rodrigo Granda), a key member of the FARC's International Committee, by Venezuelan agents of the Colombian government; and the activities in the 1970s and 1980s of DINA, the Chilean secret police, throughout other American countries, have all shown that being granted political asylum in another country is no guarantee of protection.

The other major source of insecurity for those seeking sanctuary at a distance is that of being ejected from the place of sanctuary and returned to the one's own society to face the original threat once again. This concern always affects individuals seeking asylum in another jurisdiction. It can also affect whole categories or communities of sanctuary seekers and involve large numbers of people who become political refugees. The insecurities posed by the possibility of being sent back seem to be ever present when large numbers of individuals seek distant sanctuary, although there have been cases where this danger has been minimized. The extent of the danger of return depends largely on attitudes within the host society.

Any preliminary lessons to be learned from the record of sanctuary at a distance—for example, the sanctuary sought by the nineteenth-century underground slave railroad or the late-twentieth-century sanctuary movement for refugees from Central America—have to be treated as *very* preliminary. However, some ideas can be tentatively advanced. The first is that distance and different jurisdictions do not provide absolute security and protection, especially for prominent refugees. There are too many examples of individuals being returned or of being attacked, kidnapped, or even killed while living in countries other than their own and assuming that they were protected by being outside the jurisdiction of their own rulers. Prominent adversaries pose threats to embattled regimes even when in exile, and these become even greater when such individuals are part of an organization or a movement that, "safe" on another's territory, continues to undertake activities that damage its home society and its rulers. In the eyes of nineteenth-century Southern slave owners, members of the underground railroad would inevitably help and encourage more slaves to escape, protect runaways from capture or return, and—worst of all—link up with the movement to abolish slavery altogether, thus attacking the economic and social foundations of society in the southern United States. In the 1980s members of the American sanctuary movement similarly helped Guatemalan and Salvadorian refugees (viewed by their governments as mostly left-wing supporters, if not actual members of the rebel guerrilla organizations) to escape, and also worked to end the US government's support for those regimes—or, at least, to cast serious doubts on their legitimacy. These examples lead to the hardly paradoxical conclusion that the safety and security of refugees is directly linked to their quiescence, their lack of hostile activity toward their home society once they have achieved a place in their host country. The more refugees become absorbed into their host societies as unorganized individuals, content to remain inactive and therefore harmless—as opposed to becoming an organized and active diaspora—the less likely rulers in the home society are to seek their silencing or return, and the greater the level of security they will enjoy in their sanctuary, at least at a personal level.

The other major influence that plays a part in this whole security issue is the nature of the relationship between rulers in the host country and those in the society from which the refugees are seeking sanctuary. Clearly, in the case of the 1980s sanctuary movement in the

United States, relations between the US government and the governments in Guatemala and El Salvador were positive and friendly, to say the least. Hence, refuge and safety would not be offered easily, if at all, to refugees from those countries. The threat of deportation was inevitable and only frustrated to some degree by the activities of individual US citizens, churches, and other local organizations (see Crittenden 1988; Davidson 1988; Matters 1994). The reverse situation also seems likely to be true. Hostile or unfriendly relations between host and home governments would be likely to increase the welcome afforded refugees fleeing to that host and minimize the chances of their being returned as undesirables. Whether this necessarily would increase the security of those heading for distant sanctuary is another matter, however, and depends upon the degree of hostility evinced by the host's rulers. In situations of very high hostility there is inevitably a chance that refugees—especially large numbers of refugees—could be organized by the host government as part of a serious effort to undermine the home society's rulers.

This suggests that one important factor in evaluating the effectiveness and durability of sanctuaries must be the existence of clear and accepted rules about the treatment, behavior, and, above all, use of refugee sanctuary seekers and about ways of dealing with them once they have succeeded in traveling to sanctuary. Overall, four factors appear worth further analysis as important influences on the durability of this—and probably other—types of sanctuary. The durability of distant sanctuaries appears likely to be helped by the physical distance itself (neighboring sanctuaries being more vulnerable than those far overseas or separated by several other countries); by the quiescence of those within the sanctuary; by the host ruler's disapproval of the nature or policies of the home ruler; and by the existence of firm, enforceable, unambiguous, and generally recognized rules about the provision of sanctuary.

Sanctuaries in Civil Wars—
Peace Zones and Peace Communities

Of all the environments within which it is difficult to establish and maintain any form of sanctuary, that imposed by a civil war is perhaps the most difficult and offers the most problems to the long-term maintenance of inviolability for the sanctuary and for the security of those inside it. And yet it is during such situations that there is often the greatest need for some place—or form—of safety for those not directly involved as combatants. The circumstances of civil war make it supremely difficult for people threatened by the violence to leave and find sanctuary in non-involved countries or societies.[10] This frequently leaves them with the sole option of creating their own sanctuaries, physically within the territory where the war is being fought. Historically, such wars have frequently produced more or less successful efforts to create neutral sanctuaries for noncombatants or for those wishing to "stand aside" from the struggle, neither taking sides nor taking up arms in the conflict. During the twentieth century and in earlier epochs the dilemma of being, and wishing to remain, uninvolved has been particularly acute in multi-ethnic societies, where ethnic minorities have found themselves caught up in a struggle that seems remote from their interests and way of life, and thus something to be avoided—if at all possible. Hence, the frequent adoption of a strategy of establishing and trying to maintain a ZoP or peace community as a sanctuary where those within are safe from the violence without. Even in relatively homogenous societies, civilian noncombatants have sought refuge from violence in safe havens and sanctuaries as an alternative to flight. Earlier, mention was made of the protection afforded by sacred sites in classical Greece for local populations fleeing the effects of war. This pattern of behavior remains common today.

Given the nature of civil wars and their attendant violence, the establishment of a successful sanctuary, peace territory, or peace community would appear a hopeless task, at least at first sight, and it is true that the inviolability of such a sanctuary and the safety of those inside is always problematic. There are many examples of such forms of sanctuary being ineffective or collapsing or simply being ignored by combatants who see no reason to respect self-declared neutrals or neutral territory. However, there is clearly much variation in the success of efforts to maintain the inviolability of a sanctuary during a civil war and in the durability of these initiatives. What factors might explain this variation?

One starting suggestion might be that we are dealing with two subtypes of sanctuaries that often exist within a society at peace but can also exist within a society at war with itself—what this chapter has termed intra-societal or domestic sanctuaries, deliberately constructed to provide security. The key distinction revolves around the question of who or what is contained and thus "safe" within the sanctuary, and what kind of temptation these people or things represent to any outsider (revenge seeker, slave owner, government representative, combatant party) considering the breaking of sanctuary and the seizure of those within. Again, returning to the examples provided by classical Greece, sanctuaries there provided refuge for inhabitants, supplicant individuals, or local refugees fleeing violence (in modern terminology IDPs, seeking refuge). In these and other cases, then, sanctuaries in general, and also during a civil war, can contain *individual* supplicants (opponents, offenders, war criminals, deserters), *categories* or *communities* (indigenous groups, *campesinos* wishing to get on with their lives, self-declared neutrals), or both.[11]

Analyzing the influences on inviolability leads to a line of thought that can be exemplified by two queries:

1. Does the sanctuary contain a potential target (someone or something that is valuable or dangerous), thus making it more likely that the security it affords will be undermined? (Apart from persons, the target could be goods, treasure, supplies, strategic access, tactical advantage, or symbolic success.)
2. Is the sanctuary itself a potential target because its continuing existence *in and of itself* presents outsiders with an insult, a challenge, a cost, or a major foregone advantage?

The logic underlying the first query seems reasonably straightforward. Why should the inviolability of any sanctuary be respected if it contains a person or set of persons who continue to constitute a danger? Such considerations surely explain why Antipater, who ruled Macedonia after the death of Alexander the Great, carried out such a relentless pursuit of Macedonia's Athenian opponents, led by Demosthenes and Hypereides, even after their defeat in battle. The Athenians finally sought refuge at the sanctuary in Aiakeion in Aegina,[12] only to have the sanctuary broken and the leading democrats killed, in spite of their status as supplicants (Schumacher 1993, 76).

Similar considerations are likely to influence the durability of past and current peace zones and communities, some of which contain what local combatants regard as opponents in hiding or offer sanctuary to the wounded from all parties.[13] The wounded recover, and then what? There must be some strong reasons for *not* breaking into a sanctuary that contains wounded or incapable adversaries. As I point out in Chapter 7, one of the major reasons for the collapse of UN safe zones in former Yugoslavia was the fact that they contained not just key individuals but large numbers of Bosniac opponents of the Bosnian Serbs, who, not unnaturally, regarded the former as dangerous and their removal (one way or another) well worth breaking into such sanctuaries, despite tacit agreements and the likely wrath and reaction of their protectors.

Similarly, the argument that sanctuaries and safe zones containing valued things are less likely to remain inviolable than those without such temptations seems understandable. Many Greek sanctuaries that had successfully remained inviolable during the fifth century BC were looted later because they had become repositories of rich offerings to their specific deity. Temptation offset fear of divine sanction. In a similar fashion, the longstanding Coptic Christian sanctuary on the island of Metraha was casually looted by the Emperor Tewodros in 1867 in order to pay his armies and for his armaments. Over time, the sanctuary had become a bank and a storehouse for valuables, and it seems that the search for safety for goods had actually made the place less safe for humans. For sanctuaries and safe zones the rule seems to be the more valuable, the less durable. As Krista Rigalo and Nancy Morrison emphasize in Chapter 9, the relief and medical supplies contained in those allegedly safe corridors in Sudan became, in themselves, sufficient reason for armed factions to break into the corridors intent upon seizing the goods for themselves and using the supplies as part of the ongoing struggle. The dilemmas posed in such cases may be resolvable but perhaps only on a temporary basis.

A full discussion of the circumstances in which the very existence of sanctuaries becomes a challenge to the adversaries in a civil war, and the zones or communities themselves become a target, must wait until the final part of this chapter. However, enough has been said up to now to indicate that sanctuaries—even those containing valued goods or "dangerous" persons—do survive and continue to offer some protection even in civil wars, as do peace zones or communities that, for some reason, themselves become targeted by combatants. Chapter 4 on peace zones and communities in Colombia by Catalina Rojas and Chapter 3 on the Philippines by Kevin Avruch and Roberto S. Jose offer further clues as to what factors might help to maintain inviolability. Another case that seems to offer some distinctive features might also provide some lessons as to factors that help to preserve sanctuary, even in the midst of social breakdown and civil wars. This is the case of the Christian sanctuaries in China during the early twentieth century, a period that contained a very violent civil war and a later invasion of large areas of China by the Japanese military. In fact, this case may prove to be an extreme one, at least in the sense of the degree of external interest in and direct and indirect protection of the sanctuaries by powerful outside governments. However, in this respect at least, it can provide a benchmark of sorts for other peace zones and sanctuaries that have enjoyed lesser forms of protection from outside their society but have survived to offer security during violent and protracted civil wars.

Missionary Compounds in Revolutionary China

The position of foreign missionaries, their compounds, and their converts within the Chinese Empire during the late nineteenth and early twentieth centuries was always an ambiguous one, largely because it was so closely associated with the extraterritorial privileges enjoyed by European and American commercial interests in that country; by the existence of sizeable parts of key Chinese port cities that were effectively outside the jurisdiction of the Imperial Chinese government; and by the influence wielded by foreign consuls over Chinese government officials (Wakeman 1975, 131 et seq.). During this period of Chinese history the most obvious places offering sanctuary to threatened foreigners and to the Chinese themselves were the foreign concessions at Tientsin and Hankow and the settlement at Shanghai, to which numerous individuals—hunted revolutionaries, deposed officials, overthrown leaders—fled for safety and for protection from capture and vengeance.[14] However, the numerous Christian mission stations scattered throughout the country also were able to offer sanctuary and security to large numbers of the local populations threatened by the effects of civil war, revolution and—ultimately—Japanese invasion. Furthermore, protection was not merely afforded to Chinese Christian converts but eventually (and within limits discussed below) to anyone seeking shelter from the armies fighting one another or from the activities of local bandits. In fact, by the start of the twentieth century, missionaries had come to be perceived as persons of great influence, at least in the sense of being able to shelter their Christian converts from their neighbors and also from Chinese government officials.

This last perception was to persist for some years and to play a significant role in the missions' subsequent ability to provide protection to Christians and non-Christians alike. It was enhanced during the Boxer Rebellion (1898–1901), when it was widely observed that the missions were willing to offer sanctuary to anyone who was under threat from violence, and later still, when missions offered protection to non-Christian Chinese threatened by the—often indiscriminate—violence dealt out by Western and Japanese punitive expeditions, as these spread out along the Yellow River valley and beyond (Quale 1957, 58). In later periods many local people recalled the lesson that missions would—and could—protect Chinese from foreigners as well as protecting foreigners from Chinese.[15]

The Protective Functioning of Mission Compounds

The extent to which Christian missionary compounds could serve as sanctuaries for their own converts or for local people varied greatly as the country moved into the twentieth century. Roughly speaking, missionaries faced three very different challenges during the first two decades, as the Manchu Dynasty came to an end and the struggle over its successor took an increasingly violent form.

In the decade immediately following the Boxer Rebellion and the foreign punitive expeditions, the situations facing the Christian missions reverted more or less to those that had existed previously within the empire. The central government appeared to be in control of the country, the Imperial Dynasty continued to rule, and its local authorities could be relied upon to protect the missionaries, their converts, and their property against attack, although it was still necessary—perhaps even more necessary—for the missionaries to remind governors and magistrates of their obligations, to request action for local infringements of the protocols, and to seek compensation for damage and destruction when this occurred.

After the Western reaction to the Boxer Rebellion, it hardly needed to be emphasized that the mantle of protection for Western Christian missions was based almost directly on the obvious willingness of outsiders to use unstoppable military force, if the safety and security of the missionaries and their property were not respected. The fear of this possibility on the part of the Chinese central government translated into clear and repeated instructions to provincial and local authorities to act against any threat to the inviolability of the missions and into dismissal and disgrace for those who failed to carry out their protective role effectively. After 1901 this sanction was reinforced in many areas by local memories of the military consequences that followed attacks on foreign property, all of which served to make the most hostile Chinese—peasant, politician, or official—wary of infringing norms regarding the treatment of foreign missionaries or missions. What one writer has characterized as "fear of foreign wrath" continued to operate in this period and maintained the effective protection enjoyed by foreign missionaries, extended this protection to their converts, and maintained—relatively effectively—the inviolability of their mission compounds and possessions (Quale 1957, 22).[16]

This situation changed markedly in 1911, once the republican flag of rebellion was raised against the Imperial government in Peking and a full-scale civil war, with its attendant banditry, looting, impressment of civilians for soldiers or carriers, destruction, and reprisal, became widespread throughout the country. The period between 1911 and 1917 presented new challenges for the Christian missionaries and their refuges, and in many regions of the country they passed from being the disliked and despised representatives of foreign intrusion into those providing rare oases of stability and security in a country torn by violence among rival factions struggling for military and political control.

By and large, however, the basic sources of protection for foreign missions and their inviolability during this early period of the civil wars remained the same: fear of detrimental outside reactions or the erosion of existing foreign support for their side's position in the civil war. Neither the Imperial government nor the nationalist revolutionaries (nor many of the warlords, in later years) wished to do anything that would offend foreign governments and switch their support— or end their neutral stance—to the other side or even—in an extreme case—bring about damaging sanctions.[17] It was this fear rather than the token "tripwire" forces of protective national troops or gunboats that were occasionally dispatched to guard missionary sites that helped missions continue to fulfill their roles as sanctuaries. This continued to be the situation even when the civil war intensified with the establishment of Sun Yat-sen's nationalist government in Canton in 1917, and the struggle over, and prosecution of, the northern campaign that followed.

What finally brought an end both to the privileged position of foreign missionaries and their missionary compounds and to the ability of missions to act as sanctuaries was the changed attitudes and policies of the Kuomintang as the struggle developed during the mid and late 1920s. As the gradual northward extension of nationalist control took place between 1923 and 1929, it was accompanied by an erosion of the positions of Western missionaries and a taking over of their properties wherever the Kuomintang were successful. Partly this was a working out of the longstanding Chinese resentment of foreign intervention in Chinese affairs, and partly it was the increasing influence of Soviet agents and ideas on Kuomintang doctrines and policies (at least until the nationalist purges of 1927 and 1928 returned the KMT to its nationalist roots), and partly it was the increasing realization that the likelihood of massive military retaliation by foreign powers had diminished or virtually vanished (with the possible exception of the Japanese). Whatever the reasons, the effects were unmistakable. In KMT areas mission property was occupied and used by nationalist forces as barracks, headquarters and hospitals and often taken over—or taken back, as many Chinese were beginning to see it—without any talk of compensation. This was especially so when the property had been abandoned by its occupants, but there were numerous cases reported of missionaries being ejected from compounds, schools, and hospitals and of local Chinese employees being covertly encouraged to protest and strike to provide an excuse for the property being confiscated by local KMT officials. On the other hand, given the Kuomintang policy of not billeting troops on the local population in areas the nationalists controlled or captured, there were many fewer cases of fleeing civilians seeking refuge from nationalist soldiers in missionary compounds, although they continued to do so when faced by troops from other armies. Moreover, soldiers from both sides tended to seek protection as military fortunes altered and territory changed hands.

Sanctuary and External Patronage

One finding that emerges with great clarity from the experience of Christian missionary compounds' role as sanctuaries during the protracted conflicts that afflicted Chinese society during the early decades of the twentieth century is the importance of foreign interest, influence, and patronage in providing indirect protection for the missions. While local officials from both Imperial and revolutionary regimes often provided direct protection for the missions in the form of deterrent warnings and subsequent punishment for violations, and occasionally with the presence of local police and soldiers, it was the fear of foreign wrath (often transmitted by higher level officials) that ultimately increased whatever inviolability those missions enjoyed. Not only were powerful foreign governments involved in protecting their own citizens and their property through diplomatic pressure and protest, but channels of communication to key levels of Chinese governments were many, open, and constantly used in ensuring that protection. Moreover, diplomatic pressure was backed up by an implied but very real threat of sanctions, both military and economic, and the knowledge on the part of Chinese officials that major offenses against foreign interests, including the missionaries, would simply provide the Western powers and Japan with an opportunity to extract further concessions beyond those already surrendered. Even toward the end of the nineteenth century memories remained of Western reactions to the Tai Ping rebellion, and in the early twentieth century these were reinforced after the Boxer Rebellion and the resultant punitive expeditions.

The case of the sanctuaries established by the Christian missionary compounds in China might possibly be regarded as unique. After all, it is rare that sanctuaries have been protected by the knowledge that outside governments might use military or economic sanctions against those carrying out—or permitting—the violation of those sanctuaries. However, the example does emphasize the possibility that outside interest and patronage well short of military sanctions may indeed play an important role in preserving the inviolability of some sanctuaries and ensuring their survival over time. The question then becomes who might be the most effective sources of such outside interest and what might be the nature of the influence that could be most effectively brought to bear to support initiatives in providing sanctuary. What range of potential sanctions, positive as well as negative, might be available to outsiders in order to preserve sanctuaries within other societies? Can more recent examples of successful sanctuaries offer any lessons about this and other questions that help to analyze the factors that help to maintain inviolability in volatile and violent circumstances such as civil wars?

Local Zones of Peace in the Twentieth Century

The civil wars in China at the start of the twentieth century were merely the precursor to others that followed during that century. Innumerable wars, civil wars, and protracted, violent conflicts up to the present have meant that the search for sanctuary from threats and violence has become a constant feature of life in almost every region of the world. Even if one examines only the latter part of the violent twentieth century, which followed the bloodletting of the Second World War, the number of cases of people fleeing violence and seeking distant sanctuary seems endless, as does the frequency with which individuals, families, and communities have tried to find or construct safe havens for themselves within their own societies. In 1948–49 large numbers of Palestinians fleeing from or ejected by Israeli forces (many of the latter having fled Europe for the illusory sanctuary of the Holy Land) sought safety across the borders of Mandatory Palestine in Jordan, Lebanon, and Egypt, forming the first major "refugee problem" after World War II. At almost the same time Hindus fled from Pakistan to the safety of India and Muslims fled from India to Pakistan. Similar patterns of cross-border flights of refugees in search of safety and security were repeated over and over again during the next fifty years—in Asia, Africa, and Central and South America. Refugee camps grew up on the borders of Thailand and Cambodia, of Rwanda and the Congo, of the Sudan and Chad, and of Colombia and Panama, to name only some examples.

In other cases, when countries faced protracted and violent conflicts within their own borders, sanctuary seekers became IDPs, those who had been driven out of their homes and had sought safety and protection in other parts of their country, often by moving from battlegrounds in the countryside to slums and *favellas* surrounding major cities, such as Khartoum or Medellín. Whole communities became displaced, either by general violence or by violence specifically aimed at forcing them to move. In most cases of protracted and violent conflict, individual leaders and civilian representatives were also targeted and had to seek safety as best they could, in much the same way that prominent individuals in classical Greece had been forced to seek sanctuary in temples and other sacred sites.

The last two decades of the twentieth century saw a major revival of the practice of establishing recognized local sanctuaries in the midst of violent and protracted intrastate conflicts—neutral, disarmed sites, where people could live in some degree of safety, protected from the depredations of the warring parties and able to carry on some form of "normal" existence separated from the surrounding violence. Often, as in the pioneering initiatives in the Philippines, these local peace zones or peace communities were based upon indigenous peoples who saw themselves as very different from those engaged in waging the violent struggle and whose interests were not the same as those of the rival combatants. Sometimes, as in some of the peace *experiencias* in Colombia, those attempting to establish some form of sanctuary were simply local people who had been fought over to the point where local leaders said "Enough!" and sought some relief from the seemingly endless death and destruction. In other cases local people attempted to establish a building or a cluster of buildings as an inviolable sanctuary, immune from attack—a church, a school, a hospital or a clinic. In rarer cases outsiders attempted to establish various forms of protected space to help local people—a safe corridor for food or essential supplies, as in the Sudan and a number of other war-torn countries, or a vulnerable town or city, protected from attack, either directly by the presence of troops or indirectly by the implied threat of sanctions, as in the case of the mission compounds in China or the UN safe zones in former Yugoslavia.

As many of the other chapters in this book note, some form of international interest has helped maintain the inviolability of some local ZoPs as sanctuaries, but is this a general pattern? The query returns the discussion to the issue of what can be learned about the likely success of sanctuaries from the diverse examples provided by historical and contemporary practice. What factors might help increase the inviolability and the durability of various types of sanctuary in diverse environments when such initiatives face a wide variety of challenges? Can historical examples, such as those discussed thus far and those presented in the following chapters, help us move toward some theory of sanctuary?

We return to this central conundrum in the final chapter of this work and take it up again in the light of both the historical examples of sanctuary building mentioned above and the contemporary cases reviewed by the authors of the following chapters. These cover a wide range of sanctuary-building efforts, mainly locational and intra-societal but with sufficient variation to suggest general lessons that might be learned, even if they do not provide a full-blown theory of sanctuary.

Notes

[1] The seven cities were Derby, Launceton, Manchester (later Chester), Northampton, Wells, Westminster, and York. Henry may have wished to limit the practice of sanctuary in England, as he simultaneously removed the right from all churches and monasteries in the kingdom.

[2] The inviolable nature of sanctuaries helped some to develop other important functions. Some became sites for competitive games or, like the Sacred Island of Delos, major trading centers and markets. The sanctuary of Artemis at Ephesus was one of a number of sanctuaries that also functioned as banks.

[3] Given the difficulties of this role, it is not surprising that the burden of sacred immunity often proved too much for a sanctuary's priests, and various devices could be used to drive away dangerous and embarrassing supplicants, even if this meant driving them into the waiting arms of their pursuers. Another strategy was to prevent "undesirables" from entering the sanctuary in the first place; in the second half of the fifth century BC the Athenians, for example, set up a "police station" at the entry to the Acropolis for just this purpose (Sinn 1993, 92).

[4] Theodosius granted this right for the Eastern Empire; in the West a similar right was granted by Honorius. Later laws were passed limiting the right of sanctuary for individual wrongdoers who sought to escape revenge or justice by taking refuge in a church. Theodosius excluded public debtors from such protection, while Justinian later decreed that all murderers, adulterers, kidnappers of women, and rapists could be taken from church premises. Later still, Gratian's law granted asylum to all criminals save "night robbers, highway robbers and those guilty of grave crimes in churches" (Cox 1911, 4–5). The church commonly refused to surrender fugitives unless those apprehending them took an oath freeing them from mutilation and death.

[5] At the end of the seventh century King Ine of Wessex produced a code of laws for a realm where blood revenge and feuds were undoubtedly common that included this provision: "If anyone be guilty of death and he flee to a church, let him have his life and make satisfaction as the law may direct him. If anyone put his hide in peril and flee to a church, be the scourging forgiven him." Alfred the Great's code of AD 887 stated that "sanctuary seekers were to be protected for seven days and, under certain circumstances, for thirty days" (Cox 1911, 7).

[6] There was undoubtedly less need for such a social institution in societies where revenge and "self help" as responses to wrongs had been replaced by a system of laws, law enforcement by civil authorities, and centralized redress and punishment.

[7] In general, this is another example of sanctuary being afforded to a category of people—political refugees—and denied to other categories—criminals, for example. Problems always arise about who gets to define the status of a sanctuary seeker and according to what criteria.

[8] Another facet of the modern practice of affording asylum to sanctuary seekers is the practice of using the extraterritorial nature of embassies to provide refuge to those seeking protection, usually for political "offenses." Perhaps the best known twentieth century example was that of the Hungarian primate, Cardinal Mindzenty, who spent many years in the US Embassy in Budapest. On other occasions embassies have been used as sanctuaries by large numbers of people seeking safety from widespread local violence. The French Embassy in Phnom Pen provided a refuge for large numbers of non-Cambodians during the Khmer Rouge takeover of the country.

[9] For example, most of the political leadership of the Free Aceh movement (GAM) lived in exile in Sweden and continued its campaign to win independence from Indonesia from the relative safety of its Scandinavian base.

[10] In many wars and civil wars one common practice has been to send children to safe places outside the war zone. For example, during the Second World War some British children were sent to foster homes across the Atlantic in Canada and the United States. However, this kind of sanctuary is usually open only to a relative few.

[11] It seems reasonable to argue that sanctuaries that contain individuals who support one side or the other as well as communities wishing to remain uninvolved in the struggle pose the greatest danger to continuing inviolability and safety for those within. While local combatants may be persuaded to respect the neutrality of (and lack of threat from) an uncommitted peace community, sanctuaries that also contain perceived enemies (continuing threats) pose an open invitation to violation.

[12] By 322 BC Demosthenes had fled finally to Poseiden's sanctuary at Kalaureia, but he was pursued there by Archias who attempted to persuade the Athenian leader to leave the sanctuary and surrender. Demosthenes refused but took poison, finally dying outside the boundaries of the sanctuary to avoid polluting the sacred place by his death. Archias seems to have been equally reluctant to violate the sanctuary by directly seizing Demosthenes within its boundaries.

[13] One particularly acute problem, exemplified in many of the local peace communities in Colombia, is the dilemma of having former combatants (ex-guerrillas and ex-paramilitaries) prominently involved in the establishment and continuing activities of peace zones. How might it be possible to demonstrate convincingly to the "other side" that such individuals are genuinely no longer associated with a combatant organization—are indeed *former* guerrillas or *former* paramilitaries—when the logical reaction to such claims is to assume a "worst case scenario" and act on the belief that they continue to be members of the enemy organization, masked by a pretense of withdrawal. The dilemma raises the question of how one can "retire" convincingly and become recognized as a former anything in the midst of a protracted civil war.

[14] The most prominent figure to avail himself of such protection was nationalist leader Dr. Sun Yat-sen.

[15] For example, Protestant missionaries in areas subject to the punitive activities of foreign troops provided Christian converts with multilingual

"passports" and similar documents to local villages, provided the latter had recompensed Christian losses. On occasions they interceded directly to save communities that had provided restitution from the attentions of punitive forces (Quale 1957, 57–58). Such activities undoubtedly impressed local communities with the power and influence of the missionaries.

[16] This inviolability should not be exaggerated. The period also saw the rise of much more anti-Americanism in China, particularly as a result of the harsh imposition of immigration laws by the US government after 1905, and the growth of a boycott movement, especially in the south of the country, where most emigrants to the United States originated. Requests for protection against riots and violent attacks, for compensation for resultant damage and destruction, and for the punishment of ringleaders were frequently made both on behalf of missions and individual Christian converts. These requests indicate that the safety and security of categories of persons (missionaries and converts) and of safe spaces (mission compounds) were never complete and that missionary-activated and government-implemented punishment for sanctuary breaking was never an unfailing deterrent (Quale 1957, 60–63).

[17] As early as October 1911, the revolutionaries in Wuhan had proclaimed that only members and supporters of the Manchu regime were to be harmed, and the penalty of decapitation (the same as that for concealment of Manchu officials) was to be imposed on all who injured foreigners. The Imperial government was equally unwilling to offend or injure foreigners.

Works Cited

Benet, Francisco. 1957. Explosive markets: The Berber highlands. In *Trade and markets in the early empires*, ed. K. Polyani, K. Arensberg, and H. W. Pearson. New York: Collier-Macmillan.

Cox, Rev. Charles J. 1911. *The sanctuaries and sanctuary seekers of medieval England*. London: George Allen.

Crittenden, Ann. 1988. *Sanctuary: A story of American conscience and the law in collision*. New York: Weidenfeld and Nicolson.

Davidson, Miriam. 1988. *Convictions of the heart: Jim Corbett and the sanctuary movement*. Tucson: University of Arizona Press.

Lewis, William H. 1961. Feuding and social change in Morocco. *Journal of Conflict Resolution* 5 (1): 43–54.

Marinatos, Nanno, and Robin Hèagg. 1993. *Greek sanctuaries: New approaches*. London: Routledge.

Matters, Michael D. 1994. The sanctuary movement 1980–88: An organizational analysis of structures and cultures. PhD diss., University of Illinois at Chicago.

Quale, G. Robina. 1957. The mission compound in modern China; The role of the United States Protestant mission as an asylum in the civil and international strife of China, 1900–1941. PhD diss., University of Michigan.

Schumacher, Rob W. M. 1993. Three related sanctuaries of Poseidon: Geriastos, Kalauria, and Tainaron. In Marinatos and Hèagg 1993.

Singer, Isidore, and Cyrus Adler. 1925. *The Jewish encyclopedia: A descriptive record of the history, religion, literature, and customs of the Jewish people from the earliest times to the present day*. New York: Funk and Wagnalls.

Sinn, Ulrich. 1993. Greek sancturaries as places of refuge. In Marinatos and Hèagg 1993.

Tomlinson, R. A. 1976. *Greek sanctuaries*. London: Elek.

Wakeman, Frederick J. 1975. *The fall of Imperial China*. New York: The Free Press.

Westermarck, Edward. 1909. Asylum. In *Encyclopedia of religion and ethics*, ed. J. Hastings. Edinburgh: Collier.

2

THE NATURE, STRUCTURE, AND VARIETY OF PEACE ZONES

LANDON E. HANCOCK AND PUSHPA IYER

Introduction

Many times, in a protracted, intractable, and violent conflict, it is more useful to initiate measures to mitigate that conflict—short-term violence reduction—than to resolve or transform it. One of the most important methods of conflict mitigation is through what is called institutionalizing conflict, that is, allowing conflict to continue within rules. A concrete example of this is through the establishment of zones of peace (ZoPs) (Mitchell and Nan 1997).

ZoPs are usually defined territorially (although there are instances where the concept is more abstract, such as a whole community of people). Within them, by agreement, certain acts are prohibited and/or other acts encouraged. It is important to mention that while ZoPs are visualized in many different contexts, such as interstate border zones (such as the one between Peru and Ecuador), maritime trade zones, and nuclear free zones, the zones on which we focus here are those that are created within states in areas where there is or has been an armed, violent conflict. This excludes the intrastate contexts of intermittent, urban violence (such as gang violence or riots) and contexts in which the purpose is something other than a way out of the violence.

In this context of intrastate violent conflict, it is possible to create a typology of ZoPs on various dimensions—by whom they have been initiated, the degree of formalization of the zone, its geographical extent, or other criteria. We believe that another useful means of classification is to examine ZoPs in a temporal context. This implies that

29

we should examine the creation, implementation, and sustainability of these zones with reference to their relationship to the level of peace or violent conflict in the surrounding society. While this classification does not cover all instances of ZoPs, it does provide a broad overview through which most instances can, to some extent, be categorized.

Zones of Peace, before, during, and after Peace

If we think about a ZoP in this temporal fashion, it seems reasonable to examine three different time frames within which a zone might be created. The first is a ZoP created or maintained during a period of violent conflict. The primary purpose of this type of zone is to ameliorate or remove the effects of the conflict from the local population. The characteristics of this type of zone are, in general, marked by the goals of protecting noncombatants, attempting to establish policies and practices of neutrality with regards to both (or all) sides in a conflict, and seeking to prevent or restrict the types of violent activities taking place within the zone. Short-term versions of this type of zone may be established for the purpose of delivering aid or conducting humanitarian operations, such as administering vaccines.

The second temporal type of zone is one that is established during a peace process or its implementation. This type of zone may be used as a safe area for one or more of the combatant groups. It may also serve as a safe zone for the disarmament, demobilization, and reintegration (DDR) of former combatant forces. Such a zone is often limited in duration, either to the period of peace talks or to the period intended for the demobilization of forces. One example that lasted for some time was the area turned over to the FARC in Colombia during its negotiations with the Pastrana regime—the Zona de Distensión.

The third temporal type of zone is one that is established in the post-conflict environment. This type of zone attempts to address a number of issues, including those created by ongoing civil violence short of the type of civil conflicts that engender the first type of temporal zone. Some of the issues that can be addressed by a post-conflict ZoP include continuing human rights violations, criminal and gang related activities and a lack of economic and social development. The Local Zone of Peace in El Salvador (LZP) briefly described below (and covered more fully in Chapter 6) is a prime example of this type of temporal zone.

Finally, we examine those zones that do not fit clearly into the three categories described above. While most of these "special" zones do exist during violent conflicts, we have chosen to place them in a separate section due to their focus on specific elements and individuals affected by conflict, such as children, sacred spaces, or temporally limited zones used for aid distribution or provision of health care to affected populations.

Safe Havens and Zones during Violent Conflict

ZoPs during violent conflicts and civil wars are the main focus of the ICAR Local Zones of Peace project. This is primarily due to the incongruity of having a location or zone of nonparticipation in the midst of a modern interstate or civil conflict. This section focuses on the structure and some of the successes and failures of attempts to create these zones in recent conflicts.

The Failure at Bosnia: UN Safe Havens

The UN declaration of a number of "safe zones" in Bosnia-Herzegovina came about largely as a result of efforts by Bosnian Serb forces to "ethnically cleanse" Muslims from the Drina Valley as a part of their strategy of eliminating all such communities from Eastern Bosnia. The first safe zone was authorized for Srebrenica on April 16, 1993 (UNSCR 819), demanding that "all parties and other concerned treat Srebrenica and its surroundings as a safe area which should be free from any armed attack or any other hostile act." Subsequent safe zones were created for Tuzla, Sarajevo, Zepa, Gorazde, and Bihac on May 6, 1993.

The UN safe zones were designed to be protected areas where civilian populations, largely Muslim, would be safe from attacks and "acts of genocide" by Bosnian Serb paramilitary forces. Unfortunately, like their counterparts in Croatia, the safe zones in Bosnia provided only limited safety for their inhabitants and, in the case of Srebrenica, failed to prevent the massacre of nearly seven thousand Muslim males in 1995. Another major failure of the safe zones was their inability to protect the inhabitants from the actions of Serb paramilitaries, who often shelled the zones from nearby hills or stationed snipers to shoot at civilians. The United Nations attempted to address the former problem by declaring "weapons exclusion zones" around each of the safe zones and by interning some heavy weaponry around Sarajevo.

The most notable failure of the UN safe havens started with Serb retaliation for NATO air strikes designed to force Serbs to return heavy weapons removed from their internment areas. In retaliation, Serb paramilitaries took UN peacekeepers hostage, in effect nullifying their ability to protect civilians from Serb forces. Following this, the United Nations and NATO refused to reinforce the peacekeepers and, within weeks, Serb forces stepped up attacks on the safe areas. These attacks culminated with the July 1995 capture of Srebrenica by the forces of Bosnian Serb commander Ratko Mladić, who rightly believed that NATO would not use air attacks to stop him from brushing aside Srebrenica's Dutch UN peacekeepers. Following this, several of the other safe zones fell before the United Nations and NATO vowed to draw the line, protecting Sarajevo and Gorazde with more troops and air power.[1]

The Philippines

For many years the Philippines has been torn by armed internal conflict, the roots of which go back to the exploitative policies of the colonial powers. Since independence, successive governments have succeeded in alienating entire populations by failing to respond to their needs, the result of which has been that the poor have gotten poorer while wealth and power continue to be held by the privileged few. Economic and social discontent exploded into full-scale armed conflict in the late 1940s and early 1950s. Although the government crushed the insurgency, the roots of the conflict were not addressed, and in the 1970s the conflict revived. In 1972 martial law was imposed throughout the Philippines, but the economic deprivation of the majority continued. In 1986 the dictatorship of President Marcos was brought down by a nonviolent people's revolution. Since that time the country has been making a difficult and painful transition to democracy. The new government of President Aquino launched peace initiatives, but there were many hurdles to cross on the way (Garcia 1989).

It is in this "people's power" experience that one can trace the beginnings of the idea of local ZoPs in the country. In September 1988 the first such zone was declared in Naga City. Later, in 1992, the Sangguniang Panlungsod (Legislative Assembly) of Naga City passed Resolution No. 92–169 declaring the city a peace zone. This was followed by a series of peace zones being declared from the north to the south of the country. Some of the better known ones are those in Tulunan, Maladeg, Barangay Bituan, and North Cotobato.

In many ways the Filipino experience in developing ZoPs has been a pioneering one. In the Philippines the concept of ZoPs has always been that of a geographical area that community residents themselves declare to be "off limits to war and other forms of armed hostility" (Garcia 1997). In most of the initial ZoPs, the church had a major role to play in initiating and maintaining them. The church was powerful in standing up to the government and the Armed Forces of the Philippines (AFP). The peace zones succeeded in creating a space for dialogue and in keeping the violence out, but more important, they achieved some success as a link between local and national peace efforts. This was especially made possible with the support that the peace zones achieved during the time of President Fidel Ramos. However, over a period of time these "first wave" peace zones became more distanced from the peace process at the national level between the government and the leftist New People's Army (NPA) (Arguillas 1999).

The peace zone in Tulunan recently celebrated fourteen years of existence. The church in Tulunan was actively involved in its creation and is still active today. There are other peace zones in the Philippines that have been sustained by the community for long periods of time (Elusfa 2004). Clearly, the Filipino experience is something of a success in terms of how communities can negotiate peace for themselves and thus make an important contribution to achieving durable and general peace through the establishment of peace zones. However, this experience has also shown that care must be taken to ensure that the zones remain the property of their local inhabitants and not the government or other forces, which would use them for strategic or tactical gains.[2]

Colombia: Zones and Communities; Associations and National Movements

Like the Philippines, Colombia has been held hostage by more than fifty years of civil violence. Also like the Philippines, one of the responses of ordinary Colombians living in the countryside to the constant civil war and the endemic corruption that always seems to follow has been a movement to withdraw from the conflict by creating a host of ZoPs, municipalities of peace, and even communities of peace that focus more on the people than on their geographic location. In fact, the use of peace zones in Colombia has become so extensive that it is possible to discern and describe them on two levels. The first is a traditional zone, which is confined to one locality and serves the population of one community. The second is an outgrowth of the first, namely, the creation of associations of local zones, which then use their combined power to support and educate one another and to influence the processes of conflict and peacemaking on a larger scale. Within this second level are nationwide organizations that provide support to municipalities and zones.[3]

Zones and Communities

Colombia currently has over a hundred individual zones or municipalities, with more being formed. Two of the most notable examples of individual or local ZoPs are the Samaniego Territorio de Paz, first established in 1998, and the Mogotes Municipal Constituent Assembly, established in 1997. Although these two zones are more recent than some others, they are distinguished by their association with REDEPAZ (the Network of Initiatives for Peace and against War), discussed further below.

The Samaniego Territory of Peace came about as a result of a confluence of events. In 1998 the town of Samaniego was holding both mayoral elections and participating in a national voting process by which citizens could register their preference for a negotiated solution to Colombia's armed conflict—the Citizen Mandate for Peace. The newly elected mayor was kidnapped by the ELN (National Liberation Army), one of the main leftist guerilla groups, but the following outcry among the town's residents forced his release. The mayor then invited the citizens to participate in the creation of a ZoP and contacted the national body coordinating local ZoPs, REDEPAZ, for organizational assistance (Rojas 2000, 16).

Like Samaniego, the triggering event for the creation of a ZoP in Mogotes was the invasion of the town by leftist guerrillas, who intended to try the town's mayor on charges of corruption. In response, two hundred people from the town and surrounding area gathered to form a Constituent Assembly and requested that the guerrillas release the mayor so he could be judged by the citizens. The mayor was subsequently dismissed, and the new mayor, José Angel Guadrón, implemented a series of communal reforms suggested by the new Constituent Assembly (Rojas 2000, 13).

The creation of the Constituent Assembly in Mogotes and its plan for peace was considered innovative and successful enough so that this community received a number of national awards and some level of international recognition. In addition, the success of Mogotes inspired REDEPAZ to propose an initiative entitled "100 Municipalities of Peace in Colombia," a project funded by the European Initiative for Democracy and Human Rights. This initiative was designed to expand the number of different types of ZoPs *experiencias* across Colombia as a method for combating the long-running civil war.

Associations and National Movements

In addition to the many local ZoPs, those created both before and after the REDEPAZ initiative, there are areas in Colombia where groups of local zones have banded together to create associations to share information, generate moral support, and address issues on a province-wide basis. One zone, the Asociación de Municipios de Alta Ariari, was established close to the Zona de Distensión and consists of the municipalities of Castillo, Dorado, Guamal, Frente de Oro, Lejana, Cubarral, and San Martin. Another is the Asociación de Municipios de Antioquia Oriente, comprising twenty-three municipalities, including Sonson, San Luis, Carmen, and El Retiro. This association has held meetings with representatives of FARC and the ELN to discuss issues like the release of the governor of Antioquia and safe passage for peasants through roadblocks to get their produce through to markets in Medellín.

At the national level, in addition to REDEPAZ, formed in 1993 to coordinate peace efforts throughout Colombia, a number of institutions exist that promote the development of peace zones. These include Justicia y Paz (Justice and Peace) and the government-sponsored initiative REDPRODPAZ (the National Network of Development and Peace Programs). With the exception of REDPRODPAZ, these regional and national initiatives are institutions that respond to the wishes of localities that want to either establish ZoPs or to request assistance with coordination or other peace-zone-related activities. They help to ensure that the peace-zone movement in Colombia remains rooted in the principles of citizen-based peacemaking.

Peace Implementation: Disarmament, Demobilization, and Reintegration Zones

The creation of DDR zones may not seem at first to be a part of the focus of our original project. However, we observed that many of the characteristics of a typical ZoP created during a conflict also serve to describe these cantonment zones designed for military or "rebel" personnel.

El Salvador's Designated Assembly Zones

While safe havens or conventional ZoPs were not established during the implementation of the Chapultepec peace agreement, some actions taken by the UN monitoring force did constitute something similar to the creation of safe zones for the disarmament and demobilization of Farabundo Martí de Liberación Nacional (FMLN) combatants. These zones, known as designated assembly zones (DAZs), were monitored by UN observers and members of El Salvador's military forces (Fishel and Corr 1998).

The DAZs were established as a part of the Chapultepec Accords, which were signed on January 16, 1992. Fifteen DAZs were established to oversee DDR activities by FMLN forces and were matched by a number of UN observers assigned to monitor the cantonment and the demobilization of a number of the Salvadoran military units.[4]

The DDR component was envisioned as facilitating the complete reintegration of the FMLN into civic life. Successful aspects included the induction of former FMLN members into the new National Police, of which they would make up 20 percent of the total (de Soto and del Castillo 1995). However, the slowness of the land-reform program, designed to redistribute land to former combatants, seriously endangered the DDR scheme. By September 1992 the failure of land reform had caused the FMLN to suspend its implementation of the demobilization agreement.

Although this type of monitoring and designated assembly zones for DDR were not the principal focus of our study of peace zones, it is worth noting the varied uses of safe areas, havens, and zones of peace and development employed to promote peaceful solutions, implement peace agreements, and as we describe below—and discuss in more detail in Chapter 8—support some of the long-term peace-building necessary to ensure the survival of peace agreements.

Aceh: Peace Zones before Peace

The peace zones or disarmament zones in Aceh appear unique in our analysis. Instead of being created during conflict by local communities or as part of the implementation of a comprehensive and concluded peace agreement, the peace zones in Aceh were established as an integral part of the ongoing peace process and were designed to be a confidence-building measure to help ensure the success of that process. Aceh's peace zones were established as part of the Cessation of Hostilities Agreement (COHA) signed at the end of 2002 between the insurgent Gerakan Aceh Merdeka (GAM) and the Indonesian government. COHA, however, was mainly an agreement for a cease fire and a framework for further negotiations; it was much less than a detailed and final peace agreement.

Our studies indicate that in other cases in which the main goals of establishing peace zones have been disarming, demilitarization, and demobilization, a formal cease fire has preceded the establishment of such peace zones. In Aceh, in contrast, the peace zones were to be together with the cease fire, although their main goals were still demilitarization and demobilization. The peace zones in Aceh would, therefore, be a prelude to DDR, for all of these activities were to take place after the establishment of the peace zones but within those zones before they were to occur elsewhere in the province. The COHA contained a whole section on the establishment and maintenance of the peace zones in Aceh. Representatives of GAM, the Indonesian government, and Henri Dunant Centre representatives were appointed to special committees to monitor and administer sanctions should either party break any of the provisions of the agreement (Iyer 2003).

In the period between the signing of the COHA and February 9, 2003, when GAM was supposed to begin a phased disarmament process, seven peace zones were established. They were announced with great fanfare, and in the beginning it seemed they had served the primary purpose for which they had been set up. The violence in the peace zones dramatically decreased. In the meantime, international donors pledged that they would contribute to reconstruction and development in the peace zones first. Thus there was every motivation to get the parties committed to maintaining the peace zones. However, closer to the day when the disarmament of GAM was to begin, violence once again erupted on a large scale. In the following months leading up to May 2003, the cease fire and every other agreement between the parties were broken. Neither side showed any commitment to COHA. The Henri Dunant Centre was attacked and international peace monitors were hounded out of Aceh. COHA had failed, and the peace zones had collapsed.[5]

Zimbabwe/Rhodesia's Assembly Points

The 1979–80 assembly points in what was then Rhodesia are another example of the establishment of safe areas within which armed insurgents could hand in their weapons. The Rhodesian assembly points were small, geographically concentrated areas whose main purpose was the cantonment of insurgent armed forces leading to a cease fire, a political settlement, and final disarmament and demobilization.

Toward the end of 1979 the British government, which at that point continued to be formally responsible for the governance of Rhodesia, chaired peace negotiations between the insurgent Patriotic Front (consisting of the Zimbabwe African National Union and the Zimbabwe African People's Union) and the white-settler-dominated Rhodesian Front, which had actually—if illegally—governed that country since 1964. Independence for Rhodesia was the chief issue, together with the movement of power from the ruling Rhodesian Front to the majority-supported Patriotic Front. Accordingly, the first two phases of talks were devoted to the issue of independence and the transition of political power. The third phase of negotiations focused on the issue of a cease fire. Part of the cease-fire agreement was the decision to create assembly points (Ginifer 1995).

Assembly points (also known as rendezvous points) were to be the concentration points for all guerrilla groups.[6] In the meantime, the security forces would withdraw to their own bases. A period of one week was to be given to the forces to assemble, after which the cease fire would come into effect. Sixteen assembly points were agreed upon (a few of them located in the heart of Rhodesia) and the Patriotic Front forces began to assemble at these locations. At the same time, Rhodesian security forces began to concentrate at forty different bases spread all over the country. The cease fire was to be monitored by the Commonwealth Monitoring Force, which was composed of British, Australian, New Zealand, Kenyan, and Fijian troops (Davidow 1984).

There were, of course, minor skirmishes in the assembly points (the troops were never asked to disarm there), the cease fire was broken on occasion and ZANLA (the Zimbabwe African National Liberation Army—the armed wing of the Zimbabwe African People's Union) seemed to have moved some of its troops into Mozambique. ZANLA fighters were also suspected of burying many of their arms and walking into the assembly points with just a few. However, the establishment of assembly points, the containment of troops within the assembly points, and the declaration of the cease fire all went according to plan. The goal of containment before the cease fire was relatively successful (Renwick 1997).

Thus, in Rhodesia, the success of the assembly points can be evaluated in the light of their being set up as short-term, localized ZoPs with very specific objectives. Most important was the fact that, unlike in Aceh, demilitarization and demobilization were not included in the objectives of the assembly points. In short, the assembly points in Rhodesia, unlike the peace zones in Aceh, were not meant to be a part of the confidence-building measures.

Post-Conflict Peacebuilding and Development

There are very few examples of post-conflict peacebuilding efforts that explicitly call for the creation of a "ZoP." One example revealed by our research was the LZP in El Salvador. We treat this example briefly here (it is covered in depth in Chapter 6). However, we believe that the uniqueness of this zone holds promise for other countries attempting to recover from the ravages of violent and protracted conflict or—perhaps with some modifications—in zones of poverty and crime in advanced industrialized states.

The LZP, centered on the southern coast of El Salvador, was declared in August 1998 by the Foundation for Self-Sufficiency in Central America and a campesino movement, La Coordinadora, which works to address poverty, violence, and other social issues in eighty-six Salvadoran communities. The overarching goal of the LZP was to create a culture of peace throughout the zone. In order to do this, the organizers of the LZP developed a comprehensive program aimed at (1) restoring human rights, (2) promoting peace and indigenous methods of conflict resolution, and (3) fostering the transformation of the organizational culture to reflect the aims of peace and democracy (Chupp 2003, 96).

According to both Mark Chupp and LZP publications, there are two primary peacebuilding activities that take place within the LZP. The first consists mainly of training to create a culture of peace. Using elicitive models of conflict intervention, the culture-of-peace program has held a large number of workshops to provide training in conflict mediation, transformation, and prevention for local community leaders, women's groups, and numerous others (Chupp 2003; Foundation for Self-Sufficiency in Central America 2001).

The second peacebuilding activity of the LZP's program focuses on involvement in a number of direct conflict interventions. The most notable has been a series of interventions with members of two local gangs whose members had been "repatriated" from Los Angeles. These interventions, conducted by Chencho Alas, resulted in an end to violent conflicts between the two gangs, community projects involving gang members, and a redefinition of those members as "youths" instead of "gang members" (Alas 2000).

Economic development activities are also one of the main foci of La Coordinadora's efforts, with the LZP having been created to foster the conditions in which economic and social development can take place. However, it also seems clear that the culture-of-peace program, instituted as a component part of the LZP, has had an effect on the types of development engaged in by La Coordinadora. In some sense the focus on green technologies and sustainable development may be seen as complementary to the grassroots, elicitive focus of the peacebuilding initiative.

Overall, the complementary nature of the peacebuilding initiatives and the economic development initiatives may serve to strengthen each process. A peaceful environment allows for economic development to take place, and the ability of La Coordinadora to provide resources for economic development may assist in bringing parties to the table for peacebuilding and to encourage "buy in" to the culture-of-peace program.

Specialized and Limited Zones

In addition to what might be described as conventional ZoPs, designed to mitigate the conditions of conflict for a particular geographic community or to assist in the implementation of peace or post-conflict reconstruction, there are a number of types of activity that resemble peace zones but have nontraditional foci. Although we cannot review all of these in this chapter, three that are interesting for our purposes include the ideas of *personal* ZoPs, centered on particular persons or categories of persons; *site-specific* ZoPs that seek to protect particular geographic locations rather than the communities that inhabit them; and *limited* ZoPs that have specific goals and a limited duration, just long enough to enable those goals to be achieved.

Personal Zones: UNICEF and Children

The phrase *Children as zones of peace* is over two decades old, and the concept extends to providing for a variety of children's rights and protections. However, these rights assume a special meaning in a war situation. Hence, on our temporal scale we would tend to locate these personal zones as an unusual occurrence in the violent conflict phase.

The idea of children as a conflict-free zone emerged in the 1980s. This concept was first formulated by Nils Thedin of Sweden in a proposal to UNICEF. Even if the idea seemed idealistic in the beginning, it caught on, and the idea of protecting children from harm and providing them with humanitarian assistance became part of negotiations in many bloody conflicts (Bellamy and UNICEF 2000, 42). Subsequently, UNICEF appointed a special commission to investigate the situation of children in regions suffering from protracted armed conflict. As a result of the report published by this special commission in February 2002, UNICEF's Optional Protocol on the involvement of children in armed conflict came into force as an amendment to the UN Convention on the Rights of the Child. The Optional Protocol addresses the issue of forced conscription in two ways:

1. Prohibiting armies and armed opposition forces from involving children under eighteen years of age in armed conflict.
2. Banning the compulsory military recruitment of children under eighteen (Lendon 2001).

The 1996 report and the Optional Protocol have spurred the creation of many programs for dealing with the issues of children in armed conflict, but the ways in which they are translated into action differ from program to program. The ways in which the concept of children as a zone of peace is executed often fall into one of four broad areas: (1) as an abstract or general statement supporting the idea of protecting children during armed conflict; (2) as a part of short-term, temporary ZoPs; (3) as a type of activity or process designed to protect children during conflict; and (4) through the creation of physical sanctuaries for children during conflict.

Two practical examples of such abstract principles arise in Sri Lanka and Nepal. Sri Lanka ratified the Convention on the Rights of the Child in 1991. Initiated by the UNICEF office in Colombo, the idea of children as a zone of peace was discussed with a wide range of actors—the LTTE (Liberation Tamil Tigers of Elam), the Ministry of Defense, religious leaders, teachers, NGOs, and people affected by conflict—and a coalition of NGOs and prominent individuals was formed. This coalition decided that the initiative should be promoted as a concept but not as a program. After five months of consultation a best-practices booklet was created to explain the concept. Published in English, Tamil, and Sinhala, the booklet was widely circulated, and in 1998, when the UN special representative on children in armed conflict visited Sri Lanka, the initiative was launched. Since then, there have been many advocacy campaigns to promote the concept. The objectives of this program are noble, but its activities have been limited largely to advocacy and dissemination of information (Lendon 2001).

Another initiative is Child Workers in Nepal (CWIN). This initiative too has a long list of objectives and dos and don'ts where children and child-related institutions are concerned. Its activities include information dissemination, campaigning for consensus among warring parties, negotiating days of tranquility and promoting peace education in schools. Again, its concept of children as a zone of peace remains somewhat vague, and there have been no concrete actions in pursuit of such a goal (CWIN Nepal).

CWIN's biggest problem is translating the concept of children as a zone of peace into action. Overall, the initiative has had little success in getting the commitment of all or any of the armed actors. Those who support the idea cannot articulate it, for it is still abstract. Many others have not heard of the concept. A best-practices booklet is distributed to parents, children, and teachers who may be interested in the topic, but they are hardly members of the target audience of government officials, military officers, or members of insurgent groups.

While most temporary ZoPs are created for humanitarian aid or for health initiatives—and are discussed below—a few have been designed specifically to benefit children directly, and will be briefly covered here. As with temporary zones, most of these zones have been negotiated by UNICEF or some other international third party.

UNICEF's first experience was in El Salvador in 1985. Extended negotiations with the government and the rebels resulted in securing three days of tranquility—both sides agreeing to a cease fire—during which a campaign was conducted to immunize children. More than twenty thousand health workers immunized 250,000 small children. These three days of tranquility became a regular feature in consecutive months and were repeated every year until the end of the war, six years later. This temporary "zone" benefiting children was replicated in Afghanistan during its civil war; in Uganda during the conflict between the government and the Lords Resistance Army; and in Sudan as a part of Operation Lifeline Sudan.

Two other instances of activities for children, described as zones of peace, have taken place in the Philippines and in Sri Lanka. The general idea behind these activities was to provide for recreation and safe spaces where children could also express their feelings about the conflict and achieve some measure of healing. Workshops in a camp in Davos City in the Philippines have been held to provide such opportunities for children. In addition, UNICEF supports a program in Colombia known as the Return of Happiness program. In this program more than four hundred institutions support and provide access to communications media so that children can voice their ideas directly. Through recreation and play the program helps children express their feelings and analyze events.

The final type of "zone" for children—the creation of sanctuaries—is best exemplified by the Butterfly Peace Garden project in Batticaloa, Sri Lanka. This project, initiated by McMaster University, developed a space where children could indulge in a variety of activities and still be safe. The concept was designed not only to provide a safe place to play, but also to use that play for trauma healing. Approximately fifty children—chosen by their schoolteachers as being in emotional distress—arrive each program day and take part in therapeutic play over a ninety-day period. A bus, known as the Butterfly Bus, picks up the children from the school and takes them to the Butterfly Peace Garden (The Butterfly Peace Garden 2005). The organizers of the project garnered support from all of the warring parties, who allowed the bus to travel free of harassment and security checks (Chase 2000). This helped to make the project a success in terms of the sheer relief and enjoyment it brought to the children of Batticaloa and the surrounding area (Senanayake 2001).

Sacred Sites and Localities

A second type of specialized peace zone stems from efforts by various groups and institutions, both local and international, to protect sites considered to be of significant cultural or religious value. Members of these organizations argue that conflict and civil war take their toll not only on the people in the region but also on religious and spiritual places that have historic value and cannot easily be rebuilt or replaced. One organization advocating establishing this type of zone is the Zones of Peace International Foundation (ZOPIF), located in the state of Washington in the United States. ZOPIF is a nonprofit organization with the long-term vision of an evolving global culture of peace and a strategy of working closely with local people and in partnership with religious and spiritual leaders and with government authorities, all of whom recognize the importance of preserving certain historic sites for the future. ZOPIF has been successful in promoting the creation of protected sites in Bosnia and has proposed creating others in Sri Lanka.

One interesting case is that of the Madhu sanctuary in the Mannar district of northern Sri Lanka. The Catholic church in Madhu had become a place of refuge and sanctuary for Tamils displaced from their villages. For a long time this church was a symbol of safety for the residents of northern Sri Lanka. Interestingly, the church was considered sacred not just by Catholics but by people of all religious faiths because of its historical and spiritual significance. However, during a fresh outbreak of violence in December 1999 the church was attacked and destroyed. The LTTE and the Sri Lankan government blamed each another for this attack. Over forty people who had taken refuge in the church were killed, and many others were injured. This is an interesting but tragic case, where all the warring parties and the local people had an unwritten commitment to maintaining the church in Madhu as a sanctuary and a ZoP. Unfortunately, that unwritten commitment eventually proved inadequate (Rajendran 1999).

Limited Duration or Purpose: Operation Lifeline Sudan

Among the most prominent examples of limited ZoPs were the days of tranquility fostered by the UN-sponsored Operation Lifeline Sudan (discussed in detail in Chapter 9). This program focused on the use of two types of limited peace zones—corridors of peace and days of tranquility—in order to provide humanitarian relief supplies and health services to refugee populations affected by the second civil war in Sudan.

The corridors of peace program was established initially for one month to facilitate the unhindered delivery of relief supplies to needy areas. At first, the United Nations asked for a month-long cease fire, but this was rejected by the Sudan People's Liberation Army (SPLA), which did allow, however, the creation of eight corridors through which humanitarian aid and food relief supplies could move unhindered. This effort was successful enough to be followed by another initiative in 1994 in order to establish new corridors to transport vaccines and medical supplies to children following an outbreak of polio and measles (Galli 2001, 67). These were modeled on earlier efforts designed to create periods of peace in the civil war in El Salvador during which children could be vaccinated against disease (Shankar 1998, 32–33). As such, the aims and goals were limited to ameliorating conditions in Sudan that could lead to famine or outbreaks of disease, especially among children. Although many of these conditions were no doubt exacerbated by the thirty years of civil war between north and south, it does not appear that the goals of these peace corridors and days of tranquility extended beyond an effort to address immediate needs.

Such temporary zones were created essentially by pressure from the United Nations and the international community, but they were not forced on the local political actors. Instead, these groups were persuaded by the focus on purely humanitarian purposes, especially the later effort targeting the health of children, and by the limited scope and duration of the zones themselves. Although some have thought that these zones might prove useful in promoting broader peacemaking activities, the evidence to date is that little if any transference has taken place (Galli 2001; Shankar 1998). Indeed, one critic of Operation Lifeline Sudan has labeled the effort an inadvertent accomplice to the conflict, arguing that both the Sudanese government and the SPLA have manipulated the flow of supplies to enhance their own strategic objectives (Martin 2002). The context of this argument is mostly moral, and it confronts humanitarian aid organizations the world over. Essentially, the choice is often whether to persist in the delivery of aid to relieve suffering in a war zone or to accept that lives will be lost and hope that the burden of caring for the civilian population will force embattled parties to the negotiating table.[7]

Factors Influencing Success or Failure

In looking at each of these different types of ZoPs, it is possible to discern some of the factors that have contributed to their successes—limited in most cases—or to their more obvious failures.

Sponsorship/Ownership and Commitment

In terms of failure, the UN safe zones in Bosnia-Herzegovina are notable for a number of reasons. That they were instituted by international political authorities rather than by the inhabitants of the zones themselves is notable, but the fact that the warring parties to the conflict—especially the Bosnian Serb forces—were uninvolved in the decision to institute the zones seems more than likely to have contributed most to their instability and eventual failure.

The creation of the UN safe havens was an admirable project, brought to fruition by the concern of the international community. However, if there are any lessons to be learned from the failure of the majority of these zones to provide the promised safety, it must be that a ZoP established by outsiders may suffer from either a lack of will on the part of the outside implementer or—just as important—a lack of respect on the part of local combatants. Without these, especially the latter, it is unlikely to survive for long.

By contrast, the peace zones established in the Philippines and in Colombia were largely, if not wholly, driven by grassroots processes, with some logistical, practical, and symbolic support from national and international NGOs or funding organizations. The contrast between this grassroots support and ownership as opposed to the externally mandated zones in Bosnia and some of the examples of limited disarmament zones discussed earlier seems significant in terms of success.

In summary, then, an important difference seems to be the level of "buy in" the organizers of these zones obtained from the various warring parties. It is clear that the lack of buy in in Bosnia was a key factor contributing to the failure of the safe zones there, while the high level of local support obtained in the Philippines and Colombia contributed to success in terms of the ability to create a peace zone and to maintain it over a period of time. While the buy in for these citizen-based zones was never complete, unwavering, or long lasting for all of the peace zones and communities, it was clearly a key element and something all those involved worked hard to achieve and maintain.

Some of the same issues that affected peace zones established in the context of an ongoing, violent conflict also had an impact on the disarmament zones set up during negotiation stages in Aceh, Zimbabwe/Rhodesia, and El Salvador. Most important, the issue of buy in by the affected armed actors was a component that distinguished failure in Aceh from successes in the other two cases. That this was a key factor involves two aspects. The first was the degree of completeness of the peace plan created *before* the setting up of the zones. The second was the degree to which the zones attempted to fulfill their main functions of disarmament and reintegration *before* an overall political settlement was achieved (this will be discussed in greater detail in Chapter 8).

Another aspect of the ownership/sponsorship question that we can point to with some certainty is that localized zones that are established as part of a general peace process require the fully engaged efforts of the parties to the conflict. By contrast, the localized zones created by grassroots efforts and separate from any general peace process only need the buy in of local-level armed actors, such as local guerrilla leaders or army officers, as is often the case in both the Philippines and Colombia. Given that the main goal of zones established as part of a peace process is to affect all the armed forces of each party to the conflict at a national level, this higher level of necessary commitment is not surprising.

In each of our cases of specialized zones with limited goals and duration, the major factor determining success or failure seems once again to be the almost ubiquitous need for buy in by the warring parties. This, in turn, is most likely to be influenced by the notion that these zones do not present a major threat, given their limited purpose or duration. Also influential is the level of local, indigenous participation in the creation of the zone. A third factor that apparently influences buy in by armed actors—exemplified in the case of the Butterfly Garden in Sri Lanka and some of the zones centered on religious sites—seems to be the degree to which local initiatives address local needs and values that are also held by the parties to the conflict. With this point in mind, however, it is difficult to say why there have been different levels of success attending efforts to immunize children in El Salvador compared with similar efforts in Sudan. While one can clearly say that on some level Operation Lifeline Sudan has been a success, later efforts have at times been blocked by both government and insurgent forces. We are unable to determine why either party to this conflict would see a benefit in stopping or redirecting this aid, except for the possibility that each side might want the aid to benefit its own military forces rather than the civilian population.

Goals and Duration

One major difference between zones that appear successful and those that are clear failures is in their overarching goals and, linked to this, the duration that each seeks to achieve. In terms of our study's primary focus on peace zones set up during the violent stages of a conflict, it appears that the most successful zones are those that seek to address not only problems of external violence, but also many of the social problems that nurture violent conditions, such as corruption, cultures of violence, and lack of economic or educational opportunity. ZoPs in the Philippines and Colombia are notable for not only addressing the long-running civil conflicts but also dealing with some of the issues—for example, of corruption—that gave birth to those conflicts and that, at times, have invited intervention from armed actors. This focus on the larger social structure and its connection to violence is best exemplified by the LZP in El Salvador, where the link between socioeconomic well-being and freedom from violence is made clear and explicit.

These examples involve ZoPs that are designed to endure for some considerable time with the hope that the existing situation—consisting of either civil conflict or grinding poverty and crime—will be ameliorated and eventually corrected. To some extent we can say that some of the examples we have examined have been successful to some degree, certainly so in terms of their ability to endure as ZoPs. Moreover, when we compare such examples to the UN safe havens in Bosnia, we can see some interesting comparisons. While many examples of peace zones and communities from the Philippines and Colombia were designed to address a host of problems, it is clear that the UN safe havens in Bosnia were designed to address only the issue of sanctuary from the civil conflict. One similarity between the two was the open-ended nature of their creation. Both are examples of zones that had no expiration date; they would exist for as long as the conflict existed. However, while the ZoPs in the Philippines and Colombia attempted to empower their constituents by addressing a large number of issues, the UN safe havens were barely able to maintain security, much less address issues of empowerment or psychological well-being.

On the other hand, peace zones that were set up as part of peace processes with the limited aim of aiding disarmament, or which had other limited and specific goals during ongoing violence, also involved limited duration—and in many cases can be viewed as successful. The DDR zones in El Salvador and Zimbabwe/Rhodesia sought to provide a safe space for the limited goal of concentrating combatants prior to disarming them and beginning to prepare them to return to civil society. They had definite start dates and were designed to be limited in duration (usually existing for between six months and two years). And yet there is the hardly encouraging example of the peace zones in Aceh, which were a poorly designed hybrid of a conventional ZoP and a DDR zone, with an unspecified number of goals—many of them lofty—plus an extended duration time.

One conclusion seems to be that—with the possible exclusion of the Butterfly Garden in Sri Lanka—there is a direct connection between the range of goals for a ZoP (limited or expanded) and the optimum duration for that ZoP (short term or long term). Practically speaking, one should try to match the goals with the preferred duration when attempting to create a peace zone, bearing in mind that it may prove more difficult to establish a limited zone over a long period of time or to promulgate expanded goals for a zone whose duration is by its nature short—such as days of tranquility for health programs or safe zones for disarmament.

Conclusion

Returning to our initial argument that ZoPs can be seen as one attempt to mitigate violence in an ongoing conflict or to assist in the process of ending a conflict, one can clearly see that the cases mentioned above have had varying degrees of success. Some have managed to mitigate the effects of the conflict over a short period, while others have had a longer effect.

However, it is also apparent that many of these zones have aimed to achieve more than just withdrawal from or mitigation of existing conflicts. Some of the more intensive efforts in places like Colombia, the Philippines, and Aceh attempted to create social change or social justice and to expand the principles of positive peace beyond their limited borders. It is in connection to these issues that we believe another set of questions becomes important for study—questions of who initiated the zone, who participated in its creation and maintenance, and what governance structures and leaders existed in these zones.

In addition, we conclude that these factors of creation, structure, and direction play different roles depending on the temporal context of a ZoP. It seems clear that in peace zones during violent and destructive stages of conflict, a high level of participation and ownership is required by the local population, while it appears relatively less important to have considerable government support or direction. In fact, government involvement may prove detrimental to the zone's goal of maintaining neutrality among warring parties. The situation for disarmament zones is quite different, with such initiatives requiring active governmental and/or insurgent support, and possibly less support from local populations. Finally, recalling our single example of a post-conflict peace zone, it appears that a coalition of governmental and local actors is required to make the zone viable and allow it to carry out its activities successfully.

Hence, in beginning to answer questions about what makes for a successful peace zone or community, we would propose a combination of factors such as the ownership, leadership, and goals of a peace zone, combined with the temporal position of that zone in relation to conflict and peace processes. Temporal position helps to determine the extent to which one factor might be more important than others in determining likelihood of success, even though we recognize that each situation is likely to be somewhat different from others.

We believe that the idea of a ZoP where ordinary people can stand up against the violence that affects their lives is an idea whose time has come. From the earliest days of searching for sanctuary, people have understood and yearned for places where they might be safe from violence. It is to be hoped that our analysis of these zones can assist in creating a sense of how that sanctuary might be established in many places and even in the most unpromising circumstances.

Notes

[1] For more details on UN safe havens, see Chapter 7 herein.

[2] For more details on the Philippine ZoPs, see Chapter 3 herein.

[3] For more details on the Colombian experience, see Chapter 4 herein.

[4] All references to the Chapultepec Accords are to the English version available on the www.usip.org website.

[5] For more details on peace zones in Aceh, see Chapter 8 herein.

[6] The rendezvous points were temporary places; the assembly points were permanent ones.

[7] For more details on Operation Lifeline Sudan and the debate among humanitarian aid organizations, see Chapter 9 herein.

Works Cited

Alas, Chencho. 2000. The road to hope. In *Foundation for Self-Sufficiency in Central America Newsletter* (Fall/Winter). Available online.

Arguillas, Carolyn O. 1999. Enlarging spaces and strengthening voices for peace. In *Compromising on autonomy: Mindanao in transition*, ed. M. Stankovitch. London: Conciliation Resources.

Bellamy, Carol, and UNICEF. 2000. *The state of the world's children 2000*. New York: UNICEF.

The Butterfly Peace Garden. 2005. The Butterfly Peace Garden Media Unit. Available online.

Chase, Rob. 2000. Healing and reconciliation for war-affected children and communities: Learning from the Butterfly Garden of Sri Lanka's Eastern Province. Available online.

Chupp, Mark. 2003. Creating a culture of peace in postwar El Salvador. In *Positive approaches in peacebuilding: A resource for innovators*, ed. C. Sampson, M. Abu-Nimer, and C. Liebler. Washington, DC: Pact Publications.

CWIN Nepal. "Children Are Zones of Peace." Available online.

Davidow, Jeffrey. 1984. *A peace in Southern Africa: The Lancaster House Conference on Rhodesia, 1979.* Boulder, CO: Westview Press.

de Soto, Alvaro, and Graciana del Castillo. 1995. Implementation of comprehensive peace agreements: Staying the course in El Salvador. *Global Governance: A Review of Multilateralism* 1 (2): 189–203.

Elusfa, Romy. 2004. Tulunan folks celebrate 14th year of "Peace Zone." *Mindanews 2004.*

Fishel, Kimbra L., and Edwin G. Corr. 1998. UN peace operations in El Salvador. In *The savage wars of peace: Toward a new paradigm of peace operations,* ed. J. T. Fishel. Boulder, CO.: Westview Press.

Foundation for Self-Sufficiency in Central America. 2001. *Culture of peace update* by Estela Hernández. Available online.

Galli, Guido. 2001. Humanitarian cease-fires in contemporary armed conflicts: Potentially effective tools for peacebuilding. Master's thesis, University of York, York.

Garcia, Edmundo. 1989. Conflict resolution in the Philippines: The quest for peace in a period of democratic transition. *Journal of Peace Research* 20 (1): 59–69.

———. 1997. Filipino zones of peace. *Peace Review* 9 (2): 221–24.

Ginifer, Jeremy. 1995. *Managing arms in peace processes: Rhodesia/Zimbabwe.* New York: United Nations.

Iyer, Pushpa. 2003. Peace zones in Aceh: A prelude to demilitarisation. Research Paper No. 3. ICAR (April). Available online.

Lendon, Sarah. 2001. Sri Lanka: Children as zones of peace. UNICEF-Australia.

Martin, Randolph. 2002. Sudan's perfect war. *Foreign Affairs* 81 (2). Available online.

Mitchell, Christopher, and Susan Allen Nan. 1997. Local peace zones as institutionalized conflict. *Peace Review* 9 (2): 159–62.

Rajendran, S. 1999. Dozens of Sri Lankan refugees killed in artillary attack on church. *WSWS News* (December 10).

Renwick, Robin. 1997. *Unconventional diplomacy in Southern Africa.* New York: St. Martin's Press.

Rojas, Catalina. 2000. The People's Peace Process in Columbia: A preliminary review of peace zones in Mogotes, Samaniego, and San Pablo. Arlington, VA: ICAR.

Senanayake, Renuka. 2001. Sri Lanka: "Peace Garden" for children in war zone. *World News—Inter Press Service.*

Shankar, Ram Anand. 1998. Analyzing health initiatives as bridges towards peace during complex humanitarian initiatives and the roles of actors and economic aid in making these bridges sustainable. Doctoral diss., Dalhousie University, Halifax, Nova Scotia.

3

PEACE ZONES
IN THE PHILIPPINES

Kevin Avruch and Roberto S. Jose

Introduction:
Defining Filipino Peace Zones

Zones of peace in the Philippines—or peace zones, as they are known there—are among the first examples of the phenomenon in general and, as predominantly "bottom up" expressions of local activism and empowerment, have provided a model for similar undertakings in other countries. Officially, they date back to the declaration of a Zone of Peace, Freedom, and Neutrality (ZOPFAN) in Naga City in September 1988, closely followed by declarations of peace zones in Sagada (November 1988), Tabuk (April 1989), Bituan (November 1989), and Cantomanyog (February 1990). Each zone was triggered by different events, and each took its own form, faced different obstacles, and enjoyed varying degrees of success in implementing its goals (Jolob 2001). However, they share many features, and thus it is possible to say that a peace zone is defined by the following six characteristics:

1. A Peace Zone is a geographical area within which war and any other forms of armed hostility may no longer be waged, and where peacebuilding programs will address roots and manifestations of conflict in the community.
2. A Peace Zone is declared by an agglomeration of groups and concerned citizens in the community which organizes itself as a constituency for the peacebuilding agenda.
3. A Peace Zone ranges in size from the area covered by a "purok" or neighborhood block (kapitbahayan) to a province.

4. A Peace Zone is declared and sustained by citizens with a firm conviction rejecting war and warmaking as a tool in political contest, and upholding peacebuilding as the most desirable option for enhancing human and civil rights and recreating a more humane social order.

5. A Peace Zone's citizens identify the manifestations of violence in their community, which are then the targets of peacebuilding actions within the Zone.

6. A Peace Zone is reinforced by the community's sustained, creative expressions of commitment to peacebuilding. On the national level, this means support for national peace efforts. On the local level, this means peace and justice programs within the Peace Zone, development programs which are otherwise obstructed by armed conflict, and community peace symbols and rituals. This would also entail openness to linkage with adjoining Peace Zones. (Garcia and Hernández 1989, 226–27)

One is struck by how normative, prescriptive, even idealistic, this definition is. For example, no peace zone anywhere in the Philippines has ever covered an entire province—except in theory. Nevertheless, the definition contains not only the core component of a ZoP anywhere, namely, the rejection of armed hostility within a circumscribed area (a local cease fire), but it also suggests the characteristics that help us understand the dynamics of Filipino peace zones more generally. These characteristics include the following:

1. Peace zones are multi-sectoral, that is, they combine citizens from and with a variety of local peoples' organizations and supra-local organizations—NGOs and other peace constituencies (including the church at both local and supra-local levels).

2. Although they recognize relations to regional and national level organizations and constituencies, and accept support from them (more on this below), they are essentially "bottom up" projects—locally organized, locally driven, and locally sustained. The word *community* is key.

3. Although they arise to address first and foremost the problem of local, direct violence, they are conceived more broadly, not only eventually to connect their own efforts to a larger, national peacebuilding process, but also initially to address issues of social justice, human rights, political corruption, and "right living" within their own communities—for example, by banning the sale and consumption of alcohol within the peace zone (as

in Tulunan), or by promoting respect for indigenous culture and practices (as in Tabuk).

Background and Sources of Filipino Peace Zones

Although officially established in 1988, Filipino peace zones must be understood within the context of the People Power movement that brought down Ferdinand Marcos's dictatorship by peaceful means two years earlier (Garcia 1997). This was accomplished by ongoing processes of consciously nonviolent political action predating the EDSA People Power Revolution (Blume 1993) and by the strength and resilience of Filipino civil society. This especially emanated from within the church, but also from universities, politically centrist "business councils," and other NGOs that date back to the 1950s and 1960s (Jolob 2001).[1]

Although many individuals and groups deemed radical were driven underground when martial law was declared in September 1972, other groups proliferated as anti-Marcos and anti–martial law social protest increased. The impetus for the first peace zones came directly from the political energy generated by the EDSA revolution, the sense of empowerment felt when the people banded together with the military to topple the regime, and the democratic space subsequently opened up under Marcos's successor, Corazon Aquino. Of course, the immediate impetus came from the tragic fact that violence, mostly from conflict among the Philippine government and its armed forces, the Armed Forces of the Philippines (AFP) and the constabulary or national police, and the communist New Peoples Army (NPA) did not abate with Marcos's fall. In fact, it intensified after the Communist Party of the Philippines-National Democratic Front (CPP-NDF—the political arm of the NPA) broke off peace talks with the government after police and marines fired on a crowd of protesters heading toward the Presidential Palace in Manila, killing thirteen and injuring hundreds. This act took place in January 1987, barely a year after the new administration had taken office on a wave of popular enthusiasm and hope, having promised sweeping reforms, especially agrarian ones, the immediate object of the crowd's protest.

In the wake of the breakdown of talks, a newly formed movement, the Coalition for Peace (CfP), comprising a network of NGOs, community groups, academicians, religious leaders, and other activist individuals, attempted to act as an intermediary between Aquino's government and the National Democratic Front-New Peoples Army in order to get all sides back to the negotiating table. But the CfP could not act as a third party as effectively as it wished. Although as the center of a network it was well connected, the CfP was perceived to lack a wide constituency base and so its mandate to act as a third party was questioned by both sides. Therefore, the CfP decided to reorient its peace efforts toward what it called direct peace action. This included peace education, mass campaigns, aid for populations displaced by violence, and explicit support for the nascent peace zones—"concrete community forms of action"—that were already making their appearance.[2] The specific community initiative that may have inspired the CfP to draft parameters for a peace zone occurred in 1986 in Hungduan, Ifugao:

> One day the inhabitants of Hungduan in the Philippines did a brave thing. They succeeded in getting the guerrilla New People's [sic] Army to withdraw from the locality. The next thing the municipality did was prevent the army from setting up a detachment in the town. From this experience, the Coalition for Peace developed the concept of Peace Zones. It [sic] would be established by local communities wanting to protect their residents from the violence of armed conflict. Communities would declare those areas off-limits to armed operations by both sides of the conflict. The idea sparked a new impetus for peace-building in the country.[3]

Inspired by this, the CfP proceeded to draft guidelines for peace zones, working with Hearts of Peace, a peoples' organization based in Naga City and Camarines sur Province. In September 1988 the first zone was declared in Naga City as part of a cease fire during the annual feast of Nuestra Senora de Penafrancia. It was officially called the Zone of Peace, Freedom and Neutrality (ZOPFAN). Less than two months later, in November 1988, a second zone was declared in the Municipality of Sagada, Mountain Province. In what some have called the first wave or the pioneer stage in this movement, between 1988 and 1991, an additional seven zones were declared. The nine pioneer zones were Naga (September 1988); Sagada (November 1988); Tabuk (April 1989); Bituan (November 1989); Cantomanyog (February 1990); New Alimondian (February 1990 in Bituan and February 1992 on return of displaced residents to New Alimondian); Nabundasan (December 1990); Miatuab (February 1991); and Tinoc (May 1991).[4]

We now describe some of these early zones in greater detail, and then move on to consider the more numerous zones set up in the second wave, from roughly 2000 to 2004.[5] Many of the eighty-two second wave zones are in the south, in Mindanao, in response to the violence occurring between the AFP and armed Muslim groups, particularly the Moro Islamic Liberation Front (MILF).

The First Wave (1988–91): Selected Case Studies

Although the peace zone in Naga City was the first one named, it was in some ways uncharacteristic. First, compared to other places, Naga was not at the time an active war zone; it was, in fact, already viewed as somewhat neutral territory by combatants, and a festival cease fire was already (by tradition) in place. Second, it was declared a peace zone by Hearts of Peace, the CfP, and the city's mayor, but it did not appear to enjoy widespread support among the city's residents, among whom it was viewed as a "top down" endeavor. Nevertheless, it did receive international attention, and hence it became a source of inspiration for similar endeavors elsewhere. In contrast, the declaration of Naga as a peace zone was not formally accepted by the local army or constabulary commanders.[6] In many ways the peace zones declared in Sagada and Cantomanyog, among others, were much closer to the spirit of the endeavor, especially as they were community-focused and "bottom up" projects.

Sagada, Mt. Province

In contrast to Naga City, Sagada was very much in a zone of active combat and violence between the AFP and the NPA. The original proposal, issued November 15, 1988, from "the people of Sagada" to both the AFP and the NPA, called for a cease fire and a complete demilitarization of their territory:

> On November 11, 1988, Benito Tumapang, Jr., a 12-year-old pupil at the Sagada Central School became the unfortunate victim of a war between your contending forces. He got shot and died so young, not even knowing what the war was all about. He is but one among others, like 4-year-old Hardy Bagni, Jr. and 17-year-old student Kenneth Bayang, who died October 28, 1988 after having been shot by drunken soldiers of the 50th Infantry Division. Previously there have also been incidents involving the New People's [sic] Army that caused consternation among the Sagada people. (Santos 2005, 84)

What followed was the twelve-point delineation of the proposed Sagada Peace Zone, including the banning of all "operations, patrols, checkpoints and meetings" within the "entire municipality of Sagada," as well as asking for sanctuary for the wounded, the banning of alcohol, and respect for tribal customs. The resolution was signed by twenty-seven municipal leaders, representing the church, civil society, and the tribal elders' council. But it was not just the local elite who demanded action. Women were particularly active in the community and in calling for a cease fire and an end to violence. "Residents held rallies in the municipal building area. . . . Local peace leaders sent letters to government leaders, and visited Camp Aguinaldo [the headquarters of the Department of National Defense in Quezon City] to gain governmental support for the Peace Zone. . . . The national government formally recognized Sagada as a Peace Zone in 1989" (Sta. Maria 2000, 51).

Sagada was the home of an indigenous Kankana-ey–speaking Igorot community with strong traditions of kinship, community, and an articulated code of righteous and proper living (*inayan*). It possessed a long history of effective internal conflict management and community action, even supporting neighboring Kalingas (another indigenous ethnic group) in their opposition to the World Bank–sponsored Chico Dam project. Earlier, it had refused to organize government-sponsored (anti-guerrilla) Civilian Armed Forces Geographical Units, and their predecessors, the Civilian Home Defense Units (Blume 1993, 159–61). In 1993, under President Fidel Ramos, who had supported the Sagada Peace Zone earlier as secretary of defense, the Sagada zone was among seven Philippine peace zones awarded special development area (SDA) funds, entitling it to 5 million pesos.

Sitio Cantomanyog, Candonia, Negros Occidental

Like Sagada, the village of Cantomanyog was a center of fierce fighting between the AFP and the NPA in the late 1980s, particularly in the wake of Operation Thunderbolt (April-October, 1989) launched against the NPA with the objective of flushing the guerrillas from their mountain encampments through heavily armed AFP incursions and heavy bombardments. Due to these bombardments, approximately thirty-five thousand residents of the region—more than eleven thousand from Candoni Municipality—were displaced and put into evacuation centers where food shortages and health problems were common. Upon returning to their homes after defying military orders—the only group to do so—they found their crops and belongings burned and their livestock slaughtered or missing (Blume 1993; Briones 2000). Residents of Cantomanyog believe that their village was spared the worst of the experiences at evacuation centers, where hundreds from other localities died of malnutrition and disease. "Miraculously, not a single person from Cantomanyog died. The residents attributed this 'miracle' to divine intervention" (Briones 2000, 87–88).

The divine intervention, residents believed, was the result of the very strong role played since the 1970s by the community's local basic ecclesiastical community (BEC) or *Gagmay'ng Kristohanong Katilingban* (GKK) in the local Kinaray-a language. The BEC is in some sense separate from or parallel to the more hierarchical and inclusive national-level organization of the church in the Philippines. It is truly a grassroots phenomenon, emphasizing and built upon the local community rather than the traditional diocesan notion of a geographical territory. Although local clergy was deeply involved with the BECs (and this was true for Cantomanyog, especially with its formation), much of the energy for their sustainability came from the active involvement of the laity. The BEC in Cantomanyog was very strong. It not only sustained the residents when they were displaced, but it also helped them respond when, after returning to their ravaged village vowing never to be moved again, further violence was visited upon them. Like residents of Sagada, those of Cantomanyog refused to participate in AFP-sponsored "defense" (militia) groups. They were to pay a price for this.

The triggering event was the murder in October 1989 of a resident, probably by local militia, whose brother was suspected to be a member of NPA, and a rumor spread that more than a dozen others were similarly targeted. At the same time, unknown armed men conspicuously visited the village almost nightly. In this tense and dangerous atmosphere residents (once again women played a large role here) convened and invited the respected village priest to help them deal with the situation. The idea of declaring a peace zone was discussed for weeks and was actually declared the day after Christmas, though the zone was not made public (presented to the authorities) until February 1990. At that time, as part of a week-long "peace caravan," the zone's declaration was rebuffed by military authorities, who halted the peace march as well. The villagers and other marchers (along with parish priests and a respected bishop) held a Mass elsewhere, and after the Mass the declaration of the Cantomanyog Peace Zone was read aloud in public.

But the declaration did not win support from the AFP, which, through statements of various commanders to headquarters, expressed doubts that the peace zone was truly a community-driven initiative and instead suspected its leadership of hidden motives, including support for the NPA (Santos 2005). However, the community persevered. It declared itself, first of all, free from armed men and their violence. Despite the lack of support or recognition from the local military authorities, in 1995 Cantomanyog, like Sagada, was awarded SDA status, along with the 5 million pesos that accompanied this status (Lee 2000). Along with strong leadership, clerical and lay, Briones (2000) attributes the success of the Cantomanyog Peace Zone in the face of opposition to the organizing role played by the BEC in empowering a strong tradition of community-based and faith-based decision-making.

Tulunan (Barangay Bituan), North Cotobato, Mindanao

Like the residents of Cantomanyog, those of Tulunan (Barangay Bituan) suffered displacement as result of the violence around them. Even before conflict between the NPA and the AFP, the region was subject to ongoing violence (especially violence stemming from the indigenous notion of blood vengeance or *rido*) between Southern Christian migrants, longstanding Muslim residents, and indigenous Lumad.[7] Many targeted victims were church workers. In fact, the town of Tulunan suffered tremendous violence during the Marcos regime, as it was the site of predatory vigilante groups named Tadtad (from the verb meaning "to chop into smaller pieces"). After the seventh forced evacuation of the *barangays*, members of three villages met and, with the support of local parish priests, declared a Zone of Life in North Cotobato in November 1989. They subsequently passed a resolution declaring Bituan a peace zone (February 27, 1990) and calling on all armed actors—AFP, NPA, and local militias—to respect the zone, which was declared arms and alcohol free (Blume 1993, 154–56).[8] The zone was supported by the church and the North Cotobato governor and its member of Congress. After a period when the zone was respected, on April 14, 1990 (called Black Saturday locally), the NPA launched an attack on the AFP stationed near the *barangay* of Bituan, killing three soldiers and burning their corpses. The NPA announced that this was not meant to "jeopardize" the peace zone. Nevertheless, the AFP strongly counterattacked and even instituted a food blockade of Bituan. This was lifted through the good offices of the church and the national-level (civilian) Office of the Peace Commission. The military did not support the zone—which complicated the efforts of the Office of the Peace Commission to represent the community's interests fully, since it had to maintain good relations with the AFP—and there were serious doubts raised on all sides about its viability. However, residents resolved never to evacuate again and to continue their peace efforts. Once again, despite considerable instability, in 1993, under President Ramos, the Tulunan Peace Zone was awarded SDA status and the considerable funds—20 million pesos in total, 5 million for each of the four zones making up the Consolidated Peace Zone of Tulunan—that accompanied this award.

Tabuk, Kalinga Apayo (Mountain Province)

In Tabuk, Kalinga, a peace zone arose from, and was organically connected to, the traditional modes of conflict management and resolution among the Kalinga people, that is, the *bodong,* or indigenous peace-pact system. Tabuk, in the Central Cordillera region, was situated in the heart of the battle between the AFP and NPA in Northern Luzon, "one of the most highly militarized and least developed areas in the Philippines" (Blume 1993, 154). For some, the triggering event went back to 1981, when a respected local elder was killed by government troops for leading the opposition against the construction of the World Bank–funded Chico Dam project. This project would have submerged ancestral burial grounds and land used by various indigenous communities along a major tributary that crossed different provinces. In the end, protest by the Kalinga and others in other provinces effectively halted construction and led to the World Bank abandoning the project. The murder of the elder as well as the success in halting the dam project were remembered when, in April 1989, the Kalinga Bodong Council (a council of elders) declared Tabuk to be a *Matago-an* (zone of life)—a place of peace, refuge, and security. It also signified a place where the culture and identity of the people could be protected not only from direct violence but also—as the formal declaration of the zone on April 14–15, 1989, asserts—from "the intrusion of outside influences and alien cultures and lifeways" (in Santos 2005, 102).

The Zone of Life was organized according to the parameters of the traditional *bodong,* guided by the *pagtas* (the norms and bylaws of the peace-pact system) and overseen by the *pangat* (customary guardians of the peace pact) and *mansasakusak* (elders acting as mediators or arbitrators, drawn from the Kalinga Bodong Council). The Kalinga Zone of Life qualifies as a peace zone, but it is distinct in its cultural form and is certainly seen by its residents as something more—part of a larger struggle, using traditional, indigenous cultural resources for conflict management and resolution, to maintain their cultural integrity and perhaps even their survival.

Special Development Areas

Soon after becoming president in 1992, Fidel Ramos created the National Unification Commission, charged with consulting different sectors of Filipino society and making contact with various rebel groups on such matters as amnesty in order to further the peace process. By July 1993 the National Unification Commission issued a large report that included "Six Paths to Peace," concrete actions or projects that might be undertaken by the government in pursuit of lasting peace. The six-paths concept became part of Ramos's Comprehensive Peace Policy and was carried forward in succeeding administrations.

Meanwhile, even before the report was formally issued, in May 1993 Senator Rodolfo G. Biazon sponsored a resolution passed by the Senate urging that seven already declared and established peace zones be recognized as SDAs. President Ramos, attaching the SDA notion to the Comprehensive Peace Plan, agreed. This had the effect of legitimizing the entire notion of a peace zone, according special status to the seven pioneer zones so named, and entitling each of the seven to 5 million pesos for community development under the National Program for Unification and Development Council (now under the Office of the Presidential Adviser for the Peace Process). The seven peace zones named SDAs were Sagada (Mountain Province); Bangilo (Malibcong, Abra); Cantomanyog (Candonia, Negros Occidental); and the four zones in the Tulunan Municipality of North Cotobato.

On the one hand, of course, such legitimation of peace zones from the presidential level of government was a welcome development, and the level of fiscal support that came with the recognition could only be dreamed of by other zones of peace struggling merely to survive in other places and conflicts. But the linkage of SDA status with peace zones proved a mixed blessing.

First, it was not always clear to the other pioneering peace zones why those particular seven were chosen. Second, recognition at the presidential level did not guarantee support by the military, especially the local units of the AFP (as in the case of Cantomanyog). In other cases—Tulunan's, for instance—such large governmental support was resented by the NPA, which did not want to see the government succeed in winning over the people in this way. Indeed, because the funds were disbursed at first by the National Program for Unification and Development Council, which also supported "rebel returnee" programs, many residents of the zones feared it would be interpreted by the NPA as part of the government's counterinsurgency campaign.[9] In some cases local or regional governmental support was not as effective as it could have been. Finally, the influx of such large amounts of funds led to rivalries within communities, or between communities and local/regional governments, leading to instability, waste, and, in the end, community disempowerment—the exact opposite of what successful peace zones had begun to accomplish.[10]

Lee analyzed the effects of SDA status and funding in two zones, Tulunan and Cantomanyog, and found strikingly different results. In Tulunan the communities were not internally well organized from the start, and a local parish priest (who believed the church had played the predominant role in founding the zone and thus deserved a pre-eminent role in determining the uses to which the funds were put) joined forces with local government officials and others in the zone to take control and marginalize other local activists. As a result of this internal conflict, Lee writes, "equipment and projects became ill-maintained and the money was unproductively wasted" (Lee 2000, 117). More important, the peace zone's sense of autonomy and self-reliance was diminished, and morale declined.

In Cantomanyog, by contrast, the local church, in the form of the BEC, worked closely with the community. Moreover, from the start the community itself enjoyed very strong internal organizational structures and decision-making processes, comprising monthly *asemblea* meetings where important matters were discussed, as well as weekly Bible study and reflection sessions *(panimbahon)*, wherein community voices could be heard and common problems raised and addressed. Lee notes that Cantomanyog also was fortunate in its external relations and power centers, in that the provincial governor, the conduit for the funding, "has seen to it that there is transparency and full cooperation in the actions and operations of the provincial government" (Lee 2000, 120). Indeed, in the face of strong church, NGO, and local community solidarity, the NPA (and later the People's Revolutionary Army), in contrast to the situation in Tulunan, "did not enter the area nor attempt to influence the implementation of the SDA projects in any manner" (Lee 2000, 120).[11] The residents of Cantomanyog kept control of the funds, community solidarity was enhanced, and the people were further empowered.

In sum, the awarding of SDA status was seen by many to be an important legitimation of the peace-zone concept by the highest civil authority in the land, but it did not succeed in protecting all the zones (even the ones declared to be SDAs) from further violence, and it came with other drawbacks. For those zones not awarded SDA status, the SDA program was detrimental. It was seen by some to take away "the integrity and independence of the peace zones," especially when it was done "in a high profile manner and . . . used for propaganda purposes by the government." In other cases (as in Tulunan), after the pesos were disbursed, "the first thing to collapse was community unity" (Santos 2005, 23).

The Second Wave (2000–2005)

After the first wave of peace zones, what Santos called "the long interregnum stage from 1991 to 2000" occurred, when perhaps an additional nine zones were established. Santos saw this middle stage as a sort of "stalemate" in the peace-zone movement along with a general loss of momentum in the larger Filipino peace process. But after 2000, as the main arena of armed conflict shifted southward and the primary armed actors changed from the AFP and the NPA to the AFP and the MILF (from communist insurgents to Muslim secessionists), the number (and variety) of peace zones soared to over eighty.[12] Then too, the conflict has broadened dimensionally (if not quite along "civilizational" lines) to encompass the main communal division separating entire communities of residents in the south, namely Christians (mostly settlers and migrants from the 1930s on), from (long-resident) Muslims.[13] Because of this, much peacebuilding in the south, even as it addresses the problem of direct violence and incursions by armed actors, is focused also on concerns with inter-communal harmony and peaceful coexistence, concerns taken up and reflected by many (though not all) of the peace zones there (e.g., Mercado et al. 2003).[14]

The many peace zones created after 2000, especially in the south, are characterized by their diversity and the range of their goals or aims. This diversity is underlined first by the number of different terms used by residents to name them: *spaces for peace* in Pikit, North Cotobato; *sanctuaries for peace* in Central Mindanao; *light of peace*, the alliance of peace zones in Mindanao; and such lesser used terms as *zone of peace, freedom, and development* or *buffer zone*.[15] The range of goals or aims usually revolves around the difference between those zones that simply want the minimal or core component of all the zones—to make the village or hamlet off limits to armed conflict (characteristics of the zones in Pikit) and those zones whose goals are more inclusive (such as Nalapaan), either embracing programs of local development, education, agrarian reform and health, or lesser, focused goals such as banning alcohol. Santos notes, "One difference between SOPs [sanctuaries for peace] and SFPs [spaces for peace] is the former's provision of no AFP or MILF presence such as camps, detachments or foot patrols inside the area and surrounding areas" (2005, 8); SFPs do not make this demand. In 2005 there were fifty-six communities (more than two thousand households) in the spaces-for-peace program.

Although the demand that all armed conflict cease within the zone is understood to be the minimal requirement in all the zones, the second-wave zones, especially in Mindanao, revealed another perhaps implicit but crucial necessity: that the zones be established by the communities involved as a result of local activism and effort. Santos reports some "distortions" of the peace-zone movement when, under President Estrada, some twenty towns and one city in Central Mindanao were unilaterally declared to be peace zones—ironically, during the height of the April-July 2000 offensive against the MILF by the government. These were, in fact, areas taken over by the AFP after intense combat with the MILF. They were thus "pacified" (to use military vernacular), but they were hardly "peaceful." At least one newspaper referred to the declaration of captured MILF camps as zones of peace as making a parody of the whole idea of peace zones (Santos 2005, 9).[16]

Analysis

In the foregoing discussion we have tried first and foremost to be descriptive of peace zones' major features and development, but we could not hope to do justice to the entire range of their diversity, especially across the time and physical space of the long and violent conflict in the country. We have noted some essential commonalities—the demand for an end to armed violence within the zone, or negative peace—and some differences—how much beyond the minimal demand selected peace zones hope to go toward what Galtung referred to as "positive peace" (1969). We have also noted that the movement stemmed from a basis in Filipino civil society that dated back to the 1950s and 1960s and took its impetus from the sense of empowerment experienced by the Filipino people as a result of the successful EDSA revolution that overthrew the Marcos dictatorship. In this section we briefly reflect on some other findings that have emerged from our descriptions.

First, one can almost always point to "triggers" that involve some specific act or an accumulation of acts of violence, murder, assassination, or pillage that zones refer to in their formal declarations (many of which are collected in Santos 2005). In many cases residents of zones have experienced displacement as a community and seek to return, also as a community, to their former homes and villages. But displacement by itself tells us very little. Some communities disintegrate under it, while some (like Cantomanyog) find new solidarity in its residents' desire to reestablish themselves.

Successful peace zones often derive their internal cohesion or solidarity from their religious faith—particularly if the faith is instantiated in local institutions like the BECs. But once again, the Filipino church (though generally very supportive of peace zones) can play a negative role as well, as happened in Tulunan when it was awarded SDA status. Another source of local cohesion, available to Filipino indigenous communities particularly, is the resource of local tradition and culture, as in Tabuk or Sagada, that provides indigenous and time-tested (and emotionally satisfying) modes of decision-making and conflict management and resolution—what Avruch (1998) has referred to as the internal resources of "ethnoconflict theory and ethnopraxis."[17] In all matters relating to internal cohesion, leadership is crucial. Leadership can be vested in an individual (for example, the mayor or parish priest), but we more often find it diffused in councils of elders, members of BECs, or women's groups.

As noted above, authentic peace zones must be "bottom up," locally organized and driven endeavors, but this is not to say that they can survive long without supra-local—especially regional or provincial level—support. An enlightened provisional governor (as in the case of Cantomanyog) can make all the difference between success and failure; one who is opposed to the presence of a zone, or, even if supportive, hopes to appropriate it for his own political purposes (as in the case of Tulunan), can do much harm.

NGOs, whether Filipino or international, have an important role to play as well, though in the Filipino case one must recall that there is a clear distinction made between NGOs and peoples' organizations. The latter are localized and community based. They "draw cohesion and legitimacy by building on existing forms of social organization and adapting their procedures to traditional norms of reciprocity" (Jolob 2001, 10). Ideally, NGOs support peoples' organizations in their endeavors (whether in the areas of development or in forming peace zones), and this regional-national-international linkage to local activism is what makes development and positive peace a possibility. Recall, as well, that in the late 1980s the CfP needed the peace-zone idea to reinvigorate its own efforts in peacebuilding, after its legitimacy to play a perceived direct third-party role was rebuffed by both sides of the conflict. The CfP needed those pioneering peace zones as much as the zones needed the national-level support that the CfP could bring to them.

The question of national-level support is difficult to analyze in "black and white" terms. The civilian side of the government has in the main been supportive of the idea, up to the president himself or herself. But the support of the military (or the national police) has been more lukewarm. Santos writes, "For the most part, especially during the first stage of pioneer peace zones of 1988–91, the defense and security establishment has been mainly opposed to or wary of peace zones, though there were also some positions supportive of or at least open to [them]" (2005, 29). The awarding of seven peace zones with substantial funds through their designation as SDAs might be taken as the ultimate recognition of the idea by national-level officials (and the object of envy by ZoP activists in other countries). In fact, we have seen that this was a mixed blessing, and sometimes led to serious problems and dissension in the zone. Finally, as under

President Estrada in 2000, sometimes national-level support was used cynically, or was seen as a propaganda ploy by a government that was otherwise intent on pursuing the fight through armed hostilities.

Among the government's adversaries the response was also mixed. Santos characterizes their responses to the pioneering zones, especially at the "local and lower levels," as "ambivalent and even flip-flopping" (2005, 31). Eventually the national leadership of the leftist armed opposition took a hard line and came out against the zones as "anti-people and counter-revolutionary." In short, it viewed them as pawns of the government's counterinsurgency campaign. Nevertheless, the zones were often able—again, at the local level—to secure the cooperation of local insurgent commanders, since they did not want to appear to be acting against the wishes or interests of the very people whom they were pledging to defend and liberate.

In the second wave Santos reports that the response of the MILF has been on the whole "typically vague or diplomatic" regarding support of the zones in their areas. Still, the general effectiveness of the AFP-MILF cease fire in Central Mindanao, at least (since July 2003), and the progress of peace talks ongoing in Malaysia, as well as Christian-Muslim dialogue and inter-communal peacebuilding efforts, have all helped to sustain the many sanctuaries-of-peace, spaces-of-peace, and lights-of-peace efforts in the south, even if the MILF formally refuses to affirm local peace agreements that are separate from a comprehensive, national one.

Comparing (very broadly) the two main parties that peace zones must deal with in order to survive—the government side and the insurgent side—one sometimes finds a paradoxical situation. At the highest levels of government (at least on the civilian side) there is support for the peace zones; at the local level where army and police commanders work this support is often lacking. On the insurgent side, the NPA national leadership is publicly opposed to the zones, while MILF national leadership is at best publicly noncommittal verging on non-supportive. Yet at the local level insurgent commanders often cooperate with them. Whatever the case, leadership and residents of peace zones are always and forever engaged in delicate negotiations and in constant "adjustments" with changing local events and armed actors from all sides of the conflict. Very little is assured. Everything appears contingent.

Conclusion: Peace Zones in the Philippines

"The Peace Zone," writes Madalene Sta. Maria, "may be viewed as a representation of a community's decision to assert its sovereignty over other existing political forces in the country." The community asserts that it does not wish "to side [with] or be used by any of the warring factions or by representatives of these factions" (Sta. Maria 2000, 72). For such a decision to result in a viable peace zone, there must be internal community cohesion and solidarity, effective leadership, and support (or at least "non-active opposition") from regional-level and national-level actors—and, of course, from the very armed combatants whose activities make the zone necessary in the first place. But above all—something not yet explicitly mentioned in this chapter but of crucial importance—it takes tremendous courage on the part of local individuals. All the sources we have used here talk about targeted killings, kidnapping, torture, pillage, and intimidation of all kinds, used by all the armed actors at one point or another in this conflict. Courage is hard to quantify as a discrete variable, but in situations like these one can see it existentially "operationalized" all the time, in each of the zones we have discussed and in the scores whose names we haven't even mentioned in this brief review.

In speaking to the validity of the peace-zone concept, Santos points to the more than eighty zones (under a variety of different names) constituting the second wave and formed after 2000. This, he says, constitutes a true peace-zone movement—in Mindanao, he suggests, even part of a "mass movement" for peace—one that moreover has become part of the broader peace process in the Philippines (Santos 2005). This is perhaps the ideal outcome: a locally-based and inspired movement "owned" by the people themselves that can in turn invigorate a national-level constituency for peace and justice, at the same time that it draws important support from the latter. This is the lesson given to ZoPs everywhere by the Philippines.

Notes

[1] Marcos had ruled the Philippines as its president since December 1965. EDSA is the abbreviation for the major thoroughfare in Metro Manila—Epifanio De los Santos Avenue—where, on February 22–23, 1986, a large crowd of civilians formed human barricades and prevented a force of marines sent by Marcos from arresting some 200–300 military mutineers who opposed the Marcos regime. In the face of massive nonviolent resistance, the marines turned back, the military's support for Marcos evaporated, and the generals pledged their support to Corazon Aquino, the widow of assassinated opposition figure Benigno Aquino. Marcos and his family left the Philippines on February 25, 1986, from Clark Air Base, under US protection and was welcomed in Hawaii by President Ronald Reagan. If any one event emboldened civil society to imagine that it could oppose the direct violence of the state and change political "facts," it was this event. In essence, EDSA

and the surrounding streets around Camp Aguinaldo and Crame from February 22–25, 1986, predicated the features of the peace zones in the Philippines.

[2] Jolob writes, "The CfP is a loose network of more than 30 organizations and local communities with a presence in key regions of the Philippines, and continues to be a national point of convergence for local communities and organizations to integrate into the national level peace process" (Jolob 2001, 13).

[3] "Continuation of People's Power Revolution in the Philippines," in *People Building People II: Successful Stories of Civil Society*, ed. Paul van Tongeren et al. Available on the www.gppac.net website. The Hungduan experience is not widely known, but it is cited by Ging Quintos-Deles, who was executive director of the Gaston Z. Ortigas Peace Institute, the secretariat of several major Filipino peace organizations, including the CfP. Ed Garcia also mentions a news report about Hungduan as an "inspiration" for the idea, and says that the CfP subsequently "took up the call" (Garcia 1997, 221).

[4] Initially a wide variety of terms was used, including *demilitarized zone, cease-fire zone, free zone,* and *neutral zone.* As will be seen in the case of Kalinga-Tabuk, below, and in discussing the so-called second wave of peace zones in the south, a variety of terms is still in use. The move to call these efforts peace zones seems to be due to "the influence of the CfP, which was the main support NGO for the pioneer Peace Zones" (Santos 2005, 7).

[5] Santos also describes a "long interregnum stage," from 1991 to 2000, between the first and second waves, when perhaps nine other zones were established (Santos 2005).

[6] For original documents relating to the Naga Peace Zone, see Santos 2005, 62–79.

[7] Large-scale migration and settlement from Christian Luzon and Visayas between 1930 and 1970 reduced the Muslim population from almost 98 percent to about 40 percent by the mid-1970s. This set the stage for the Christian-Muslim conflicts in Mindanao today.

[8] Collectively, one can speak of the Consolidated Peace Zones of Tulunan, North Cotobato, which consisted of four communities—two villages *(barangays)* and two hamlets *(sitios)* in the municipality of Tulunan. These communities were the Zone of Life in Barangay Bituan, Barangay Nabundasan, Sitio Miatub in Barangay Tubran, and Sitio New Alimonian in Barangay Banayal.

[9] This is the main reason the program was eventually switched from the National Program for Unification and Development Council to directly under the Office of the Presidential Adviser for the Peace Process.

[10] To give some idea of the scale of money brought in by SDA funding, Lee notes that the 5 million pesos given to each of the four separate peace zones of Tulunan totaled 20 million pesos, while the entire internal revenue allotment of the whole municipality was only 13 million pesos (Lee 2000, 115).

[11] This underlines the fact that there was often little or no consistency or predictability in how local AFP or NPA units would relate to the peace zones in their areas of operation. In addition, relations, positive or negative, were never entirely stable.

[12] The original adversary was the Moro National Liberation Front (MNLF) and its military arm, the Bangsa Moro Army, founded in 1968 and issuing a manifesto (from Libya) in 1974 declaring the goal of establishing an independent Moro Homeland composed of about a dozen Muslim ethnolinguistic groups from Mindanao, Palawan, and Sulu. The MILF broke away from the MNLF in 1977 to more vigorously promote the Islamic character of the struggle and its goals; the MILF is now the main armed adversary of the Philippine state. In 1987 the MNLF signed an accord with the government relinquishing its goal of independence. The MILF rejected the accord and launched an offensive soon after. After a month or so a truce was declared, and a more formal cease fire followed in 2001. The MILF is now engaged in productive talks with the government (in Kuala Lampur, hosted by Malaysia) as part of a broader peace process in the Philippines. Other armed groups, notably the Islamicist Abu Sayyaf, remain outside the peace process.

[13] See note 7, above. It should be noted, however, that additional peace zones have been declared in this period in the north as well, in Luzon, as the AFP-NPA conflict continues there.

[14] Along with Christians and Muslims a third communal group, indigenous Lumads are part of the inter-communal dialogues and peace efforts in Mindanao.

[15] The term *sanctuary* might be preferred to *space* in Muslim areas because the former is more resonant with the Islamic notion of Dar es-Islam (House of Peace, or Islam).

[16] For a more generally critical view of this phenomenon, see Sales 2004.

[17] Of course, the BECs are also indigenous resources of ethnopraxis.

Works Cited

Avruch, Kevin. 1998. *Culture and conflict resolution*. Washington, DC: United States Institute of Peace Press.

Blume, Francine. 1993. The process of nonviolent politics: Lessons from the Philippines. PhD diss., University of Hawaii at Manoa.

Briones, Alfredo V. 2000. The Cantomanyog zone of peace: The role of the grassroots church in local peacemaking. *Philippine Journal of Psychology* 33 (7): 77–111.

Galtung, Johan. 1969. Violence, peace, and peace research. *Journal of Peace Research* 6 (3): 167–92.

Garcia, Ed. 1997. Filipino zones of peace. *Peace Review* 9 (2): 221–24.

Garcia, Ed, and Carolina G. Hernández. 1989. *Waging peace in the Philippines: Proceedings of the 1988 International Conference on Conflict Resolution*. Manila: Ateneo Center for Social Policy and Public Affairs; Quezon City: Ateneo de Manila University Press. Garcia and Hernández are quoting from the *Peace Zone Primer* (Manila: Gaston Z. Ortigas Peace Institute).

Jolob, Natasha. 2001. *The peace movement in the Philippines*. Quezon City: Gaston Z. Ortigas Peace Institute.

Lee, Zosimo E. 2000. Peace zones as special development areas: A preliminary assessment. In *Building peace: Essays on psychology and the culture of peace*, ed. A. B. I. Bernardo and C. D. Ortigas. Manila: De La Salle University Press.

Mercado, Eliseo R., Margarita Moran-Floirendo, Ryan Anson, and Southern Philippines Foundation for the Arts, Culture, and Ecology. 2003. *Mindanao on the mend*. Manila: Anvil Pub. Southern Philippines Foundation for the Arts, Culture, and Ecology.

Sales, Peter M. 2004. Reinventing the past or redefining the future? An assessment of sanctuaries of peace in the Southern Philippines. Paper presented at the Oceanic Conference on International Studies, July 14–16, Australian National University, Canberra, Australia.

Santos, Soliman, Jr. 2005. *Peace zones in the Philippines: Concept, policy, and instruments*. Quezon City: Gaston Z. Ortigas Peace Institute and the Asia Foundation.

Sta. Maria, Madalene. 2000. Managing social conflict: The Philippine peace zone experiment. *Philippine Journal of Psychology* 33 (2): 48–76.

Tongeren, Paul van, et al., eds. *People Building People II: Successful Stories of Civil Society.*

4

ISLANDS IN THE STREAM

A Comparative Analysis of Zones of Peace within Colombia's Civil War

CATALINA ROJAS

Introduction

Colombia's conflict is the oldest armed conflict in the Western Hemisphere, with nearly four decades of armed confrontation among FARC, ELN (left-wing guerrillas), AUC (right-wing paramilitaries), and the Colombian army. Historically, Colombia's state has been a fragile one, currently disputing political and territorial sovereignty with a number of violent actors including guerrillas, drug traffickers, self-defense units, paramilitaries, and common criminals.[1] Within this complex association of violent actors, civilians have become the most vulnerable population for a number of reasons, including:

- Government authorities, such as the police and military, do not protect the lives and integrity of their citizens.
- Colombia's territory is partially controlled by non-state armed actors, endangering the lives of civilians who currently occupy those areas.

This chapter is partly based on Catalina Rojas, "The People's Peace Processes: Local Resistance Processes and the Development of 'Zones of Peace' in Colombia," *Reflexión Política* (Journal of the Political Studies Institute of UNAB University, Bucaramanga, Colombia) (2004), 70–87. This chapter would not have been possible without the collaboration, comments, and field research over the years of my Colombian colleague Diana Angel.

- Violent factions forcibly recruit civilians, exposing them as targets for massacre, disappearance, torture, or murder.

The effects of the conflict on civilians are immense. Since 1985 nearly 2.9 million civilians have been forcibly displaced, creating the largest humanitarian crisis in the Western Hemisphere (CODHES 2003, 124).

Civilians are usually the primary victims of violence and are often "trapped" in the middle of confrontations among the armed actors. In sum, it is important to support empowering processes and interventions by which civilians can declare themselves to be actively neutral if an enduring, sustainable peace is to be achieved in Colombia.[2]

Colombia's civil society is complex and rich; its actors include peasants, students, union workers, women's groups, and associations of relatives of kidnapped and disappeared people. Likewise, peace initiatives vary from pressuring the national government to start a negotiation process to organizing thousands of women marching the streets of Bogotá and Putumayo in 2002 and 2003 and supporting local processes of peace. One of the many local resistance processes conducted in Colombia in the last few years has been the One Hundred Municipalities of Peace, organized by REDEPAZ, the oldest national peace network in Colombia.[3] One of the important aspects of this project has been its special focus on the most vulnerable civilian sectors currently suffering the consequences of the armed confrontation in remote regions of Colombia, often under the control of armed actors and historically abandoned by the Colombian state.[4]

The objective of this chapter is to illustrate the case of three municipalities that are part of the above-mentioned project. In the 1990s Mogotes, Samaniego, and San Pablo declared themselves ZoPs. In illustrating the process, development, obstacles, and current challenges of establishing a ZoP, I address the following themes:

1. *resisting violence:* the process of developing active neutrality.
2. *neutralizing the war machine:*[5] the process of reacquiring spaces for peace.

The leading argument of this chapter is that ZoPs are capable of producing identity-transforming changes regarding the notion of being victims of the conflict. Thus, a ZoP contributes to modifying a victim-centered perspective toward one of resilience, in which local communities foster conditions for reconciliation and resolution of the conflict on their own terms. The project is thus based on the notion that unarmed civilians are not solely victims of armed confrontations but can be actors for peace within their own communities. Much has been said about the need to complement the formal negotiation process between the elites of the parties with democratizing, "bottom up" processes. ZoPs such as Mogotes, Samaniego, and San Pablo are concrete examples of citizen, governmental, and nonprofit organizations cooperating to protect the life, the land, and the dignity of unarmed civilians. This chapter is an attempt to contribute to our knowledge of ZoPs by learning from field experiences and, hopefully, initiating a deeper understanding of what makes a ZoP more durable and successful under conditions of extreme violence.

Peace Communities:
Resisting Pain While Reconstructing Life

Colombian international humanitarian rights expert Alvaro Villarraga argues that since 2002 the peace movement in Colombia has manifested itself in three areas:

> (1) the women's movement; (2) indigenous resistance as a cultural and territorial movement; and (3) community resistance processes as humanitarian flags. Those are the three bastions. I believe it is only these most importantly that could let us affirm as a fact—as a real, material fact—that there is still a peace movement in Colombia.[6]

The process of building local resistance initiatives is an interesting one because it exemplifies how communities can restore their social fabric by working on humanitarian goals in conditions of high levels of violence. Some of these local resistance processes are led by women. As Magdala Velazquez explains:

> The civil resistance done by women is very strong here . . . but Colombia doesn't have the eyes to see it or to value it. After Uribe won last year [2002], the humanitarian struggle has been led by women. I mean the only humanitarian agreements that have been accomplished in this country are done by women. . . . The vanguard of the humanitarian movement is in the hands of women.[7]

Local resistance processes have been largely ignored by Colombian society in general and by the social sciences in particular. However, there is an increasing interest in the topic, as shown by the efforts of several research institutes. One of the more recent reports—*El conflicto, callejón con salida* (UNDP 2003)—was compiled by a team of researchers who spent more than a year talking with over four thousand people across the country. In one chapter the researchers explored community-oriented processes for restraining violence. It is precisely in regions that are most affected by the incursion of guerrilla or paramilitary violence that resistance and coexistence practices are becoming "keys" to confront violence and resolve conflicts. The UNDP report offers some examples of these local resistance practices:

> To protect ethnic reservations in El Cauca, communities are creating indigenous "guards." Processes of civil resistance to armed actors in Micoahumado (Bolívar) succeeded so that paramilitaries and ELN guerrillas respected their village; Constitutional assemblies were established in Mogotes (Santander) and Tarso (Antioquia) and in some parts of Tolima. . . . In the Valle region, land has been given to 10,000 Internally Displaced Peoples (IDPs), thanks to the humanitarian accords achieved between armed groups and communities. (UNDP 2003, 17)

The process of local resistance has an intrinsic value in itself, as citizens are able to organize themselves in peace communities. Villarraga defines peace communities as

> spaces into which armed actors are not allowed to enter. The only protection is symbolic, with signs and everything, but obviously this is symbolic, and reduces the risk to the community as well as distancing them from the violent actors.[8]

Without the use of arms, entire communities have prevented the incursion of violent actors or partially negotiated with insurgents, with some degree of success. Those local resistance practices are not exempt from failure, and some leaders have been assassinated by guerrilla organizations (for example, a key indigenous leader in El Cauca). However, in some peace communities, like Mogotes, the process has endured for some years and has gained national recognition.

Moreover, these processes help to answer the question of how civilians, who are clearly victimized by the civil war, can make a transition from victims to leaders in the reconstruction of their community's social fabric. In other words, local resistance efforts, either in the form of zones or communities of peace, are examples of how to move effectively from pain to resilience as a form of resistance.

Such local resistance processes support the concept that an eventual peace process in Colombia has to take into account regional differences in how the conflict manifests itself. For example, in areas where forced displacement has occurred, many returnees have established peace communities. According to the research done by the

Foundation for Democratic Culture on the returnee community of San Francisco de Asís:

> In 1999 [the community] ratified a document with a framework for defining individual membership to the peace community. [In the document, the community] stipulated what it meant not to provide the armed actors with any logistical, strategic, or tactical assistance to any of the warring factions. [The document also stipulated] the types of penalties that could be incurred within the peace community to prevent such assistance from happening and to enforce any disciplinary modalities and security measures that would prevent anyone giving a false impression about the nature of the peace community. (Fundación Cultura Democrática et al. 2003, 76)

One reason it is important to study ZoPs is in order to understand the Colombian conflict in its regional dimension. Hence, the perspective of the conflict in Colombia varies depending on whether a person is in the capital, Bogotá, or in an area that is in dispute or controlled by armed actors. Regional resistance processes are being organized in places like Tolima, Antioquia, Cauca, Barrancabermeja, Urabá, Nariño, Caldas, and Atrato among others. These regional practices are questioning two assumptions: first, that "dialogues" should only be held at the national level; and second, that negotiations should be exclusively between armed actors and the government.

NGOs and the Creation of Zones of Peace

In 1998 REDEPAZ developed the One Hundred Municipalities of Peace in Colombia project. According to the REDEPAZ grant application to the European Initiative for Democracy and Human Rights the project was an attempt to "promote, create, and/or consolidate one-hundred experiences of citizen participation in local decision making processes that foster gender equity, peaceful relationships and democracy at the local level."[9]

The project can be briefly summarized as a way of conducting civilian resistance by sealing off communities from the presence and influence of violent actors without resorting to violence itself. It consisted of a number of different approaches that gave shape to the process of creating and consolidating a peace territory, including

- an autonomous decision by the inhabitants of a municipality; or
- a decision of the local authorities; or

- a process guided by REDEPAZ (or any other domestic or international NGO); or
- a combination of the above.

According to the "Methodological Guide for the Construction of Peace Territories," the project was the result of the interaction of the following strategies: (a) citizen participation, (b) pedagogical intervention, (c) public action, (d) information and communication processes, and (e) the organization of local civil society leadership in one hundred municipalities. Its general objective was to

> foster local participatory efforts of peaceful coexistence within local communities in order to contribute to violence reduction and to strengthen citizen participation in public affairs, as a way of implementing the Citizen Mandate for Peace, Life and Freedom. (REDEPAZ 2001, 5)[10]

The project was based on the need to build and strengthen the elements of civil society that any peace requires. The intention was to provide a territorial dimension to peace and implement the Citizen Peace Mandate in the different territories and communities, reaffirming that peace is the most important public asset for all Colombians.[11]

The European Union was the main financial supporter of the project, which began as an eighteen-month-long initiative. Although the process of consolidating peace territories usually takes much longer, the goal of the project had to be to foster the initial stages of the One Hundred Municipalities of Peace during that year and a half. (In this context it is relevant to know that REDEPAZ supports only those communities that ask for advice, accompaniment, or any other form of assistance under the parameters of peaceful coexistence.) This proved a difficult task, even though the time period for support was eventually extended a further two years.

Another shortcoming in a project encompassing so many different levels of actions and actors was the difficulty of evaluating success if there was no explicit description of which level of activities was to be implemented first. For instance, the project did not clearly delineate the degree of importance between the pedagogical process and the establishment of the peace municipalities, or the creation of networks of different sectors of civilians working for peace. More clarity was needed about which strategy should be considered the most relevant for the success of the project; a systematic explanation of how these different strategies work was also needed.

The three ZoPs that are described below are part of the One Hundred Municipalities of Peace project. These cases were selected for analysis because each of them represents an experience by which a community could initiate the process of becoming a ZoP. Mogotes was originally created by a "bottom up" process of cooperation among the inhabitants of the municipality, who requested the creation of a Constitutional Assembly to deal with the ongoing conflicts of political corruption and guerrilla interference in the internal decisions of the locality. In Samaniego the mayor initially developed the peace declaration in something of a "top down" process. Last, the population of San Pablo pressed for a peace declaration because of its geographical location. San Pablo is located in southern Colombia, close to Putumayo, and is near the target zone for the US-backed Plan Colombia's drug-eradication efforts.[12]

All three municipalities are in zones that suffer from active guerrilla operations: FARC in the San Pablo area, and the ELN in the Mogotes and Samaniego areas. In addition, prior to their recent "disbanding," right-wing paramilitaries affiliated with the AUC also operated in all three areas. Furthermore, these zones can be characterized as deprived areas, where there is little or no state presence represented by official forces of law and order, educational facilities, health services or basic infrastructure.

While there is a significant number of ZoPs in Colombia that are not part of the REDEPAZ project, this chapter examines only the three territories just described, which are important parts of this project. Since scholarly sources on the topic of local ZoPs in Colombia are scant, much of the data for this analysis is based upon primary sources such as interviews, internal documents, and newspaper archives.

Mogotes: Peace in Spite of Adversity

Mogotes is located in the province of Guanentá within Colombia's Santander Department, north of Bogotá. Estimates of its population vary from 11,800 to around 12,400. It is a largely rural area located thirty-three kilometers from Santander's capital, Bucaramanga, and during the period of this study the ELN, FARC, and the AUC had a presence in the region. The Municipal Constituent Assembly was formed on September 13, 1998, making Mogotes one of the longest enduring of Colombia's ZoPs.

History of the Process

On December 11, 1997, 150 armed guerrillas from the ELN took control of Mogotes with the stated intention of judging, and presumably executing, the municipality's mayor on charges of corruption.

In response to this action, in which three policemen and one civilian were killed, communal leaders called for the creation of a Municipal Constituent Assembly, which was formed by two hundred citizens from Mogotes and its adjoining rural villages. The assembly members unanimously requested that the guerrillas return the mayor, Dorían Rodríguez, to the town so that he could be democratically judged by the citizens. After a popular vote, the town decided to remove the mayor and called for new elections. José Angel Guadrón was elected the new mayor. He intended to implement the governance program suggested by the Municipal Constituent Assembly together with the process of municipal reform also suggested at the forum.

The experience of Mogotes is one of citizen participation for social change and nonviolent conflict resolution. In 1999 Mogotes received national and worldwide recognition by receiving the National Peace Prize. Diplomats, union leaders, nonprofit leaders, Catholic priests, and members of the media have all visited Mogotes. A year after receiving the award, an event was organized by the Municipal Constituent Assembly, REDEPAZ, and the Catholic Offices in Santander to write a "commitment letter" with the objective of strengthening Mogotes's engagement in peace.

The Challenges

The Mogotes experience was so powerful that it led REDEPAZ to initiate the One Hundred Municipalities of Peace project in order to replicate the process across Colombia. However, as in any process that is not based on force or coercion, the intent to isolate any community from the territorial, political, social, and economic influences of violent actors confronts a myriad of challenges. In Mogotes, the ELN later killed the mayor originally charged with corruption. In retaliation, the mayor's relatives publicly accused one of the leaders of the Municipal Constituent Assembly of collaboration. Consequently, the process of political renovation and citizen power started to show signs of fracturing. After a while the process regained strength, and the community began gaining cohesiveness after a Catholic father engaged in a four-day hunger strike, offering his life to the process. The community requested that the violent actors show respect for the process. The hunger strike was stopped when insurgents, paramilitaries, and REDEPAZ went to the town, and Mogotes reiterated its commitment to peace.

The people of Mogotes are indeed remarkable. For example, they modified the title of mayor to manager, thus transforming the whole concept of public service, moving away from clientele-based politics to a more efficient, merit-based method of handling public affairs. Periodically the manager has to present a report to the inhabitants in the public plaza. Long question-and-answer sessions with the manager and the Municipal Constituent Assembly are examples of some of the dynamics of social change taking place in a town that remains characterized by unemployment and minimal presence of the state. According to Diana Angel, a Bogotá REDEPAZ staffer who visited the village, "Mogotes is the living example of a small Athens in the middle of nowhere in Colombia."

Recent Events in Mogotes: 2004–2005

According to Sara Ramírez, our field researcher for the ICAR-USIP project on local ZoPs in Colombia:

> Up to July 2003, 44 assembly meetings have taken place over the last five years of the existence of the process. Of all these assemblies, records have been kept, and in addition, in order to guarantee the good behavior of the constituents, a manual was created entitled: "The Profile of the Public Servant." (Ramírez 2003a)

Mogotes is still under threat from ELN forces. However, a much more deadly threat—the paramilitaries—has entered the area. The ELN and the paramilitaries are fighting for control of the surrounding province of García Rovira. In 2004 the paramilitaries directly threatened some of the leaders of the Municipal Constituent Assembly. In addition to these threats the process in Mogotes has been publicly discredited by politicians who—much like President Alvaro Uribe—tend to associate citizens' initiatives for peace with the insurgency and see their leaders as guerrilla collaborators. Despite pressure from the paramilitaries and its previous crisis, Mogotes still defines itself as an autonomous peace community. Given the economic and social crisis that Mogotes is facing, leaders of the Municipal Constituent Assembly are working to develop a strategic economic plan in order to improve the social and economic situation of their municipality.[13]

Samaniego: The Effectiveness of Power Localities

Samaniego is located in the department of Nariño in the southwest region of Colombia. From 1993 to 2003 the population grew from around fifty-one thousand to over sixty-five thousand; much of this increase appears to stem from the influx of IDPs from the Putumayo region. Samaniego is located four hours from Nariño's capital city of Pasto and reportedly has been affected by the aerial fumigation associated with Plan Colombia. A July 1, 2001, article in the newspaper *El Espectador* reported that a local high school, protected national regional forest, and a fish hatchery had all been repeatedly sprayed with defoliants designed to kill coca crops.

Establishing Samaniego's Zone of Peace

According to Francisco Angulo, former REDEPAZ member in charge of the southern Colombia region, Samaniego is "a very special case." In his words: "Samaniego is an example that local authorities can be committed to peace, and it breaks the myth that it is only in civil society where change lies. In addition, the most important lesson is that it is possible to work jointly with local representatives for peace and reconciliation."[14]

In Samaniego two processes overlapped in 1998: the mayoral elections and the Citizen Mandate for Peace. When the elected mayor was taken by the ELN, the entire town protested, demanding his release. After his liberation the mayor committed himself to work toward transparency in his actions and the implementation of the mandate. He then invited the citizens of Samaniego to participate in the process of declaring the village a ZoP. The initiative was welcomed by the people, and the process of building a peace municipality started. The mayor contacted REDEPAZ for advice on the process of declaring Samaniego a peace territory. On January 1, 1998, the process was completed. However, Samaniego remained under the direct influence of the ELN, which monitored the process of elections.[15]

The mayor pursued one of the programs of the President's Office for De-mobilization, graduating two hundred adults with high-school degrees including a minor in peace coexistence. Moreover, the mayor authorized these two hundred adults to train other members of the community, creating a multiplier effect for peaceful coexistence. This gesture was taken as the mayor's commitment to direct participation processes and generated support within the community.[16]

Samaniego has now been a ZoP for several years. Its main problem remains the influx of IDPs from Putumayo, a direct result of the humanitarian crisis created as a byproduct of Plan Colombia's effort to eradicate coca production, started under former President Andrés Pastrana. In response, the departmental Nariño Peace Table sought support and advice from organizations such as REDEPAZ and the Catholic Church.[17] The people of Samaniego had already contacted the governor of Nariño to assure the continuity of the process and to provide solutions to the continuing IDP crisis. In general, some of the biggest problems have been the total absence of a humanitarian accord with the violent actors present in the region; people's loss of faith in past peace processes such as that between FARC and former President Andrés Pastrana, and continuing violence targeting civilians.

The process of establishing Samaniego as an accepted ZoP has been paralleled by the efforts of the Peace Table of Samaniego, an organization consisting of twenty-five representatives of private and public institutions, youth groups, children, and other community members who support Samaniego's efforts to maintain itself as a ZoP. This process, as stated above, had the complete support of the then mayor, who was convinced of the need to transform the culture of confrontation and fear. The activities initially planned by the Samaniego Peace Table included:

- The establishment of an information system for the vulnerable populations of the municipality.
- Creation of municipal social policies to improve the situation of children, women, homeless, seniors, disabled, and other vulnerable sectors of the population.
- Design, creation, and implementation of TV, radio, and publicity campaigns intended to shift the perception of the communities toward the affected populations of Samaniego.
- Networking with institutions that target at-risk populations in order to implement and jointly evaluate programs and projects envisioned in a coherent social policy for the municipality.[18]

Samaniego was, as are many municipalities in Colombia, a territory in which the insurgents controlled the area and local politicians were corrupt. The people of Samaniego, under the leadership of its mayor, were committed to changing public and private institutions so that they could contribute to the municipality's peace process.

Recent Events in Samaniego: 2004–2005

Despite the steady increase in paramilitary attacks against the population, as well as retaliatory acts by left-wing guerrillas, Samaniego continues to exist as a ZoP. However, the lack of institutional support from the current municipal administration and a lack of financial assistance from external NGOs and the local government have slowed the development of the programs that were part of the peace program. According to Sara Ramírez, "The greatest obstacle that 'Samaniego: Territory of Peace' faced has been the lack of continuity in the programs by subsequent administrations which led to stagnation and the termination of the majority of the programs" (Ramírez 2003b). The main problems that, in turn, escalate the conflict situation are those stemming from continued drug production, indiscriminate chemical fumigation under Plan Colombia and Plan Patriota, and the steady arrival of IDPs from Putumayo.[19]

A recent sector that has gained community recognition is the youth sector. In 2003 the Movement of Children for Peace in Samaniego started a nonprofit organization called the Foundation for Children and Youth for Peace. The foundation is engaged in a wide range of activities, from implementing campaigns to exchange war-based toys for recreational toys to conducting peace workshops in various villages and participating in radio talk shows. In addition, members are involved in assisting the displaced populations with housing, food, and healthcare.

Overall, Samaniego's peace community survives amid the following challenges:

- the security challenge resulting from continued incursions by the AUC and guerrillas, together with drug production and trafficking;
- financial problems resulting from difficulty in acquiring funds; and
- the humanitarian challenge resulting from the influx of IDPs in need, who mainly rely on public assistance; many have environmental/health problems due to US-sponsored fumigation, which damages food crops and poisons natural resources.

On a positive note, social actors such as children, youth, and women have started to gain recognition as agents of social change, which can influence—in the long term—the current culture of war and violence as the preferred strategy to deal with crisis, uncertainty, and disagreement. However, the situation is far from easy, given that ELN guerrillas recently kidnapped the peace leader of the youth movement and there are accusations that the current mayor of Samaniego has close ties to paramilitary units in the area.

San Pablo: Striving for Peace in the Midst of War

Like Samaniego, San Pablo is located in the department of Nariño in southern Colombia. Its population is reported to be over twenty-five thousand, and, like Samaniego, an unknown number of these are IDPs fleeing the conflict in Putumayo. One major difference is that San Pablo is well known as a coca-growing area. This has generated interest from, and the presence of, guerrillas from both FARC and the ELN, as well as paramilitaries from the AUC, making the initiative to establish a ZoP in San Pablo truly remarkable.

San Pablo's Story

The story of San Pablo's ZoP highlights the complexity of the war's dynamics in southern Colombia. Being an illegal crop–cultivation area, control of San Pablo is currently disputed by all of the armed actors who seek to cash in on the profits generated by growing coca. There were hostilities between FARC and the ELN, and subsequently the paramilitaries started to appear on the scene. In addition, the consequences of both Plan Colombia and the later Plan Patriota are clearly seen in this municipality. As in Samaniego, IDPs are coming from Putumayo, and a general escalation in armed interventions is a direct product of President Uribe's strategy for the southwestern part of the country.[20]

According to Francisco Angulo, the history of San Pablo reveals six attacks from insurgents belonging to FARC and the ELN.[21] The population decided to declare itself a ZoP in order to protect the community from further attacks by the violent actors in the conflict. In November 2000 the population publicly declared San Pablo a peace municipality. Unfortunately, on March 9, 2001, FARC again attacked the town. San Pablo's citizens, together with the Nariño Peace Table and REDEPAZ, expressed to FARC, the government, the paramilitaries, and everyone else their unwillingness to stop the process of being a peace territory. Most important at that time was the determination of the community and supporting institutions to make it clear to the violent actors that they should respect the voluntary and popular decision of San Pablo to declare itself a ZoP. This process was very difficult, in part because San Pablo's community is not homogeneous, with some civilian sectors aligning themselves with one or another of the violent factions. There were conflicts between the civilians supporting FARC and those supporting the ELN. During an interview in 2001, Francisco Angulo affirmed that San Pablo's political context was very complex indeed. The population was divided and influenced by different armed sectors, making it difficult to develop the notion of neutrality fully. This was not an easy step, given the problems of division and intra-communal conflicts among the inhabitants. According to Angulo, FARC saw the ZoP of San Pablo as a real obstacle to its goal of gaining economic, social, and political power in the municipality. FARC's stance was a real threat to the community, especially given the fact that FARC attacked San Pablo after its declaration as a ZoP, clearly indicating the insurgents' disregard for the popular will of many of the citizens of San Pablo.

At the end of his interview in 2001, Francisco Angulo stated:

> Zones of peace are posing a real obstacle to the violent actors, because war is about controlling territories, and creating zones of peace removes those territories from the war. Hence, violent actors tend to frame these zones as territories that they have "lost." This is why they are a clear military target, and this explains why FARC and the ELN insist on attacking civilians.[22]

Recent Events in San Pablo: 2004–2005

San Pablo's levels of violence have steadily increased, even after its declaration as a peace zone. As a way of reacting to the high levels of violence, REDEPAZ attempted to denounce the violent actors at both the national and international levels. It also became necessary to protect leaders working inside the communities, given the imminent risk to their lives. Unfortunately, due to this high level of violence, local organizations engaged in the process of developing the ZoP were unable to continue their work. By 2003 many leaders had been obliged to leave the area in order to survive, virtually halting the activities of the peace territory.[23]

In addition, the local leadership of the peace territory shifted the project of San Pablo from being a ZoP to working on small economic and production projects. Such changes were made by the local leadership without consultation with REDEPAZ, isolating San Pablo from the national network of peace territories. At this point the remaining community leaders have all left; local leadership also left after being accused of mismanagement. This is a case in which both internal and external circumstances contributed to a fundamental weakening of the entire process.

San Pablo remains plagued with high levels of violence, drug production and trafficking problems, and a humanitarian crisis resulting from the continued influx of IDPs from further south. With both the Colombian and US governments attempting to force a military solution to political violence and the drug problems, San Pablo's situation is likely to get even worse.

A Comparative Analysis

Given our overview of three instances of ZoPs in Colombia—two of which we can consider successful and one that has failed—this section outlines some commonalities that may help us to understand the conditions under which a ZoP tends to endure or even flourish. Likewise, it is necessary to discern the main obstacles that a ZoP faces and the primary areas that need to be addressed by any community wishing to undertake the process of creating a ZoP.

First and foremost, it is necessary to understand the conditions under which a ZoP may best be established. When is a community likely to undertake the establishment of a ZoP, and how can third parties help make that attempt successful? One of the key elements in successful establishment of a ZoP seems to be a sense of necessity born out of some sort of triggering event. In all three cases a violent act by one of the armed actors to the conflict prodded the local community—in the form of a group of citizens, a leading citizen, or the entire community—to attempt to take back control of its community and its people's lives. In each of these cases the impetus for the creation of the zone was local, even if some technical assistance was later offered by NGOs or other national or international groups. After Mogotes, one other outside input may have been the example of Mogotes and other ZoPs in showing local inhabitants that participating in the ongoing civil war was not the only way to go about their lives; Mogotes showed that there are nonviolent ways of governing and discussing differences. It is this determination, shown by the communities in all three locales and in many others, that gave the ZoP movement its real strength—a strength that is often enough to enable the communities to convince both local and national armed actors that they are serious about withdrawing from the civil conflict and are committed to applying the norms and principles of conflict resolution within their communities.

As with any other action by a civil society, there does not appear to be a single local or national actor with a preponderance of influence on this process. The creation and consolidation of ZoPs within Colombia was the result of cooperation among various sectors of civil society, including faith-based organizations, such as the Catholic Church and other religious organizations; indigenous communities; various Colombian peace-oriented NGOs, for example, REDEPAZ, CINEP, and JUSTAPAZ; human rights and women's NGOs; peasant organizations; educational organizations, such as local schools or universities; local leaders, like the mayor of Samaniego; organized groups, like Mogotes' Municipal Constituent Assembly; and complete communities like San Pablo. Each of these actors played an important role in either promoting or sustaining the ZoP.

In addition to our consideration of the creation of a ZoP, we must also ask why some of these communities were more sustainable than others. Two main things help to make a ZoP sustainable in terms of community drive or commitment. The first is the need for the community to provide some sort of protection for people and their land, especially given the fact that none of these communities has the ability to achieve such ends through the use of force. This leads to a second area of psychological strength for ZoPs. Like other civilian populations that experience a cease fire or other cessation of hostilities, members of a ZoP feel empowered about themselves and the direction of their community—a feeling that they may not have felt for decades.

Additionally, these communities can benefit a great deal from strong processes and knowledge about how to operate in ways that differ from past principles of patronage or the politics of violence. These resources enable them to confront the internal challenges that many ZoPs face, namely, the tasks of creating a unified internal voice by building decision-making structures and institutions capable of addressing intra-communal differences in a nonviolent manner. This can be extremely difficult because of a lack of knowledge or trust that communities may have in these new processes or in their collective ability to implement them.

Externally, fledgling ZoPs, or even those with a fairly long existence, can face challenges both from irregular armed actors and from organs of the state that often see the creation of the ZoP as either a challenge to their authority or as an opportunity to extend their power. While, at times, guerrillas and insurgents might be willing to respect the wishes of the ZoPs, recent efforts by President Uribe's administration to resolve the civil war through military action have reduced the willingness of guerrillas to leave the ZoPs out of the conflict. Additionally, while the right-wing paramilitaries of the AUC have recently agreed to disarm and demobilize, this process remains plagued by both a funding shortfall and lack of a legal structure to address AUC members accused of human rights violations. If faced with jail or other penal consequences, some former AUC members may elect to continue their activities.

Finally, in addressing the conditions necessary for ZoPs to survive and flourish we need to consider both the short term and the long term. In the short term ZoPs can benefit a great deal from expanded training. Even in the most remote areas people are asking for pedagogical interventions. Understanding the concept of active neutrality and knowledge of international humanitarian law can contribute to bringing communities together by giving them both a framework of knowledge for action and the strength to carry it out. These concepts help communities create a common identity and are effective in reducing the influence of violent actors on civilians. This kind of work can best be done by Colombian nationals and is exemplified by the One Hundred Municipalities of Peace project described earlier.

Another short-term need that might be met by international actors is their active support and publicizing of the ZoPs communities by speaking out to the Colombian government and by denouncing attacks on these communities. For those with a more practical bent, accompanying processes, such as those carried out by Peace Brigades International or the Fellowship of Reconciliation, can assist locals in areas where armed actors do not want their violence witnessed by outsiders.

The main long-term need of these communities is socioeconomic investment. The communities examined in this chapter—like many of the ZoPs in Colombia—have historically been abandoned by the Colombian state. This is one of the main reasons why they are areas of insurgent influence. One very good way to combat this is to provide long-term investment in their economies through sustainable development projects. Otherwise, continuing conditions of economic deprivation make it difficult to advance the cause of peace. Therefore, it seems likely that no major advance toward a lasting peace will be made until armed actors and governmental agents at all levels, local communities, and international agencies all understand these needs and take steps to address them.

Conclusion

Many local communities and municipalities in Colombia are well aware that conflict is a natural part of everyday life, but they have chosen to use dialogue as the preferred mechanism to resolve their differences. In some cases local authorities are cooperating with communal initiatives. This chapter discusses just one small sample of the almost invisible processes of local people building peace in the midst of a civil war. These peacemaking efforts continue despite the fact that Colombia is again in the process of escalating its armed conflict under the influence of the US-sponsored Plan Colombia and, more recently, with Plan Patriota. Endurable peace processes need to start at the local level, and what is happening in Colombia with the development of ZoPs and other local resistance processes is—despite the recurring escalation of the conflict—a small but significant sign of peacebuilding practices at the grassroots level. It is to be hoped that this will contribute to sustaining an eventual peace process in the country.

Notes

[1] Note that each actor can strategically ally with another if needed, for example, drug lords and self-defense units in the northern part of the country;

the military and paramilitaries against guerrillas; different guerrilla groups against paramilitaries.

[2] Active neutrality is the concept developed by several Colombian NGOs that means social actors are independent of all violent actors; oppose all forms of war and violence; and actively work for the resolution of the conflict.

[3] REDEPAZ (Network of Initiatives for Peace and against War) comprises more than four hundred organizations with different peace efforts. The network has an active presence in all the regions of the country, fostering local peace processes within these communities.

[4] Mogotes declared itself a peace territory in 1998. REDEPAZ used Mogotes as an example of a local citizens' peace initiative that could be reproduced in other locations such as municipalities, schools, and neighborhoods. This was the origin of the One Hundred Municipalities of Peace project funded by the European Union.

[5] The phrase *war machine* includes the geographical, psychological, and cultural dynamics that fuel and perpetuate conflict and conflict behavior.

[6] Alvaro Villarraga, interview by Catalina Rojas, October 17, 2003.

[7] Magdala Valezquez, interview by Catalina Rojas, October 29, 2003.

[8] Villarraga, interview.

[9] The author thanks Antonio Sanguino, the REDEPAZ project director, for access to internal project documents.

[10] The Citizen Peace Mandate for Peace, Life, and Freedom was another project directed by REDEPAZ, in which almost ten million Colombian citizens voted for a negotiated settlement of the armed conflict and the immediate cessation of hostilities among the violent actors in October 1997.

[11] This particular project defines a ZoP as a territory together with a community committed to peace.

[12] Plan Colombia was a US$1.3 billion grant from the United States to Colombia originally conceived as primarily providing counter-narcotics military-operation assistance to the Colombian army.

[13] Diana Angel, email message to author.

[14] Francisco Angulo, interview by Catalina Rojas, March 22, 2001.

[15] In the early 1990s the new constitution installed a "decentralization process," which, according to some analysts, is one of the major reasons guerrilla organizations gained so much territorial and political power in the regions.

[16] Angulo, interview.

[17] REDEPAZ has regional chapters in different zones of the country. The Nariño Peace Table guides the efforts of REDEPAZ in that specific region.

[18] This information was extracted from an official document of Nariño's Peace Table.

[19] Plan Patriota is President Uribe's initiative to send almost seventeen thousand Colombian troops to southern Colombia in the hopes of defeating both the ELN and FARC insurgencies.

[20] For a detailed analysis, see Catalina Rojas, "What is the war on (t)ERRORISM? US foreign policy towards Colombia in the post–September 11 world: The end of the peace talks, the beginning of the new-old war,

Reflexión Política (Journal of the Political Studies Institute of UNAB University) 4, no. 7 (2002): 76–94. Also available online.

[21] Angulo, interview.

[22] Ibid.

[23] Ingrid Cadena (REDEPAZ–Nariño), personal communication, June 25, 2003.

Works Cited

CODHES (Consultancy for Human Rights and Displacement). 2003. Displacement. In *The authoritarian spell*, ed. N. P. Hernández. Bogotá: National Coordination of the Colombian Platform for Human Rights.

Fundación Cultura Democrática, Colombian Ministry of the Interior and Justice, IDEPAZ, The Jesuit Peace Program, UN Development Program, and UNICEF. 2003. Peace communities and humanitarian zones in Urabá and Atrato, ed. Fundación Cultura Democrática. Antioquia: Colombia: Fundación Cultura Democrática. Translations herein are the author's.

Ramírez, Sara. 2003a. Municipal Constituent Assembly of Mogotes. Fairfax, VA: ICAR.

———. 2003b. Samaniego "Territory of Peace." Fairfax, VA: ICAR.

REDEPAZ. 2001. Methodological guide for the construction of the peace territories. Bogotá: REDEPAZ.

UNDP (UN Development Program). 2003. *El conflicto, callejón con salida: Informe Nacional de Desarrollo Humano para Colombia—2003.* Available (in Spanish) on the www.pnud.org.co website. Translations herein are the author's.

5

THE *RONDAS CAMPESINAS* OF PERU

Jennifer Langdon and Mery Rodriguez

Introduction

Anthropologist Orin Starn describes the *rondas campesinas* (peasant patrols) of Peru as one of the largest and most sustained rural movements in late-twentieth-century Latin America (Starn, Degregori, and Kirk 1995, 425). Starn and others credit the presence of the *rondas* as a significant factor in the defeat and/or containment of the insurgent group Sendero Luminoso (Shining Path) in Peru's 1980 to 2000 civil war (Starn 1995, 1999; Fumerton 2001). Today the *rondas campesinas* make up an organized force that advocates on behalf of campesinos and other oppressed populations in the country. As a significant social movement the *rondas* have potential to provide insight into how "ordinary" people are motivated to better their social environments. In this way the *rondas* can be studied in juxtaposition to other grassroots social movements, such as ZoPs.

We propose that the concept of a "ZoP" be used as a comparative model for analyzing the social significance of the *rondas campesinas*. A ZoP is defined as "an attempt to establish norms which limit the destructive effects of violent conflict within a particular area or during a particular time period or with regard to a particular category of people" (Nan and Mitchell 1996, 3). While ZoPs usually form within the context of armed conflict, the first *rondas campesinas* were "nightwatches" organized by local leaders in the towns of northern Peru to protect the inhabitants of the towns from the increasing danger caused by thievery and violent crime. These first *rondas* may indeed be considered ZoPs if the crime wave the campesinos were

91

experiencing is considered to be within the parameters of violent conflict, as Mitchell and Nan use the phrase.

Starn traces the origins of the northern *rondas campesinas* to the establishment of the first *ronda* in December 1976 in the Cuyumalca, in the department of Cajamarca (1995, 426–27). *Ronderos*, as individual members of the *rondas* are called, patrolled their towns and surrounding areas in search of potential rustlers and other criminals. The first *ronda* was successful in reducing theft, and news of its success traveled to other towns and departments. The *rondas* spread throughout northern Peru, numbering approximately thirty-four hundred in the mid to late 1980s at the peak of their success (Starn 1995, 426).

Rondas campesinas were also established in southern Peru, but their origins are quite different. In southern Peru what are now commonly referred to as *rondas campesinas* first developed as self-defense committees in the mid 1980s in direct resistance to the violence perpetrated by Sendero. The resistance groups later took the name *rondas campesinas* in reference to their predecessors in the north (Fumerton 2001). Some of the southern *rondas* were of grassroots origin, while others were formed under pressure from the Peruvian armed forces in the midst of their armed struggle with Sendero. The varied origins and development of the *rondas* in both the north and the south require complex analysis and challenge many of the assumptions inherent in the ZoP model.

While at least some of the *rondas campesinas* might be considered ZoPs, when peace and violence are conceived broadly, their varied origins and development tell different stories about the pursuit of peace in Peru. We use Galtung's (1969) concepts of positive peace and structural violence to enhance our comparative analysis of the *rondas campesinas* as ZoPs. In this sense the atypical case of the *rondas campesinas* as ZoPs provides further insight into the concept of peace itself.

Rondas Campesinas in Northern Peru

The *rondas campesinas* are one example of peasant response to the inability of the state to meet the basic needs of the Peruvian population. Specifically, the *rondas campesinas* are largely understood by scholars to be a response to rising crime in the department of Cajamarca in the northern Andes (Faundez 2003; Gitlitz and Rojas 1983; Starn 1999). In the mid 1970s, when the *rondas campesinas* first emerged, Peru was in economic crisis. In the central provinces of the department of Cajamarca, where the majority of the population were independent commercial farmers, cattle represented a family's wealth. Gitlitz and Rojas describe cattle as "a way of saving, the peasant's bank account"

(1983, 169). As a result of the economic crisis, cattle also became a main target of theft. The rise in cattle theft was coupled with a historic distrust of the official justice system (Starn 1992). Campesinos considered police and judges to be corrupt and ineffective. A third factor that provided a context for the creation of the *rondas* was the absence of the central government's authority in the remote towns and hamlets of the Andes (Starn 1992).

The theft of cattle took two forms—professional and local. Large-scale cattle-rustling rings of six to thirty-six individuals existed outside the communities that they targeted. Small-scale theft by neighbor against neighbor also existed. This petty thievery increased significantly as the economic crisis became more severe. During this time the occasional thief would work in conjunction with the larger rings (Gitlitz and Rojas 1983). The rising rate of cattle theft was not being controlled by the local police. Failure to control the theft could have been partially explained by the isolated and open terrain of the high plateaus. However, many of the residents of Cajamarca believed that the police were in league with the thieves (Gitlitz and Rojas 1983).

Whether this was the case or not, law enforcement was at best ineffective at controlling the growing problem of cattle rustling. The courts were also ineffective at convicting those who were caught and tried for this crime. Against this background of an inefficient criminal justice system, the residents of Cajamarca formed the first *ronda campesina* in December 1976 (Gitlitz and Rojas 1983).

The idea came from Regulo Oblitas, the lieutenant governor of the hamlet of Cuyumalca (Gitlitz and Rojas 1983). Lieutenant governor is a low-level government post that provides some representation for the executive branch in the more remote areas of the country. Oblitas had once worked on the sugar plantations on the coast and remembered being forced to patrol the plantations in order to protect them from theft. He proposed his idea to the general assembly of Cuyumalca in December 1976. At first his idea was rejected but, after a particularly bold burglary at the local school later in the month, the general assembly of Cuyumalca agreed, and the first *ronda* was formed.

Oblitas obtained support from the next official in the government hierarchy, the sub-prefect, to form the ronda. All men in the hamlet were recruited and organized to patrol the pastures and the trails of the hamlet. The hamlet was divided geographically, and groups of *ronderos* would patrol their assigned areas nightly in rotation. Women did not patrol, but they supported the *rondas* by preparing meals and supplies for the *ronderos*.

The success of the first *ronda* prompted other neighboring towns to adopt the same crime-control strategy, and *rondas campesinas* became a familiar feature throughout the central provinces of Cajamarca.

The *rondas* maintained the same basic structure and function as they spread to other hamlets in the department. In their officially recognized capacity the *rondas* were authorized to patrol and to turn in anyone they apprehended to the authorities. They were not officially endorsed to be armed. However, despite these official decrees, the *rondas* were armed and, at times, did not hand criminals over to the police. The disparity between the officially sanctioned function of the *rondas* and how the *rondas* actually operated created a tense relationship between the local police and the *rondas*. Each group was suspicious and cautious of the other, although they did manage to cooperate on the most basic level in their efforts to control crime (Gitlitz and Rojas 1983).

The initial success of the *rondas* in controlling cattle rustling led not only to their expansion to other communities but also to expansion of their duties. One of the additional roles that the *rondas* took on was the administration of justice. Instead of handing the apprehended cattle rustlers over to the police, often the *rondas* determined the rustlers' guilt and punishment themselves (Gitlitz 2004, 2). Gitlitz describes *justicia rondera* as being about "reconstructing communal peace" and "reintegration into a strong community, so that community life can be preserved" (Gitlitz 2004, 9). Gitlitz's use of the term *peace* leads easily to a consideration of ZoPs. Is community peace achieved through *justicia rondera* comparable to community peace achieved through declaring an area off-limits to the violence of armed actors in a social conflict? To answer the question it is helpful to refer to the distinction between negative and positive peace that is made by Johan Galtung. Galtung defines negative peace as the cessation of physical violence, while positive peace is the cessation of the conditions that lead to the physical violence (1969, 183). According to this distinction, *justicia rondera* is an example of the quest for positive peace on a local level, while declaring an area off-limits to violence is an example of efforts to achieve negative peace at the local level.

It seems clear that Nan's and Mitchell's (1996) definition of a ZoP assumes a conceptualization of peace as negative. Therefore, upon initial examination the *rondas campesinas* of northern Peru do not seem to meet the minimal criteria to be considered ZoPs. They were not an effort to stop violent conflict in the traditional sense. Through the development of *justicia rondera* the *rondas* can be understood as an effort to develop just communities. In this way we can understand the northern *rondas* as zones of positive peace.

The concept of positive peace leads us to consider another one of Galtung's core concepts, the notion of structural violence. Structural violence refers to systemic oppression that perpetuates injustice

(Galtung 1969). The Peruvian government's failure to respond effectively to the rise in cattle theft helped to perpetuate unjust living conditions for the campesinos, who were already living in poverty. In this sense crime can be seen as an indicator of structurally violent social conditions. Rubenstein's assertion that persistent patterns of crime can be understood through the lens of social conflict also supports this interpretation (2003). Following this line of analysis the *rondas campesinas* of northern Peru challenge both the concepts of peace and violent conflict that are central to Nan's and Mitchell's definition. The historical development of the *rondas* in southern Peru adds further dimensions to this discussion.

Rondas Campesinas in Southern Peru

The exact origin of the *rondas campesinas* in the southern portion of the country is not clear. It is possible, as Starn asserts, that the phenomenon simply spread from the north. However, the *rondas campesinas* of the south seem to be of a separate type altogether, merely taking on the name of their northern counterparts for strategic purposes (Fumerton 2001). The origin and development of the southern *rondas campesinas* are inextricably linked to the guerrilla insurgency of Sendero Luminoso.

The department of Ayacucho was the center of the Sendero Luminoso guerrilla insurgency, which began in 1980. The movement enjoyed initial support from the peasants in the area, because Maoist rhetoric of social justice and empowerment of the people was attractive to the poorest of the poor in Peru. However, peasant support waned over time when the promises did not come to fruition and when the campesinos themselves became targets of Sendero's zealotry. Fumerton identifies the first peasant uprising against Sendero as occurring in Huaychao, in Huanta Province, in early 1983. Seven Senderistas were killed by villagers on the morning of January 21, and the peasants' act of self-defense was met with national praise. This act marked the beginning of a new counterinsurgency strategy in the fight against Sendero (Fumerton 2001).

At the end of 1982 President Belaunde had ordered the Peruvian armed forces to enter the region of Sendero's stronghold to fight Sendero and as a result, the plight of the peasants had worsened. Not only were campesinos victimized by Sendero, but they were also targeted by the army, who considered any campesinos who did not evacuate to the district capitals as terrorists. What started as a grassroots effort at self-defense by the Iquichanos of the Huanta highlands was generally encouraged by the Peruvian armed forces. Eventually, peasants were not only encouraged to take up arms against Sendero but were left with little choice but to become members of the self-defense committees. Aquirre J. Coronel notes that the first civil-defense committee (CDC) to be organized by the Peruvian armed forces was formed in September or October of 1983 (Coronel 1996).

The extent to which the self-defense committees were compelled by the Peruvian armed forces varied widely across the south. This wide variance is the result of particular local conditions across the region. Despite the local variations the phenomenon of self-defense committees grew rapidly in the late 1980s and 1990s. The significance of peasant support in the government's war against Sendero was officially recognized when President Fujimori authorized the distribution of firearms to the groups in 1991. Arming the committees is widely recognized as a turning point in the Peruvian civil war (Degregori 1996).

How the self-defense committees came to be known as *rondas campesinas* is not known. Starn (1993) hypothesizes that Peruvian military officials renamed the self-defense committees in an effort to stave off criticism that peasants were being forced to participate. Regardless of its origins, the name *rondas campesinas* was adopted by the peasant self-defense committees of Ayacucho and is widely recognized today (Fumerton 2001). Despite the common name, however, the *rondas campesinas* of the south are quite different from those of the north.

As Fumerton documents, the *rondas campesinas* in southern Peru took three forms of resistance against Sendero. The first example Fumerton provides is that of the grassroots self-defense committees formed by the Iquichanos in the Huanta highlands. The Iquichanos are a distinct ethnic group who lived in the High Andean villages of Huanta Province. Because of intermarriage, the Iquichanos were relatives as well as fellow villagers. When Sendero began to discredit and assassinate the peasant leaders in these villages, the seeds for a grassroots uprising were planted. Fumerton argues that the Iquichanos were the first peasant group to resist Sendero because they were more unified than other peasants in the region, sharing a common language and ancestry. The Iquichanos chose a violent form of resistance because they had few connections or places outside the region to which to flee and because they were very protective of their land (Fumerton 2001).

The second and most widely recognized form of southern *rondas* were the civil-defense committees that were the result of "encouragement" by the armed forces. The first CDCs were modeled after the Iquichano village-defense groups and were organized by the Marine Infantry in Huanta Province in 1983. Although the villagers had little choice but to form CDCs, many of the groups chose their own leaders.

These government-supported *rondas* grew from seven hundred in number in 1989 to over twenty-five hundred in 1997 and hence became an indispensable part of the government's military strategy against Sendero (Fumerton 2001).

The third form of resistance against Sendero in the south is particularly interesting. Some communities in the Pampas River area and the Huanta Valley resisted both the Sendero and the armed forces in a nonviolent fashion. These peasants either chose to leave their territories or refused to take up arms against Sendero. The peasants in these *resistente* communities "focused on creating spaces of autonomy within the general climate of violence by rallying around their established community authorities and traditional social institutions" (Fumerton 2001, 487). Even though the peasants suffered greatly during times of active conflict, their high levels of resilience and cohesion allowed them to work together well, creating effective self-governance and resolving internal conflicts. Those who stayed in their territories lived close to one another under strict rules and resisted pressures by and orders from *all* of the armed actors, whether legal or illegal. The path of resistance for these communities was rejection of association with any armed actors. In this way these communities fulfill all of the criteria for ZoPs; that is, they attempted to limit violence within a context of armed conflict.

However, the first two types of southern *rondas* are also worthy of analysis from a ZoP perspective. While it is impossible to argue that either the self-defense or the civil-defense *rondas* should be considered examples of ZoPs, their different origins have implications for understanding the social significance of the *rondas campesinas* in Peru today. Fumerton notes that during the 1990s, *ronda* took on certain local governance roles in the communities with which they were associated. When the violence eventually subsided around these communities, the *ronda* CDCs formed by military pressure withered away, whereas those with grassroots origins persisted and took on roles of community building similar to those of the northern *rondas* (Fumerton 2001). Research by our colleagues points to a similar observation in examination of ZoPs; that is, those of grassroots origins have greater longevity.[1] An examination of the current status of the *rondas campesinas* in Peru (both northern and southern) provides further insight into the relationship among the *rondas*, structural violence, and positive peace.

Rondas Campesinas Today

While the northern and southern *rondas* have distinct origins and development paths, today the *rondas campesinas* are a national phenomena rather than a regional one. Currently the *rondas* make no distinction between those of northern and southern origin. The *rondas campesinas* today are constitutionally recognized groups that are locally organized to work for indigenous/peasant autonomy and collective rights. The focus of their work is to eliminate the conditions of structural violence that remain. For this reason we might consider today's *rondas campesinas* to be zones of positive peace. The transition of the *rondas* from two distinct sets of phenomena with a shared name to a nationally organized network of federations of *rondas* with a shared vision parallels Peru's own transition from a period of direct violence to one of negative peace.

During the 1990s the conflict with Sendero persisted, and the social and economic conditions of Peru worsened. In the midst of the crisis, on April 5, 1992, President Alberto Fujimori dissolved Congress and suspended portions of the constitution. Following these actions, Fujimori created an eighty-member elected Democratic Constitutional Congress to write a new constitution—the text of which passed an October 1993 plebiscite by 52 percent and was signed by the president on December 30, 1993.[2] The new Peruvian constitution recognized Peru as a diverse country in which all its peoples (from Spanish to indigenous descent) had the right to exercise their traditions. This right to traditional practices held the same status as other constitutional principles such as the rights to freedom of religion, language, and ethnic identity. However, while the right to exercise traditions was articulated in the 1993 constitution, it was not implemented for another decade, and then only after several constitutional reforms.

On December 17, 2002, after several failed attempts, the *rondas campesinas* were officially recognized by Law No. 27908 (Ley de Rondas Campesinas), signed by President Alejandro Toledo. This law defines the *rondas campesinas* as an "autonomous and democratic form of community organization" and recognizes their capacity as independent entities fundamental to the pacific resolution of conflict. It also stipulates that no community can have more than one *ronda* registered and that all its members (including minors) must have identification that recognizes them as active members of the *ronda*. In addition, no *rondero* can belong to more than one *ronda*. It is interesting that the bill, within the rights and duties section, includes rights to democratic participation, to respect for the rights of children and youth, as well as banning discrimination against women, senior citizens, and disabled people.

While some people consider this bill a triumph for the peasant and indigenous movement, others consider it a governmental strategy to keep the *rondas* within their control. In other words, by institutionalizing the *rondas*, their grassroots power may be limited. Even though the analysis of the effectiveness of Law No. 27908 is mixed, it seems clear that the passage of this bill demonstrates the social significance of *rondas campesinas* in the last thirty years of Peruvian history.

Even though indigenous recognition in the 1993 constitution was a triumph, some of the articles of the new Magna Carta proved to be antidemocratic and dangerous (Manchego 2003). Parts of the constitution opened the door for an increase in poverty and injustice in Peru. Among the new reforms were those allowing for presidential reelection, adoption of neo-liberal economic models, and the use of military courts to judge individuals for terrorism and treason *(traición a la patria)*. These reforms sowed the seeds of structural violence that would outlast Sendero's reign of terror.

The reelection provision allowed Fujimori to solidify his power, which allowed the military to continue compelling peasants in the south to take up arms against Sendero. As Manchego notes, the new provision in the constitution regarding the expanded reach of the death penalty for cases of treason gave an overwhelming power to the armed forces. Although the provision could be enacted "in case of war," it did not limit the concept to conventional war, opening it up to practically any type of armed conflict (Manchego 2003). The implications of this provision are demonstrated by the fact that massacres, displacement, and general fear did not stop in the south immediately after Sendero's defeat. On the contrary, the armed forces stayed in the region for several years. Its presence was justified by the new constitutional provision that gave the armed forces the power to charge campesinos with treason if they did not "cooperate" with the wishes of the military in the area.

The constitutional provision that provided for the adoption of a neo-liberal economic model paved the way for the exploitation of natural resources (especially mining) by foreign companies, the privatization of public services, and a free-market economy. Over the twelve years since the adoption of the new constitution, all of these changes have contributed to increasing poverty and class divisions within Peruvian society. The continued persistence of structural violence that takes the form of poverty has become the main focus of current initiatives of the *rondas*. For example, the *rondas campesinas* in the area surrounding the US corporate-run Yancocha gold mine have been active in the movement to limit its environmental destruction of the area and its harmful effects on the health of the surrounding villagers (Chatterjee 1997; Davis 2002).

Over the last five years the national unification of the *rondas campesinas* has become evident. The distinction between the northern and southern *rondas campesinas* is no longer clear. Instead, the *rondas campesinas* are identified by the name of the city or department to which they belong. There is also a national association, Asociacion Nacional de *rondas campesinas* y Urbanas, that provides organizational services to the various *rondas* across Peru. The current aims of the *rondas* focus on public works and organization against the foreign exploitation of mines and other Peruvian resources in general. The fact that the *rondas campesinas* organized and created an association that includes urban *rondas* and *rondas femininas* (women's *rondas*) demonstrates the capacity of indigenous peasant initiatives to be flexible and to evolve according to the political, economic, and social circumstances of the country. It also shows that eliminating structural violence and achieving positive peace are central to the work of the *rondas* of today.

Positive Peace and the *Rondas*

The focus of the work of the *rondas campesinas* today is mainly on improving the living conditions of the campesinos and other impoverished groups. The *rondas* have worked to limit the exploitation of Peru's resources and workers by foreign corporations (Davis 2002). We argue that despite the cessation of armed conflict, many in Peru still live in a violent environment. Galtung's concept of structural violence encompasses many of the conditions of persistent poverty that are characteristic of peasant life. The current *rondas* are working on many of the same tasks that the northern *rondas* turned to after they had effectively controlled the crime problem, that is, public works projects and other efforts to improve the living conditions at the local level. In this way we can consider both the original *rondas* of the north (which have been incorporated into the national *rondas* movement) and the current *rondas* that exist throughout Peru as zones of positive peace.

When analyzed from a ZoP perspective, the *rondas campesinas* present an interesting marginal case. The *rondas* of the north did not originate against a background of armed conflict (what Galtung would call direct violence), yet the crime they experienced was a direct result of the structural violence of poverty and their response was a grassroots attempt at restoring peace to their communities. For this reason we call the original *rondas* of the north zones of positive peace.

The *rondas* of the south provide another provocative case. They were born out of the dire conditions of direct violence perpetrated by Sendero and in response by the armed forces. Instead of declaring themselves neutral noncombatants, they took up arms as a means of survival. Yet the southern *rondas* of grassroots origins persisted beyond the presence of Sendero and the armed forces in the region. Today they, like the northern *rondas*, work toward positive peace. As

Perez writes, "The great paradox of the *rondas* is that, originating from the violence, they showed the basis for peace" (in Kay 2000, 17).

Our analysis of the historical evolution of the *rondas* in the north and the south reveals the need for a wider conceptualization of a ZoP. First, the analysis forces us to ask specifically what is meant by *peace* in terms of these zones? As defined earlier, the implication is that *peace* is what Mitchell calls "safety-from-violence peace" (2003) or what Galtung terms "negative peace" (1969), that is, the cessation of violence. However, there are broader notions of peace that are important to consider. Galtung also developed the concept of "positive peace," which is more than just the cessation of violence. It is a move to deal with the structural violence that underlies the initial causes of the conflict (Galtung 1969). The structural lens that Galtung's concept provides opens up a level of analysis that has been relatively unexplored in the ZoP literature.

Galtung's concept of structural violence also widens the lens that researchers possess to understand ZoPs. When violence is conceived broadly to include unjust and exploitative social conditions, such as poverty and oppression, then the criteria for ZoPs are also broadened. What we propose is to regard the evolution of *rondas* as an evolution of the concept of "ZoPs" as well. By analyzing the *rondas* through the lens of positive peace and structural violence, our objective here has been to highlight the structural conditions that sow the seeds for armed conflict. In this way it becomes possible to see ZoPs not only as forms of conflict *mitigation* but also as mechanisms for conflict *prevention*.

The northern *rondas* present an example of just this point. By developing effective strategies to combat crime and then expanding their social role to include building infrastructure and other development projects, the northern *rondas* built stronger communities. The existence of these strong communities has been cited as one of the reasons why northern Peru remained relatively immune to the advance of Sendero during the period of armed conflict (Starn 1995, 1999). The *rondas* of the north served as mechanisms of conflict prevention because of their work in achieving positive peace on a local level. This case raises the possibility that the expanded *rondas* movement of today may serve a similar purpose on a national level. If successful, its work for positive peace may serve to prevent Peru from becoming engulfed in another civil war.

Further Considerations

Our consideration of the case of the *rondas campesinas* poses more questions than it answers. Instead of generating a definitive answer to the research question, Are *rondas campesinas* zones of peace? we pose the question, What do we mean by peace? We also ask, What do we mean by violence? By arguing for a broader conception of both, we contend that a structural perspective is needed in the study of ZoPs. Questions that still remain include the following: What are the structurally violent conditions that lead to the direct violence that causes a zone of (negative) peace to be constructed? How might zones of positive peace serve the task of conflict prevention?

The case of the southern *rondas* is particularly stimulating in this context. The choice of the peasants in the south to take up arms (especially when they did so of their own accord) leads to still more questions. Why do some peasants choose (relatively) nonviolent mechanisms of peacebuilding while others take the route of violence? Another question that the southern zones provoke is whether violence can be considered a legitimate way to achieve peace. Can positive peace be built on a history of direct violence? Even avoiding these as yet unanswered questions, it is clear that ZoPs are complex social phenomena and that various analytical tools are needed to understand the social significance of such grassroots initiatives. Our analysis of the *rondas campesinas* of Peru provides one small contribution toward this goal of greater understanding.

Notes

[1] For more details on the Philippine and Colombian cases, see Chapters 3 and 4 herein; for a more in-depth analysis, see Chapter 10.

[2] An Agence France Presse report on December 30, 1993, reported that Peru's traditional political parties boycotted the November 1992 vote for the constituent assembly, allowing Fujimori's supporters to pack the assembly and essentially write a "made to order" constitution.

Works Cited

Chatterjee, Pratap. 1997. Conquering Peru: Newmont's Yanacocha mine recalls the days of Pizarro. *Multinational Monitor* 18 (4).

Coronel, Aguirre J. 1996. Violencia politica y repuestas campesinas en Huanta. In Degregori 1996.

Davis, William. 2002. Dynamics of growth: Building social capital. Paper presented at the Bahá'í Development Seminar, December 18, Orlando, Florida.

Degregori, Carlos Ivan, ed. 1996. *Las rondas campesinas y la derrota de Sendero Luminoso.* Lima/Huamanga: IEP/Universidad Nacional de San Critobal de Huamanga.

Faundez, Julio. 2003. Non-state justice systems in Latin America: Case studies: Peru and Colombia. Paper prepared for the DFID workshop, March 6–7. Available online.

Fumerton, Mario. 2001. Rondas campesinas in the Peruvian Civil War: Peasant self-defense organizations in Ayacucho. *Bulletin of Latin American Research* 20 (4): 470–97.

Galtung, J. 1969. Violence, peace, and peace research. *Journal of peace research* 6 (3): 167–92.

Gitlitz, John. 2004. *Justicia rondero y derechos humanos, Cajamarca: Understanding conflict resolution in the rondas of Northern Peru.* Available online.

Gitlitz, John, and Telmo Rojas. 1983. Peasant vigilante committees in Northern Peru. *Journal of Latin American Studies* 15 (1): 163–97.

Kay, Cristobal. 2000. Conflict and violence in rural Latin America. Working Papers 312. Institute of Social Studies.

Manchego, José F. Palomino. 2003. *Problemas escogidos de la Constitución Politica Peruana de 1993.* Instituto de Investigaciones Juridicas. México: Universidad Nacional Autónoma de México. Available (in Spanish) online.

Mitchell, Christopher. 2003. Differing meanings of "peace" in local "zones of peace." Fairfax, VA: ICAR.

Nan, Susan, and Christopher Mitchell. 1996. *Local zones of peace as a form of institutionalized conflict: Some introductory thought.* Fairfax, VA: ICAR. Available on the www.gmu.edu website.

Rubenstein, Richard. 2003. Institutions. In *Conflict: From analysis to intervention,* ed. S. Cheldelin, D. Druckman, and L. Fast. London: Continuum.

Starn, Orin. 1992. I dreamed of foxes and hawks: Reflections of peasant protest, new social movements, and the *rondas campesinas* of northern Peru. In *The making of social movements in Latin America: Identity, strategy, and democracy,* ed. A. Escobar and S. E. Alvarez. Boulder, CO: Westview Press.

———, ed. 1993. *Hablan los ronderos: La busqueda por la paz en los Andes.* Lima, Peru: IEP.

———. 1995. Nightwatch. In Starn, Degregori, and Kirk 1995.

———. 1999. *Nightwatch: The politics of protest in the Andes.* Durham, NC: Duke University Press.

Starn, Orin, Carlos Ivan Degregori, and Robin Kirk, eds. 1995. *The Peru reader: History, culture, politics.* Durham, NC: Duke University Press.

6

EL SALVADOR'S POST-CONFLICT PEACE ZONE

Landon E. Hancock

Introduction

So far in our examination of ZoPs we have largely focused on those instances wherein a zone has been declared either during a conflict or as part of a comprehensive—or not so comprehensive—peace process. However, given the large number of peace zones in places like Colombia, the Philippines, and Peru that attempt to address larger social issues through mechanisms of positive peace (Galtung 1969), the time seems right to examine another type of peace zone, namely one whose aims are not primarily to reduce civil conflict but rather to induce positive social change through the creation and implementation of new social institutions and cultural norms. At the beginning of the twenty-first century examples are few and far between. However, since 1998 a collection of communities in El Salvador, known as La Coordinadora has attempted to ameliorate the impacts of the post–civil war environment in El Salvador through the creation of the Local Zone of Peace aimed at both long-term peacebuilding and economic and social development.

Postwar El Salvador

El Salvador's twelve-year-long civil war between US-backed right-wing Salvadoran governments[1] and the leftist FMLN was officially ended by the signing of the Chapultepec Peace Accords on January 16, 1992. This was followed by nationwide elections in 1994 (Stalher-Sholk

1994, 3). Although hopes were high for peace, both in terms of the cessation of conflict—negative peace—and the redress of what were seen as historical inequalities in economic development, political participation, and land distribution—positive peace—many of the latter aims were not reached at the national level or were thwarted by those within entrenched power positions. Jenny Pearce notes that although the general social and economic direction of the country was not addressed by the peace accords, the ARENA government apparently decided that limited land reform was preferable to wage hikes or more structural and sweeping reforms and was more in line with its views of limited government. In addition, the National Reconstruction Plan, which aimed to rebuild the economies of former conflict areas, largely in the north and west of the country, was characterized by waste, corruption, and ineptitude (Pearce 1998, 602).

Despite poor progress on much of the economic front, some advances were made in the political and national security areas of the state. These included the reduction of the armed forces and the creation of the National Civilian Police and the disbanding of other armed security forces such as the Treasury Police and the National Guard (Doyle, Johnstone, and Orr 1997, 603). However, despite advances in the security arena—facilitated by the UN mission ONUSAL—there were a number of "hiccups" in the process that dogged El Salvador's transition to a post-conflict society based on the rule of law. Primary among these was the resumption of death-squad activities and the reluctance of the government to investigate former military personnel suspected of involvement (de Soto and del Castillo 1995, 194; Pearce 1998, 603). Additionally, there were problems with the induction and retention of former police and military officials into the new force and the initial slowness with which the old, discredited police force was disbanded. Although many of these problems were resolved with the prompting, or prodding, of the United Nations, the peace agreement failed to address other areas of public security, such as the judicial and penal systems, seriously affecting the state's ability to respond to criminal activity—an important point we will return to below—and to reverse decades of institutionally sanctioned impunity (Costa 2001, 24). This was largely due to the vague terms with which the agreement addressed these areas, creating an imbalance between a highly reformed police sector and leaving reforms of the judicial and prison sectors for later.

Accusations of judicial corruption were finally although only partially addressed in the mid-1990s when the election of a new Supreme Court allowed international efforts by the United Nations and USAID to begin implementing judicial reform through partial purges of the judiciary and the implementation of training programs for prosecutors and judges (Stanley and Loosle 1998, 136). These reforms resulted in what Pearce cited as the least politicized Supreme Court in history, but one leaving El Salvador still a long way from "enjoying a non-partisan, independent and effective judiciary" (Pearce 1998, 604).

Overall, postwar El Salvador remains plagued by elements of corruption, politicization of the institutions of government, continued poverty, and threats to public safety from demobilized combatants and gang-affiliated criminals, both the homegrown variety and those affiliated with US-based gangs who returned after the end of the war. It was within this atmosphere that a group of communities located on the southern coast of El Salvador first came together to address issues of economic development and public safety.

La Coordinadora

La Coordinadora, or more properly, La Coordinadora de Comunidades de Bajo Lempa y la Bahia de Juiquilisco,[2] was formed in 1996 in order to address the annual flooding of the Lempa River on the south coast of El Salvador. Between 1996 and 1999 La Coordinadora grew from thirteen communities to eighty-six and founded an NGO—the Mangrove Association—to professionalize its efforts at generating funding, starting development projects, and empowering self-sufficiency for its constituents and their communities.[3] As a part of its orientation toward democratic decision-making, each community elects a representative to La Coordinadora, which is then responsible for governing the Mangrove Association (Chupp 2003, 98–99). La Coordinadora and the Mangrove Association concentrate their efforts in the areas of community organization, disaster response and prevention, participatory processes, environmentally friendly development, and the Culture of Peace Program (CPP)—the cornerstone of the LZP.

Declaring the Local Zone of Peace

The LZP was established as a part of the development activities of La Coordinadora. Post-conflict El Salvador still faces a number of difficulties. These include the failure of land reform to redress historical inequalities, a poor distribution system, and endemic violence. While La Coordinadora was created to address economic and social development issues, it soon became clear that criminal violence, especially violence conducted by gang members repatriated from the United States, was seriously hampering efforts to rebuild the local economy and attain a level of economic and social self-sufficiency.

According to Chupp the LZP was developed based on a UN concept derived from the 1971 UNESCO declaration of the Indian Ocean as a ZoP and the subsequent 1990 declaration of Latin America as a ZoP by several of the region's presidents (Chupp 2003, 99–100). The creation of the LZP was spearheaded by José Alas, a former parish priest from El Salvador who had fled during the civil war, and assisted by Ramón López-Reyes, the director of the International Center for the Study and Promotion of Zones of Peace in the World, based in Hawaii. The general idea flowing from López-Reyes's experience was that in order to be successful a ZoP needed to be instituted from the grassroots up rather than from the governmental or top level down, as the Indian Ocean and Latin American zones had been (Hayes 1998). This grassroots orientation was complemented by Alas's experience as a parish priest and colleague of Archbishop Romero and his participation in the liberation theology movement in Latin America, with its emphasis on using faith and principle as a means for eradicating poverty and improving social conditions.

The LZP is territorially defined in its founding principles as "a territory occupied by a community" seeking to define its own goals and aspirations to live peacefully, using the LZP to create a foundation for "the free and full expression of rights, be they economic, social and cultural, as well as . . . civil and political rights" (Hayes 1998). This passage taken from the declaration of the LZP indicates that the members see the establishment of a ZoP as part of and precursor for the creation and maintenance of a whole series of rights, economic and political, necessary for a stable civil society. The physical area of La Coordinadora and the LZP are coterminous, consisting of eighty-six communities located at the southern end of El Salvador's Usulután Province and bounded by the Rio Lempa on the west and the Rio Grande de San Miguel on the east.

The Culture of Peace Program

For the LZP the creation of the CPP has been an essential cornerstone of both the general activities of the LZP and the democracy promotion and development activities of La Coordinadora. As described on their website, the Culture of Peace Program (CPP) is summarized as transforming a culture that promoted and rewarded violence to one that values and practices peace (La Coordinadora 2000). The components of the CPP are focused on educating for peace, using methods for transforming conflicts, and creating new organizations for grassroots participation for peace. The main goals within the CPP are peace, democracy, and self-sufficiency, which had a tremendous impact on the nature of the CPP and the methods by which it was created and implemented.

The training program used to design the CPP was developed by López-Reyes, Chupp, and others with the participation of a number of Salvadorans, including Mario Mejia, who had been hired as the program's full-time coordinator in October 2000. The design of the training program followed the tenets of Lederach's (1995) elicitive training model, emphasizing the uncovering and use of local knowledge to create positive change and sustainable peacebuilding. The local and international trainers worked to elicit the peaceful qualities of each of the communities in the project and combined this with works stemming from the Quakers and analysis models like Dugan's (1996) nested theory with the goal of assisting the communities to create a positive vision of their own future and the ability to organize to create that future.

The components of this program include knowledge of and education for peace, methods of conflict transformation, methods of organizing and creating participation, and commitment to a positive approach to social change and building peace. One of the essential features is the dialogue and reflection circles, a process created to introduce elements of the program to communities and allowing them space to discover and create their own strengths in spreading the CPP (Chupp 2003, 113).[4]

The CPP benefited from grants by the United States Institute of Peace and the Hewlett Foundation, totaling $115,000, which supported efforts to expand the dialogue and reflection circles (La Coordinadora 2000; FSSCA 2001a). The CPP continued to grow throughout 2002 and 2003, expanding to twelve communities and using the circles for dialogue and reflection to empower men and women to speak out about their feelings with regard to the war and violence as well as assisting them to organize and meet challenges due to poverty, hunger, and violence. Two specific instances of improvements included the training of teachers in Isle de Mendez to use and model conflict resolution behavior and the inauguration of La Coordinadora's radio station, Mangrove Radio, allowing for a wider dissemination of conflict resolution and peacebuilding principles (FSSCA 2002a, 2003).

In addition, La Coordinadora's US-based partner, the Foundation for Self-Sufficiency in Central America (FSSCA) has used the CPP as a springboard for the creation of a region-wide initiative known as the Culture, Spirituality, and Theology of Peace Project—also called the Meso-American Peace Project—designed to bring together the differing cultures of the region and create a force for peacebuilding based upon the values for peace inherent in local traditions, cultures, and religions (FSSCA 2004e).

As of early 2006, the main part of the training for the CPP has been completed. However, local communities continue to use the dialogue and reflection circles that have been incorporated into the governance structure of the LZP and La Coordinadora. Typically a circle includes members from between four and seven communities, who work together upon similar development alternatives or community needs. Additionally, some members of the circles and some local communities have begun to participate in the Meso-American Peace Project as well.[5]

Supporting Projects

Around this core of the partially indigenous and partially international CPP, the LZP has instituted a number of programs and initiatives designed to address social conditions that either result in violence or prevent peaceful economic development and self-sufficiency for the communities in the LZP. The two main obstacles to generating self-sufficiency and economic development, as described by La Coordinadora, are the general problem of an endemic culture of violence and the specific problems associated with the return of Salvadoran youths who had fled to the United States during the decade-long civil war.

The problems associated with an ingrained culture of violence, wherein violence became an accepted part of life and drained many resources away from poverty reduction, education, and economic development, were mostly to be addressed by the implementation of the CPP, which would allow and encourage other resources to be focused on the economic development activities described below. However, the specific problems associated with the return of youths to post-conflict El Salvador appeared early in the process of developing the LZP. In 2000 the project team implementing the CPP pilot project in Tierra Blanca found that the primary issue of concern for the local population was the high levels of violence perpetrated by members of two rival gangs.

The two gangs in question, Mara Salvatrucha (MS-13) and Calle 18, are imports from the United States. Both gangs got their start in Los Angeles' MacArthur Park area in the 1980s (Wallace 2000, 51). In the 1990s US immigration laws were toughened, increasing the range of crimes for which an offender could be deported, leading directly to the deportation of more than sixteen thousand individuals to El Salvador for criminal reasons between 1994 and 2003.[6] In Tierra Blanca the CPP team met first with members of MS-13 and then with members of Calle 18 to discuss their backgrounds and some of the problems they face as youths and as gang members in the community.

Not surprisingly, gang members described themselves as facing some of the same problems that other members of the community faced, namely, difficulty in finding work and dealing with grinding poverty, along with threats of violence from members of rival gangs and discrimination by the police and security forces (Alas 2002). The team managed to hold two meetings between the rival gangs and had started a process that seemed to hold promise of addressing some of the concerns regarding employment skills and reintegration into Salvadoran society. For their part, the leaders of the two local cliques agreed to institute a truce between the gangs and pledged to take steps forward. Unfortunately, the local police chose that moment to arrest one of the clique leaders, perhaps because reactionary forces wanted to ensure that the gangs did not reform and leave their lives of crime (Alas 2002).[7]

Several projects emerged out of the realization that the CPP by itself would not be able to address some of the structural roots driving these new conflicts. One of the first activities was the Rays of Light Youth Art Project, which was designed to give students concrete skills in drawing, painting, and silkscreening to allow them the opportunity to use these skills and to give them an alternative to gang membership. The project, formally started in 2002, has taught between seventy and one hundred students per year. In 2005 La Coordinadora sponsored the opening of an art gallery along one of El Salvador's main highways, bringing attention to the art, the artists, and the project itself. While this project does not focus on generating moneymaking skills, it does allow students to use their time productively and provides alternative venues to gang membership or just "hanging out" (FSSCA 2005b).

A second project aimed particularly at gang-affiliated youth was started in 2004. This project, named Adios Tattoos, was designed to integrate former gang members back into society by providing laser tattoo removal. Tattoo removal is an important part of signifying that former gang members are ready to reenter society; it engenders trust in the local communities, reducing the likelihood of discrimination by community members and the police and increasing job prospects for the former gang members (FSSCA 2004b).

The success of this project was confirmed in an online testimonial from a former gang member, Mauricio, who underwent the process shortly after the project began. Mauricio described the project as a key factor in his ability to reintegrate into society. Bolstered by courses offered by La Coordinadora in wood working and drafting, Mauricio works as a carpenter. He indicated that after tattoo removal he had become more trusted by members of the community who had previously feared him. When bidding on contracts for carpentry work,

Mauricio noted that he could now ask for advance payment to purchase supplies for the job, stating that "people no longer hesitate in giving me this payment because they know that I am responsible and that I won't spend it on alcohol or drugs" (FSSCA 2004a). Furthermore, although he has received some criticism for his decision to remove his tattoos, he feels more at ease in moving about the community and is more welcomed by community members, including the police, who see his tattoo removal as a concrete sign that he has distanced himself from gang membership and his former life.

By early 2006 Adios Tattoos had provided funds to remove tattoos from twelve former gang members. While this number may appear to be low, the process is both expensive and time consuming. To remove the tattoos from one former gang member—gang members often have tattoos covering much of their bodies—takes between one and one-half to two years. Demand for the removal remains high, but as with many of La Coordinadora's projects, funding is uncertain.[8]

In order to promote both the CPP and to provide modern skills to youths and community members, La Coordinadora started two associated programs in 2004. The first, located adjacent to the Adios Tattoos removal center is the Mangrove Cybercafe, which provides computer training, printing services, and Internet access through satellite connection to members of the community. The cafe is run by local volunteers, with equipment and training provided by volunteers sponsored by the Jewish Youth Philanthropy Project. The cafe is relatively small, with just a handful of computer workstations, but it provides valuable services for the community through the use of email, Internet research, and broadband audio and video links at prices far below the cost of telephone service. In addition, the interns at the cafe learn valuable business management and technical skills (FSSCA 2004d, 2004c).

A second project designed to disseminate information and promote self-sufficiency is La Coordinadora's radio station, Radio Mangrove. Located alongside La Coordinadora's main office in Ciudad Romero, the station was started primarily to give the region—largely ignored by the national media—its own voice (Weissman 2004). The station, which expanded its broadcast hours from ten to fifteen hours a day between 2003 and 2004, broadcasts music, news, commentary, health campaigns, and literacy programs (FSSCA 2003, 2004b). The literacy project, which ran from August through October 2004, was part of a national literacy campaign, but it also benefited from the high degree of infrastructural support provided by La Coordinadora. The radio portion of the program, which consisted of three twenty-minute sessions each week, was supplemented by the training of twenty-three local facilitators who provided follow-up training and organization for the project. In a country where adult illiteracy approaches 40 percent, the participation of more than three hundred individuals has added measurably to the communities' abilities to increase their levels of self-confidence and self-sufficiency (FSSCA 2005a).

In addition to the public-service component of Radio Mangrove—including programs aimed at economic development—the station serves as an educational and experiential venue for the region's young people. The station is staffed by fifteen youth volunteers, who receive professional training and are active in all aspects of running the station (FSSCA 2003). Some of the youth who work at Radio Mangrove are former gang members. The goal, as in all of these projects, is to provide alternatives to gang membership for local youths and to assist them in learning skills that they can use for self-development and to become productive members of society.

Economic Development

Although much of the focus of this chapter has been on La Coordinadora's activities in promoting the CPP, one of the underlying goals of the LZP is to address the economic factors that cause conflict (Baron 1996). Given that the founders of the LZP believed that there was a dialectical and supportive relationship between sustainable development and peace—in other words, that you can't have success in one area without success in the other—it is important to examine the projects that are more focused on the development side of La Coordinadora's mission.

Disaster Response and Prevention

In terms of one of its primary responsibilities, disaster response and prevention, La Coordinadora has initiated a number of activities. Although the devastation caused by Hurricane Mitch in 1998 came too soon after the founding of the LZP for any prevention efforts, La Coordinadora was apparently the only group in El Salvador that was organized and effective enough to collect data to present to a UN conference held in the Dominican Republic in early 1999 (Alas 1999). In addition, volunteers were able to evacuate their flood-threatened communities so effectively that there were no lives lost—in stark contrast to a region just to the north where more than 150 people died (Lehman 2001).

Taking stock of the aftermath of the hurricane, La Coordinadora embarked on a program to ensure that in future disaster situations it would transform as much aid as possible into development projects.

It reasoned that emergency assistance should be temporary assistance, otherwise it breeds dependency instead of self-sufficiency (Fernández 1999). This focus on the balance between relief and development proved useful when, in 2001, El Salvador was rocked by several earthquakes. According to FSSCA board chairman Harold Baron:

> The Coordinadora's disaster response team went into action within ten minutes. Pickups and cars fanned out to the communities. Only two hours later we saw the local disaster teams taking inventory of the damage. Within 36 hours the central office had assessments from a majority of the villages, despite major communications difficulties.

In addition to the quick response, Baron noted:

> While communities still rigged temporary shelters and hauled in drinking water, [La Coordinadora] started on permanent reconstruction for housing and production. [The people] worked with a strategy their organization had honed . . . in response to . . . Hurricane Mitch. . . . Six weeks after the first quake, Coordinadora villages are laying the foundations for homes, restoring fields, and reconstructing shrimp ponds. They have moved from disaster response to building for the future. (Baron 2001)

Following the three earthquakes that rocked the region in early 2001, La Coordinadora immediately provided temporary shelters of tents and plastic sheets, organized water distribution, assisted communities with food supplies and immediate crop cultivation, and provided for an evaluation of the damage in each of its member communities (La Coordinadora 2001).

As a part of its disaster-prevention program La Coordinadora focused its efforts on building houses that can withstand natural disasters, both from earthquakes and hurricanes, and on providing cisterns for storage of potable water. The focus on prevention led to the development of two separate housing programs, one involving the design and construction of concrete block homes, and another involving the purchase and construction of wooden roundhouses—prefabricated homes designed as permanent alternatives to tents and other temporary shelters. By October 2001, La Coordinadora—working with volunteers—had installed seventy-five of the roundhouses in its affected communities (FSSCA 2001e, 2001f). Work was slower on the larger concrete block homes, but twelve had been completed by June, with construction continuing on another forty (FSSCA 2001c). By spring

2002, more than two hundred new homes had been built, including a larger two-bedroom unit "model home" in Ciudad Romero (FSSCA 2002b).

Finally, in 2001, La Coordinadora completed a forty-eight-bed Disaster Relief Shelter and Dormitory next to its headquarters in Ciudad Romero. The structure, designed to provide temporary shelter in times of need, also serves as a meeting place and, during the annual summer tour of the LZP, as a housing facility for visiting dignitaries and interns (FSSCA 2001a).

Sustainable Development

As might be expected from an organization that insists that economic development and violence reduction go hand in hand, La Coordinadora has sponsored a large number of development projects designed to ameliorate the conditions of poverty and structural violence endemic to the region. For ease of analysis, these projects have been concentrated under three broad themes: credit and grants, education and training, and transport and marketing. Individual projects at times span more than one of these areas, with education being offered as a component of most programs.

Under the goal of increasing self-sufficiency, in 1999 La Coordinadora started a micro-credit program to help farming families grow diversified organic crops and to assist shrimp farming and fishing cooperatives. From 1999 to 2001—the only years for which data are available—the Credit Fund Project awarded loans to more than two hundred individuals and cooperatives, increasing food security for many low-income families and allowing several fishing and shrimp farming cooperatives to rebuild and restart their businesses following the destruction wrought by Hurricane Mitch. The micro-credit project, like many of La Coordinadora's projects, works through local community leaders and project technicians to identify recipients and to monitor each recipient to ensure follow through on the project. Recipients are normally granted a grace period before beginning their repayment, but they are required to sign documents indicating their agreement to abide by the terms of the loan and to guarantee its repayment (FSSCA 2000).

Unfortunately, much of the funding for the micro-credit project was diverted to disaster assistance following Hurricane Mitch, the 2001 earthquakes, a subsequent drought, and the effects of Tropical Storm Stan, which destroyed the crop plantings of more than two thousand families in the fall of 2005. Despite these setbacks, the FSSCA and La Coordinadora received approval for a grant from the Inter-American Foundation to fund the micro-credit program for three to four years at approximately US$150,000 per year. These funds will largely be directed toward helping small agro-businesses and individual farmers with disbursements scheduled to begin in the fall of 2006.[9]

In 2000 La Coordinadora began working on creating alternative irrigation systems to allow farmers to grow during El Salvador's dry season. As a method of increasing food security, dry-season growing is key, especially given the fact that crops planted during the wet season are often ruined in the frequent floods that plague the area. Several systems were implemented, all based on drip irrigation fed by cisterns raised off the ground to allow gravity to pressurize water flow. A number of different methods were implemented to pump water into the cisterns, mostly gasoline powered, but also systems using either hand pumps or converted bicycles for foot pumping the water (FSSCA 2001d).

This project feeds into one of La Coordinadora's main goals, the creation and support of sustainable, environmentally friendly agriculture. Since its inception, La Coordinadora and the LZP have focused on persuading farmers to use environmentally friendly techniques and, in 2000, established a training school to promote agricultural education. This school for food production leaders trains individuals to use appropriate technologies to irrigate their lands, fight pests, and fertilize their crops. In addition, the school promotes the gathering of seeds, both for use as fertilizer—as with pigeon peas—and to stock nurseries in order to reduce their dependence on outside distributors (FSSCA 2001b).

Other elements of the sustainable agriculture project include crop diversification to increase biodiversity, family garden plots to increase food security, a chicken project to increase calorie intake and protein consumption among campesinos, and an environmental program to rehabilitate the Bay of Jiquilisco by reforestation efforts and by helping depleted fish and turtle populations to recover (FSSCA 2004b).

The third prong of La Coordinadora's development efforts focuses on increasing direct participation by community members in markets. Some of these efforts dovetail with CPP education efforts (such as the Cybercafe) and with disaster prevention efforts (such as a project that distributes cell phones to community representatives for emergency communications) to allow farmers and other producers to have access to market prices in order to be able to price their goods competitively (FSSCA 1999). In 2002 a new project was started to purchase land and build a market center along one of El Salvador's main highways, with plans to expand the center to include a restaurant and hotel (Telleen-Lawton 2002; FSSCA 2002a). By 2003, La Coordinadora's marketing project had circumvented middle men entirely and had assembled a logistical team to transport produce to a women's cooperative for sorting and repackaging before a distribution team transported produce directly to markets in San Salvador and elsewhere (FSSCA 2003). As with other aspects of La Coordinadora's development projects and the CPP, the main goals are self-reliance and self-sufficiency. Although technical assistance and philanthropic donations are welcome, the direction and management of all projects lies in the hands of La Coordinadora, with guidance and participation at the grassroots level from all member communities.

Analysis

As we begin our analysis of the LZP we should note those things that are similar to or shared by the LZP and some of the ZoPs we have examined in areas like Colombia, Peru, and the Philippines. Foremost among these is the nature of these zones as being grassroots oriented, with democratic structures of governance. For the LZP the governance structure is explicitly grassroots and democratic, with representation for local campesinos embedded in the local peace groups, which then elect representatives for three-year terms as members of La Coordinadora's central committee.

A second similarity comes from the twin goals of the LZP, with its focus on reducing gang violence by reducing the sources of inequity and poverty that lead members of El Salvador's youth to join gangs and terrorize their communities. The nature of the violence being addressed is different, with communities in Colombia and the Philippines attempting to address civil conflict while the LZP focuses largely on criminal conduct. However, citizens in both types of zones see the conflict as a result of issues such as poverty and corruption, which can be dealt with to a greater or lesser degree by the structure and focus of the zones themselves. In other chapters we have seen how ZoPs that began by addressing civil violence by withdrawing from the wider conflict later expanded in order to address some of the underlying conditions. They created democratic structures of governance, addressing a lack of education by working to educate themselves and addressing issues of poverty by attempting to acquire resources from international bodies and by negotiating with local armed actors to ensure that farmers and other small producers could get their goods to market.

However, despite these similarities, there are a large number of differences between the LZP and the ZoPs we have examined in other chapters. The most important among these is the fact that while both types of zones were initially created to address issues of violence, the types of violence and the arena in which the zones must work are significantly different. Because El Salvador's civil institutions do function after a fashion—even with endemic poverty and issues of corruption and possible death-squad activity—the membership of the LZP can focus most of its efforts on the economic development projects that address the sources of criminal violence rather than being forced to expend its efforts on maintaining its existence in the face of competition for control among different factions of violent actors. The relationship between the LZP and the government of El Salvador is not one of enthusiastic cooperation—indeed, the then president of El Salvador, Armando Calderón Sol, refused an invitation to attend the inaugural ceremony of the LZP, instead choosing to travel to a nearby town to discuss the creation of sugar plantations with local oligarchs—but neither is it one of outright hostility, as is often the case in Colombia, for example, where the Uribe regime "forbids" local peace initiatives and local army commanders believe that anyone promoting active neutrality is merely a front for one of the left-wing guerrilla movements. The nature of this difference between struggling to survive and addressing larger social concerns is one that, in this author's opinion, has allowed the LZP to concentrate its resources on both its peacebuilding efforts and on the economic projects that often make the difference in addressing the structural sources of conflict that threaten the stability of ZoPs elsewhere.

Another major area of difference between the LZP and many of the other ZoPs studied in this volume is the degree of institutional and financial support provided to the LZP's efforts by government bodies and grant-makers in the United States and elsewhere. Although REDEPAZ in Colombia received support from the European Union and some zones in the Philippines received monies from the government when they were designated SDAs, neither locale has benefited from foreign or governmental monies to the same degree that the LZP has. The main reason for this difference is the existence of the FSSCA, which operates largely as the US-based arm of La Coordinadora and the LZP in the United States. With the exception of the Meso-American Peace Project, all of the FSSCA's efforts are directed toward assisting the peacebuilding and development goals of the LZP. The FSSCA provides a source of steady funding and a contact point for individuals and grant-making organizations, allowing US-based individuals and groups to make tax-deductible contributions to the LZP through the FSSCA. In addition, the FSSCA provides the conduit for tour groups and volunteers to visit the LZP. Volunteers have played an important part in a number of the LZP's projects, especially by providing technical expertise and equipment to set up the Mangrove

Cybercafe. In addition, the FSSCA's former executive director, José Alas, stressed the emotional and symbolic importance of visitors in validating the work of the campesinos of the LZP. The sense of solidarity gained through the visits of LZP tour members and volunteers could be compared—somewhat—to the important work done by witnesses from Peace Brigades International and other similar groups who accompany human rights workers in violent conflict situations with the hope that their presence will bring a sense of solidarity and may deter violence on the part of government or rebel forces. Although it is certainly much less dangerous to volunteer to assist campesinos in the LZP, the solidarity that is achieved through such actions can go a long way toward energizing locals to continue with the hard work of changing their lives and their communities for the better.

Another important aspect behind the overall success of the LZP is the fact that, unlike many of the other communities we have examined in this volume, the LZP encompasses a large number of communities. As noted above, the LZP started with forty-seven communities in 1998 and grew to eighty-six communities by 2005.[10] The size of the LZP allows for economies of scale in terms of both procuring grant monies and other forms of assistance and delivering services and programs to member communities and to individuals within those communities. Scholastic programs focusing on training for agriculture, civil society, democracy, and conflict resolution skills are more sustainable when larger numbers participate in them, and funders are more likely to support such programs when they feel that program impact will be distributed widely, both geographically and demographically. Some programs, such as the irrigation project, radio station, and micro-credit program can only be implemented on a region-wide rather than community-wide basis. While attempting something similar in places like the Philippines or Colombia may be impossible largely due to the ongoing civil conflicts, the structural difficulties of sharing and allocating resources may also hinder these types of efforts in areas where the zones are largely based at the community level rather than at the regional level.

In terms of our examination of ZoPs, we believe that the LZP shows us not only the promise of peace zones in developing countries, but may also point to new mechanisms that developed countries could use to revitalize urban areas blighted by economic deprivation and civil unrest. The combination of a grassroots governance structure based upon the principles of self-sufficiency and use of methods of conflict transformation and peacebuilding to address economic and social concerns of the local populations has given the LZP a solid foundation upon which to build and provides elements of a model that may be transferable to other troubled regions.

Notes

[1] The center-right Christian Democrats. led by José Napoléon Duarte, were replaced in 1989 by the far-right Alianza Republicana Nacional (ARENA) party, led by Roberto d'Aubuisson.

[2] The literal translation is "Coordinator of the Communities of the Lower Lempa River and Juiquilisco Bay."

[3] For more information, see the www.fssca.net website.

[4] For more details about the training program, see Chupp 2003. Chupp served as one of the principal trainers and participants in the creation of the CPP.

[5] José Alas, interview by Landon E. Hancock, February 20, 2006.

[6] US Bureau of Citizenship and Immigration Services—formerly the Immigration and Naturalization Service. Accessed from LexisNexis Statistical Services. Wallace notes that in 2000 there were twenty thousand full-fledged gang members in San Salvador alone (2000, 50), while Johnson and Mulhausen indicate that roughly one-third of the four thousand to five thousand yearly deportees to Central America had criminal records in the United States (2005).

[7] Wallace also notes that postwar El Salvador has become a haven for organized crime syndicates, who use the gangs, or *maras*, as a smokescreen for their own activities and that reactionary forces might want the gangs to continue as they are, both to justify their own existence and to make sure that gang members do not lift their sights from turf battles to perhaps starting a second civil war (2000).

[8] Alas, interview.

[9] Ibid.

[10] When La Coordinadora was founded in 1996, it comprised thirteen communities. By the time the LZP was founded two years later, La Coordinadora had grown to forty-seven communities, which is why the LZP's starting number of communities differs from La Coordinadora's. This nominal difference between La Coordinadora and the LZP may raise some questions regarding the degree to which these two organizations are separate or are intertwined. It is this author's view that based upon their shared governance structures and intertwining projects they can be considered one organization.

Works Cited

Alas, José. 1999. My recent visit to El Salvador. Available on the fssca.net website.

———. 2002. Youth gangs in El Salvador. Available on the fssca.net website.

Baron, Harold. 1996. ITAMA helps create a local zone of peace. *ITAMA Update* (Fall). Available on the fssca.net website.

———. El Salvador earthquake: Disaster and response. *Spring 2001 Newsletter*. Available on the fssca.net website.

Chupp, Mark. 2003. Creating a culture of peace in postwar El Salvador. In *Positive approaches in peacebuilding: A resource for innovators*, ed. C. Sampson, M. Abu-Nimer, and C. Liebler. Washington, DC: Pact Publications.

Costa, Gino. 2001. Demilitarizing public security: Lessons from El Salvador. In *El Salvador: Implementation of the peace accords*, ed. M. S. Studemeister. Washington, DC: United States Institute of Peace.

de Soto, Alvaro, and Graciana del Castillo. 1995. Implementation of comprehensive peace agreements: Staying the course in El Salvador. *Global Governance: A review of multilateralism* 1 (2) (May): 189–203.

Doyle, Michael W., Ian Johnstone, and Robert C. Orr. 1997. *Keeping the peace: Multidimensional UN operations in Cambodia and El Salvador*. New York: Cambridge University Press.

Dugan, Moire. 1996. A nested theory of conflict. *Leadership Journal* 1 (July): 9–20.

Fernández, Eva. 1999. Looking at reconstruction. *Summer 1999 Newsletter*. Available on the fssca.net website.

FSSCA (The Foundation for Self-Sufficiency in Central America). 1999. Mangrove cellular. *Fall/Winter 1999 Newsletter*. Available on the fssca.net website.

———. 2000. The Credit Fund Project. 2000. June. Available on the fssca.net website.

———. 2001a. *Annual report 2001*. Round Rock, TX: FSSCA.

———. 2001b. El Salvador agricultural school. Available on the fssca.net website.

———. 2001c. Homes for earthquake victims. June 5. Available on the fssca.net website.

———. 2001d. The Irrigation Project. April. Available on the fssca.net website.

———. 2001e. More roundhouses for Rio Roldan and Los Flores. Available on the fssca.net website.

———. 2001f. Roundhouses. Available on the fssca.net website.

———. 2002a. *Annual report 2002*. Round Rock, TX: FSSCA.

———. 2002b. Homes: El Salvador's biggest challenge. *Spring 2002 Newsletter*. Available on the fssca.net website.

———. 2003. *Annual report 2003*. Round Rock, TX: FSSCA.

———. 2004a. Adios Tattoos Project offers former gang members a more normal life. Available on the fssca.net website.

———. 2004b. *Annual report 2004*. Round Rock, TX: FSSCA.

———. 2004c. Mangrove cybercafe: Getting ready for business. Available on the fssca.net website.

———. 2004d. Salvadoran cybercafe connects people, provides information and training services. Available on the fssca.net website.

———. 2004e. *What is the Meso-American Peace Project?* Available on the fssca.net website.

———. 2005a. Mangrove Radio and Literacy Project. *Winter 2004/2005 Newsletter*. Available on the fssca.net website.

———. 2005b. Rays of Light Youth Art Project. Available on the fssca.net website.

Galtung, Johan. 1969. Violence, peace, and peace research. *Journal of peace research* 6 (3): 167–92.

Hayes, Margaret. 1998. Declaration of the local zone of peace. Available on the www.fssca.net website.

Johnson, Stephen, and David B. Mulhausen. 2005. No silver bullet for youth gangs. *The Washington Times*, August 29.

La Coordinadora. 2000. *Fall/Winter 2000 Newsletter.* Available on the www.fssca.net website.

———. 2001. Report #4 on the post-earthquake situation in the Bajo Lempa–Bay of Jiquilisco. The Coordinadora del Bajo Lempa–Mangrove Association. January 23. Available on the fssca.net website.

Lederach, John Paul. 1995. *Preparing for peace: Conflict transformation across cultures.* Syracuse Studies on Peace and Conflict Resolution. Syracuse, NY: Syracuse University Press.

Lehman, Karen. 2001. The earthquake and the Coordinadora. January 18. Available on the fssca.net website.

Pearce, Jenny. 1998. From civil war to "civil society": Has the end of the Cold War brought peace to Central America? *International Affairs* 74 (3): 587–615.

Stalher-Sholk, Richard. 1994. El Salvador' negotiated transition: From low-intensity conflict to low-intensity democracy. *Journal of Interamerican Studies and World Affairs* 36 (4): 1–59.

Stanley, William, and Robert Loosle. 1998. El Salvador: The civilian police component of peace operations. In *Policing the new world disorder: Peace operations and public security,* ed. R. B. Oakley, M. J. Dziedzic, and E. M. Goldberg. Washington, DC: National Defense University Press.

Telleen-Lawton, David. 2002. The produce of peace and hope. *Summer/Fall 2002 Newsletter.* Available on the fssca.net website.

Wallace, Scott. 2000. You must go home again. *Harper's Magazine* (August): 47–56.

Weissman, Gary. Radio Mangrove 106.9 FM: A dream growing on the air. *Summer 2004 Newsletter.* Available on the fssca.net website.

7

COMPARING SANCTUARY IN THE FORMER YUGOSLAVIA AND THE PHILIPPINES

CHRISTOPHER MITCHELL

Introduction

This chapter focuses on another—relatively unsuccessful—effort to establish a form of sanctuary, namely, efforts by outsiders to set up safe or protected zones for a civilian population in the midst of an extremely violent civil war. At least one unusual feature of this particular type of sanctuary is that such zones are often established and supervised by outsiders, that is, by governments or international organizations seeking to mitigate some of the worst effects of civil strife, frequently at the same time as they try to broker a negotiated settlement of the conflict. Specifically, the chapter discusses the establishment and later collapse of the UN Protected Areas (UNPAs) in the former Yugoslavia in the period from 1992 to 1995, and asks what lessons might be learned both about the low durability of these zones and—more generally—about the role of outsiders in the establishment of effective sanctuaries during protracted conflicts.

The analytical approach adopted is based upon two assumptions, the first being that it is possible to learn as much from failures as from successes. And there is an undoubted consensus that the Yugoslav experiments—usually viewed as experiments in peace-keeping by outside interveners (UN, NATO, UNHCR)—were, indeed, failures. At least this is the case as far as the mandates establishing them were concerned and certainly as far as bringing stable peace to the areas involved, which witnessed some of the worst massacres and ethnic cleansings of the so-called war of Yugoslav disintegration.

A second assumption is that our general understanding of peace zones will be increased by briefly contrasting those established in the former Yugoslavia with the first ZoPs established in the Philippines slightly before, in the early 1990s. When the United Nations was trying to provide sanctuary in Bihac, Sarajevo, and the rest, local ZoPs had already been established in Luzon, Negros, and Mindanao, in what many regard as the first, pioneering wave of local peacebuilding on the islands.[1] However, although the Philippine ZoPs were also set up during national efforts to end a long, drawn-out civil war, even a cursory glance at their history shows that they were very different from the zones in Yugoslavia. Hence, our comparison is very much between "un-likes," so that any lessons about relative successes have to be drawn cautiously.

This warning returns us to the issue of what constitutes a success for a peace zone. It can be argued that efforts to establish and maintain the peace zones in Yugoslavia did contribute something, both to the mitigation of the conflict and to the search for a peace settlement acceptable to the warring parties (or, at least, one that seemed so reasonable to outsiders that they were willing to force it onto the Yugoslav adversaries). In the case of some of the peace zones in Yugoslavia, at least for a time, relief supplies managed to enter, the level of violence died down (usually temporarily), and so life improved a little for those within the zones. However, the central fact that the wars continued meant that even this temporary change within the zones was precarious and liable to come to an end with the next major assault. None of the zones seems to have lasted until the final settlements, including that brokered at Dayton, with the possible exception of Sarajevo and Goradze in Bosnia. The fate of zones such as Zepa and Srebrenica is widely known.

Types of Peace Zone in Yugoslavia

Zones in which certain kinds of conflict-related behavior were outlawed were established during the various conflicts making up the overall war of disintegration. Below, I outline the five main types that have been identified and add brief details about some of these efforts before switching to an analysis of those established between 1993 and 1995 in Bosnia, which seem to be most closely akin to other types of LZPs offering some form of sanctuary against violence that are discussed in the present volume.

UN Protected Areas in Croatia

UNPAs were first established in February 1992, following the January 2 cease fire between Croat and Serb forces in Croatia, brokered by Cyrus Vance, the UN secretary-general's special representative.

Three UNPAs—areas in which there existed a substantial or majority Serb population and where tensions "had led to armed conflict in the recent past" (UN 1991, 5)—were established in Eastern Slavonia, Western Slavonia, and Krajina.[2] The UNPAs were to be fully demilitarized zones with a UN force (UNPROFOR) supervising the withdrawal of all Yugoslav army units (mainly if not exclusively Serb); the disarming, demobilizing, and disbanding of all "irregular" forces; and the handing over of all weapons, which were to be stored under a dual-key system. UNPROFOR was also to assist the UNHCR in helping to return any displaced persons who wished to go back to their homes. In addition, there were to be unarmed, UN-supplied civilian police within the UNPAs to assist local police and to ensure that basic human rights within the zones were being observed—and, particularly, that further ethnic cleansing did not take place.

One of the more difficult parts of UNPROFOR's mandate was to ensure that local administrative organs (including the police) within the UNPAs conformed to the composition of the population *before* actual hostilities had broken out. In other words, the UNPAs were supposed—somehow—to return to the status quo ante as far as population mix was concerned. More conventionally, should further violence between local Serb and Croat communities threaten, UNPROFOR was to "interpose" itself between the two sides to prevent hostilities.

"Pink" Zones

Pink Zones were areas outside but adjacent to the actual Protected Areas, which were controlled by the Serbs or contained a significant number of Serb communities. Supposed to be demilitarized as part of the Vance Plan, their monitoring also became part of UNPROFOR's mandate as a result of a Security Council decision in June 1992.

The Pink Zones increasingly became subject to sweeps and incursions by the Croat forces and were used as launching pads for nightly Croat hit-and-run attacks into the UNPAs themselves.

UN Safe Areas in Bosnia

The declaration of certain Bosniac controlled towns and adjacent territory as safe areas for the population therein (often increased by an influx of Bosniac displaced persons) came about largely as the result of the Fall 1992/Spring 1993 efforts of the Bosnian Serbs to drive all Muslims out of the Drina Valley, which was part of the Serb strategy of eliminating all such communities from Eastern Bosnia.

This strategy interfered considerably with UNPROFOR's task in Bosnia—to ensure the delivery of relief supplies—and involved local commanders on the ground with the politics of the Bosnian/Serb conflict. Eventually the problems led the UN Security Council (on April 16, 1993) to declare Srebrenica a safe area—a move which, like others, freed up Bosnian Serb forces for other activity elsewhere. Later (on May 6, 1993), under pressure to extend this idea, the Security Council added Tuzla, Sarajevo, Zepa, and Goradze to this list of safe, protected areas, together with Bihac in the northwest corner of Bosnia. (Usually these towns had originally had very mixed populations of Bosniacs, Serbs, and Croats, and in some cases were the site of much internal violence among the local populations in their various parts of the cities.) In June 1993, facing the facts that (a) to provide credible protection for the local populations from Serb attack large numbers of troops (estimated at thirty-four thousand) would be needed, and (b) that these troops were not available, the Security Council authorized the dispatch of seventy-six hundred troops. It also allowed calling in air power in order to provide a more credible deterrent against Serb assaults.

Weapons Exclusion Zones

Once the safe areas had been proclaimed, it became evident that in many cases they and their protected populations were vulnerable to long-range (or even short-range) attacks by heavy weapons. For example, during the first half of January 1994, shells killed an average of six people each day in Sarajevo. On February 5 a mortar shell landed in Sarajevo market square, killing sixty-eight people.

This incident led to a NATO ultimatum to the besieging Serbs (as well as the Bosnian government) that all heavy weapons should be withdrawn from an "exclusion zone" (ultimately set at twenty miles around the city) or face their destruction by air attack.

Enough weapons were withdrawn by the Serbs to justify the view that the desired exclusion zone had been successfully established and that at least some weapons of long-range destruction had been taken from this zone.

"No Fly" Zone over Bosnia

As early as October 1992 the Security Council had passed a resolution banning flights by military aircraft in Bosnian air space. This decision had been taken partly as a result of sporadic attacks on Bosnian and Croatian targets by Serbian military aircraft, but also as part of the sanctions package that had been imposed earlier on Serbia and Montenegro. A month later the Security Council added another resolution, insisting that all flights into Bosnia had to be inspected at Split, Zagreb, or Belgrade.

UN Protected Areas in Croatia

The rest of this chapter will focus mainly on the so-called safe areas in Bosnia, but the ideas and assumptions underlying the establishment of the UNPAs in Croatia are also worth commenting on, briefly.

The first point to be made is that the UNPAs were established after the declaration of a cease fire and as the result of a settlement (the Vance Plan) negotiated with those seen to be the main parties—that is, the warring governments of the former Yugoslav Republics. However, it is not clear whether this negotiation process involved all the stakeholders to the conflict in former Yugoslavia/Croatia, particularly the Croatian Serbs who has been responsible for driving out Croatian Croats from the areas themselves. Certainly, the subsequent behavior of the local Serbs indicated that they would do little to implement (and much to undermine) the terms of the agreement about UNPAs. The two main difficulties (apart from armed incursions into the zones by the Croats) revolved around interlinked issues of (1) disarmament and (2) return of IDPs.

Fundamentally, the ideal model of a UNPA was of an area restored to its condition before violence had broken out. However, to achieve this the more than a quarter of a million displaced Croats had to be returned to their homes. This was never achieved, and the process of ethnic cleansing (driving Croats *from* their homes) continued in the UNPAs, in spite of UNPROFOR's efforts to protest this—protests made to Serb-controlled authorities who were themselves often directly responsible for the expulsion of Croats from the UNPAs or were simply indifferent to the continuation of that process.

Actual return of Croat IDPs depended upon their security being guaranteed and this, in turn, depended upon genuine disarmament and a balance being achieved in local (security) administration—which in turn depended upon the return of the IDPs. "Disarmament" within the UNPAs frequently consisted of Serbian politico-military forces handing over their weapons to or becoming members of the local police—whom the Serbs in Croatia naturally saw as their only source of real security.

UNPROFOR therefore found itself in the position of actually preventing the return of Croat IDPs to the UNPAs on the grounds that their security could not be guaranteed once they did return. Actions that involved physically stopping Croatian attempts to return IDPs peacefully to the UNPAs simply reinforced Croat government perceptions of UN partiality as well as fears that the UNPAs would be lost forever to Zagreb. Eventually, in March and August 1995, the Croat army took over all the UNPAs, defeating local Serb forces and speeding a new outflow of IDPs, on this occasion Serbs, many of whom went into the Serb controlled regions of Bosnia.

Looking at UNPAs as sanctuaries, their main features seem to have included the following negative factors:

1. The zones contained people from one side of a conflict who were supposed to be protected from attacks by their adversaries, rather than people who claimed to belong to neither side and simply wished to be left alone, as was the case with the Philippine peace zones.
2. Those within the zone retained their arms, ostensibly as a last resort with which to defend themselves, but additionally to retain dominance over what was left of their rival community. In Philippine ZoPs efforts were made to ban all arms.
3. Those within the zones continued the persecution and expulsion of members of the rival community, who were actually left unprotected.
4. The third-party (UN) role was to monitor disarmament and to ensure appropriate treatment for the minority community, but it had no sanctions other than protest when the terms setting up the UNPAs were violated—nor did UNPROFOR have any sanctions beyond revelation when the Croats carried out incursions into the UNPAs, thus creating a self-fulfilling prophecy regarding Serb retention of arms for their own "defense."

UN Safe Zones in Bosnia

Perhaps the most interesting aspect of conflict mitigation in the former Yugoslavia, at least as far as illuminating different means of providing sanctuary is concerned, was the UN effort to establish safe zones for the inhabitants and IDPs living in key towns in eastern Bosnia (and in Bihac, near the Croatian border), which had become threatened enclaves in (Bosnian) Serb-controlled territory. Clearly, the safe zones established in Bosnia were very different entities from the ZoPs established in the Philippines or Colombia (discussed in other chapters of this book). However, it might be their very differences that can indicate something about the strengths and weaknesses of various means of trying to provide local sanctuary.

The following section, therefore, contrasts some key features of the Bosnian safe zones with those of the local zones established at about the same time in the Philippines.[3]

Setting Up the UN Safe Zones—the Philippines and Bosnia

The Bosnian UN Safe Zones (UNSZs) were established unilaterally by UN Security Council resolution. In other words, there was a declaratory act by an outside third party, without, as far as one can tell, previous consultation with the combatants or with the communities within the zones. In the case of the majority of the Filipino ZoPs, in contrast, it appears that the local community initially declared the establishment of the zone, and in some cases there may have been prior consultation with local combatants.

Trigger Events

Several of the ZoPs in the Philippines appear to have been established as the result of a key event such as an attack on a church, the killing of a youngster in the town or village, or the decision of IDPs to return to their place of origin.

In the case of Srebrenica, the trigger event was the visit of French General Morillon to the town to investigate the failure of UN relief convoys to get through Serb-controlled territory and the subsequent refusal of the local inhabitants to allow the general to leave. (This was perhaps the first example of a common tactic based on the hope that the physical presence of outsiders—UN, NATO, and so on—would either deter Serb attacks or force the outside organization to take sides against the adversary because its representatives were in the line of fire or actually being attacked.)

The other UNSZs appear to have been established as a follow up to the initial declaration of Srebrenica as a safe zone.

Objectives and Aspirations for the Zones

The early ZoPs in the Philippines appear mainly to have been established by the population living within them in order to withdraw from the fighting—with associated objectives of restoring control over their own lives and developing a more democratic, egalitarian, or traditional way of living. In other words, it was a form of neutralization, containing an element of "a plague on both your houses."

The Bosnian zones were quite different. They were in no sense neutral zones but rather zones containing a population of adversaries protected from the attentions of its own adversaries. In short, they are best seen as adversary zones, not neutral zones.

Rules for ZoPs and Sanctions for Breaking the Rules

Expressed slightly differently, the UNSZs were—justifiably—perceived as partisan arrangements in that they contained people and (armed) resources from one side of the conflict who could be (and were) regarded as wholly legitimate targets by the other side (the Bosnian Serbs). Moreover, the people within the zones were not even trying to remain neutral and inactive. The limitation on armed forces within the zones was wholly one sided, as the Bosniac forces therein were not disarmed and could—and did—use the safe zones as bases from which to launch raids on the surrounding Serb forces.

With this *caveat* in mind, the central rule concerning the Bosnian zones involved the prevention of sustained assault from the outside by one of the combatants (which could take the form of long-range shelling). Sanctions to deter this consisted of the threat (or use) of air power to strike at the forces undertaking any assault. This sanction worked on a few occasions but was countered by the Serb tactic, especially at Bihac, of taking UNPROFOR personnel prisoners and using them as hostages against possible third-party (NATO) air strikes.

It should be recalled that the UNSZs usually contained mixed populations and often substantial IDP populations "cleansed" from the surrounding countryside. This IDP presence threw a heavy strain upon resources within the zones and thus made them even more vulnerable to externally applied sanctions and blockades.

Outside Help in Establishing Zones

Clearly some of the Filipino ZoPs had outside help in starting up their zones, often from local and regional church authorities. Further, there was a strong relationship between the existence and linking of local ZoPs and the overall peace movement at the national level, especially under President Ramos.

In the case of UNSZs, the zones were the actual creation of the UN Security Council (plus UNPROFOR), so it seems inaccurate to talk about outside "help" in establishing these zones. However, there clearly had to be outside help in maintaining them—the Bosnian Serbs were undoubtedly bent on clearing all Bosniacs from eastern Bosnia and solidifying their hold on the region. All the UNSZs contained at least some third-party peace "supervisors" (although never enough to make up a credible deterrent force) whose role was to discourage attacks by (1) presence, (2) revelation, and (3) reaction by force—although the last was both remote and uncertain so that the consequences of any incursion or attack were never clear, certain, or automatic. Moreover, those determining whether to use a coercive response were linked to vulnerable agents in the field who could easily become hostages and act as a counter deterrent.

Combatants' Reactions

In the case of the Philippines, the reaction of the local combatants to the establishment of a zone from which *both* were supposed to be excluded was a complex, variable, and localized one, depending upon day to day circumstances. Clearly, for certain periods of time the local community was able to negotiate with both government and guerrillas so that they respected the "rules" of the local zone, until it ceased to be advantageous—or at least not harmful—to do so, or until some higher level command came down to stop acceding to the wishes of locals to be treated as neutrals.

In the case of the UNSZs in Bosnia, the reactions seem much less problematical, given that the zones mainly contained people (and armed forces) from one side being protected against assaults from the other. For both parties, actual (or potential) control of contiguous territories was a major value, while for one party the consolidation of a contiguous bloc of territory, the obliteration of "anomalous" areas, and the expulsion of the (enemy) population were valued goals in themselves. In Serbian eyes the UNSZs were obstacles to be removed whenever the opportunity presented itself (although, at times, the UN presence was seen as temporarily releasing Bosnian Serb forces for action elsewhere). For the Bosnian government the UNSZs and the presence of UN personnel therein provided possibilities for the closer involvement of outside parties on the side of the Bosnians, should UNPROFOR personnel be injured or killed as a result of Serb activity.

In short, there were major reasons for one side to launch attacks on what it regarded as enemy outposts within its own territory—geographical entities that possessed major strategic, material, and symbolic value; and for the other, reasons for hoping that such attacks would turn peacekeepers into allies rather than neutrals.

Regional and National Dynamics

It seems reasonably clear that the successful first-wave ZoPs in the Philippines were usually in political backwaters as far as national-level conflicts were concerned. (It is likely that there was actually no fighting between the NPA and government forces anywhere near Naga City when one of the first peace zones was declared there, although the area had been badly affected by the activities of official and semi-official "self-defense" vigilantes.) Hence, while they may have been affected by the national-level peace process and the negotiations between the government and the NPA, the ZoPs themselves did not figure significantly in processes at that level.

In contrast, the whole UNSZ issue was bound up with the Croatian-Bosnian conflict, with the Bosnian government/Bosnian Serb conflict, and with the Bosnian-Serbian governments' conflict. Campaigns in other parts of the former Yugoslavia, sanctions and blockades imposed by third-party interveners, and regional and UN politics all had an impact on the maintenance of even marginally viable safe zones and provided a turbulent environment with which those actually in the zones, their protectors, and their attackers had to deal. The issue of the UNSZs could not be ignored at national political levels.

Lessons from Bosnia?

Can one draw any lessons about local ZoPs from the Bosnian experience, beyond saying do not, in the middle of a civil war, try to set up a protected ZoP that clearly belongs to one side and is regarded as a legitimate target by the other?

Perhaps the best way of using the Bosnian experience is (1) to think of it as an extreme example of the process of establishing and maintaining a ZoP, characterized by features that contributed mightily to the probability that it would not be durable, even with a high degree of outside support and interest; and (2) to ask what those features were, precisely, what might be their opposites, and whether these opposites might contribute to greater durability in other situations.

For example, one important characteristic of the UNSZs was the degree of outside interest and support for them, but this would need to be modified by considering also the extent to which the third-party "supporters" were (a) able to threaten credible sanctions on violators of the zone (b) invulnerable to counter threats themselves. Would it make a difference if the outside third-party supporters were able to offer positive sanctions for nonviolation (plus negative sanctions for violations) as well as being impervious to the threat of counter sanctions? This argument suggests that one can contrast ZoPs according to at least three characteristics: level of outside support available; outsiders' capacity for imposing sanctions (positive or negative); and outsiders' vulnerability to counter sanctions.

Following this line of thought, I can propose that both the UNSZs experience and some early initiatives in setting up ZoPs in the Philippines highlight a number of important characteristics likely to affect the success and survivability of local sanctuaries. Some of these can be conceptualized as discrete variables and include the following:

1. Source of protection from violation
   - internal armed force
   - third-party armed force
   - supernatural sanctions
   - norms involving shame/reputation
   - international resolutions
   - internationally recognized rules or norms
   - persuasive negotiation with combatants
2. Allegiance of protected population within zone
   - partial to one side
   - mixed allegiance
   - neutral
   - not involved (i.e., different ethnicity/culture)
3. Advantages offered local combatants by zone's existence
   - release of forces for other fronts
   - area for rest, recreation
   - denial of resources to adversary
   - enhancement of reputation/credibility
   - neutral arena for contacts with adversary
   - advantages bargained elsewhere by agreeing to zone
4. Manner by which zone established
   - unilateral declaration by inhabitants
   - unilateral declaration by third parties
   - negotiated agreement with local combatants
   - general policy agreed by national/regional leaderships
5. Arrangements regarding arms
   - within zone
     –complete ban on presence/carrying
     –carrying limited to certain approved categories (e.g., police)
     –secured stockpiling within zone
   - around zone
     –complete ban on all/heavy weapons
     –limited ban on presence
     –limitations on use
6. Role of outside third parties involved in zone
   - observers of/publicists for violations
   - monitors of a (formal or tacit) agreement
   - protectors

- providers of humanitarian aid
- trainers in (requested) skills
- intermediaries

Alternatively, other characteristics can be regarded as continuous variables, such as:

1. Attitudes of combatants in local area to the existence of the zone, ranging from support through indifference to outright hostility.
2. Degree of decision-making authority retained by "legal" national authorities, ranging from continuing and unchallenged authority to complete replacement by others.
3. The nature of decision making within the zone, ranging from highly participatory to highly hierarchical.
4. The volatility of the conflict in the immediately surrounding region.
5. The nature and intensity of interactions with other peace zones.
6. Ease of access to the zone by existing or potential outside supporters.[4]
7. Importance of the zone to local combatants.

Bosnia and the Philippines

Table 7–1 represents an attempt to distinguish between the experiences of trying to set up peace zones in Bosnia and in the Philippines, simply on a compare-and-contrast basis.

A final word of caution is necessary once again, however. It can easily be argued—with some justification—that the UN's outsider efforts in Bosnia ended in a fairly resounding and comprehensive failure (with the possible exception of Goradze). In contrast, the local, insider initiatives in the Philippines seem to have been (relatively) successful, in that the ZoPs survived and flourished, in spite of setbacks and tragedies, at least for a number of years, and in some case up to the present time.

However, it should not be assumed that the reasons for the destruction of the UNSZs in Bosnia and the survival of the Philippine ZoPs can be found simply by comparing some obviously different and highly selective characteristics of the two initiatives, such as those outlined in Table 7–1. These—and many others as yet unknown—may all have contributed to the short life of the Bosnian sanctuaries and the relatively longer duration of those in the Philippines. Reviewing this and other chapters about experiences in sanctuary building

TABLE 7–1. CONTRASTING FEATURES OF TWO FORMS OF SANCTUARY

	Bosnia (UNPZs)	Philippines (first wave)
How established	Unilaterally by an external third party	Unilaterally by community or through local negotiation
Communities	Partial to one side (Bosnian Muslims)	Neutral or not involved
Local combatants	Mainly from one side (Bosnian Serbs)	From both sides: AFP and NPA
Attitudes of local combatants	Highly hostile	Mixed and variable
Importance of zone to local combatants	High symbolic and strategically important	Most remote and not of central concern
Volatility of local environment	Relatively stable; most violence focused on SZ	Volatile but low key violence
Arms in zones	Local forces from one side retained arms and ability to lauch attacks from SZ	Zones internally disarmed
Third-party roles	One-sided protection by United Nations	None involved, although national church important in some cases
Protection by	Small armed forces from outside plus (uncertain) air strikes	By negotiatied agreements and nonviolent sanctions
Politics within zones	Continued dominance of government inputs	Often divorced from national government

can only lead to the conclusion that different efforts to construct sanctuaries in one form or another can never simply be viewed as successes or failures, and accounting for the effectiveness of sanctuaries is more complex than listing half a dozen or more variables that possess a surface plausibility. With our present level of knowledge all we can do is suggest that some factors help to make sanctuaries more effective and durable, while others seem to have the opposite effect. We need to build on that beginning.

Notes

[1] The Philippine ZoPs are discussed in much greater detail in Chapter 3 and in Garcia 1993 and 1997.

[2] In most of these three areas it is probable that—because of "ethnic cleansing" tactics—the actual ratio of Serb to Croat populations had shifted heavily in favor of the Serbs.

[3] For more details of the development of LZPs in the Philippines, see Chapter 3; Garcia 1993 and 1997; and Lee 2000. I have omitted any detailed history of the Bosnian peace zones from this essay. For the events in Srebrenica, the first of the safe zones established by the UN and the scene of subsequent massacres carried out by the Bosnian Serbs, see Honig and Both 1997. For good accounts of the establishment and misfortunes of all of the safe zones, see Durch 1996 and Gow 1997.

[4] The nature of and reasons for obstacles to access will clearly be different from case to case, ranging from geographical remoteness to deliberate blockades by combatants.

Works Cited

Durch, William J. 1996. *UN peacekeeping, American politics, and the uncivil wars of the 1990s*. New York: St. Martin's Press.

Garcia, Ed. 1993. Participative approaches to peacemaking in the Philippines. United Nations University monograph series on governance and conflict resolution. Tokyo: United Nations University.

———. 1997. Filipino Zones of Peace. *Peace Review* 9 (2): 221–24.

Gow, James. 1997. *Triumph of the lack of will: International diplomacy and the Yugoslav War*. New York: Columbia University Press.

Honig, Jan Willem, and Norbert Both. 1997. *Srebrenica: Record of a war crime*. New York: Penguin Books.

Lee, Zosimo E. 2000. Peace zones as special development areas: A preliminary assessment. In *Building peace: Essays on psychology and the culture of peace*, ed. A. B. I. Bernardo and C. D. Ortigas. Manila: De La Salle University Press.

UN (United Nations). 1991. Report of the Secretary General Pursuant to Security Council Resolution 721 (1991). S/23280. New York: United Nations.

8

THE COLLAPSE OF PEACE ZONES IN ACEH

Pushpa Iyer and Christopher Mitchell

Peace Zones and Disarmament

Establishing zones to facilitate (among other things) safe disarmament or demobilization is a common feature of the ending of many violent and protracted conflicts. These zones are variously named— safe zones, demilitarized zones, assembly areas, protected zones— and have been used frequently but with varying degrees of success. Such zones are one answer to a common dilemma that arises when peace agreements are being negotiated or—once agreed—implemented: how to ensure safety for combatants whose previous security has rested in their own weaponry, but who are being required to give up those weapons while their erstwhile adversaries retain theirs.

The provision of reliable sanctuaries for armed combatants in transition toward a new status in what it is hoped will become a peaceful civil society—or in a process of "reinsertion"—thus connects to the issue of diminishing mistrust between adversaries and is fraught with problems. Some safe zones have worked well—in former Rhodesia and in Namibia, for example—and the process of disarmament been carried through smoothly and safely. Others have been less successful. The example discussed in this chapter involves the peace zones that were set up in 2003 to facilitate an end to violence and a negotiated agreement in the Indonesian province of Aceh in the northern part of the island of Sumatra. These particular zones can hardly be counted a success, and their collapse exemplifies not only the complexities and problems of bringing about a solution to this conflict, but also some of the common problems of establishing sanctuaries where disarmament can safely take place.

The Most Recent Peace Process in Aceh

Representatives of the government of Indonesia and the Acehnese separatist movement GAM signed a peace accord in Vantaa, Finland, on July 16, 2005, and GAM members began to hand in weapons on September 15, 2005; some Indonesian troops and "nonlocal" security forces began to be withdrawn from the province at the same time. Negotiations that led to this new "Memorandum of Understanding" started in February 2005, following a new initiative encouraged by the Finnish government and particularly by the former president, Marrti Ahtisaari. Between May 2003 and the end of 2004 the Indonesian government had carried out a renewed strategy of military repression to try to crush GAM and had severely curtailed its ability to operate successfully. However, many have argued that the major impetus for this renewal of the peace process resulted from the devastation in Aceh caused by the tsunami that struck northern Sumatra on December 26, 2004, leaving an estimated 150,000 dead in Aceh alone, together with over 500,000 homeless.

The Vantaa negotiations were, in fact, a renewal of previous contacts and negotiations between GAM and the government; for the peace process in Aceh has a history that goes back to the late 1990s. In fact, for the war-weary people of Aceh, the first real ray of hope came as early as December 9, 2002, when it seemed as though peace had become a genuine possibility. After twenty-seven years of bloody violence GAM and the government of Indonesia had signed a preliminary agreement to end hostilities.

Unfortunately, the negotiated cease fire held in the region for only a brief time before collapsing in May 2003. During that time, however, a number of peace zones were established in Aceh, the main purpose of which was to ensure that demilitarization took place in order to pave the way for humanitarian aid and rehabilitation. The zones set up in Aceh between January and May 2003 can hardly be counted as successes, but a review of their history can be useful. There is much that can be said about and learned from the process and the parties involved in setting up the zones and from the overall peace process itself. This stage of the peace process in Aceh was always very fragile and encountered many problems, even in its early phases. However, the peace zones did survive for a time, so this chapter outlines the process of establishing them, identifying their key features, reviewing their fortunes, and commenting on both the intended and the actual role of the zones in the overall peace process. The main sources of data for this chapter were newspaper reports; these were however supported by discussions with Acehnese, many of whom were actively involved in the conflict.[1]

Background to the Conflict

Aceh, an oil-and-gas-rich province of Indonesia, is located on the northernmost tip of Sumatra and is the westernmost point of the country. Until the middle of the seventeenth century, Aceh was an independent sultanate. From 1641 to 1824 the kingdom was at the center of British-Dutch rivalry, and finally, in 1824, Aceh achieved its independence under an Anglo-Dutch treaty. In 1873 the Dutch invaded Aceh and colonized the region. They were met with fierce resistance and the war between Acehnese and Dutch raged intermittently from then on. In 1949, when the Republic of Indonesia was created from the Dutch East Indies, Aceh was made a special region (province) of the new country. Mortified by this status, the Acehnese have since then demanded independence from Indonesia (they declared themselves independent in 1953, an act that was not recognized by the Indonesian government), and their separatist movement quickly turned into an armed struggle.[2]

In 1971 oil was discovered in the region. This changed the face of Aceh in the eyes of Indonesia and the rest of the world. Foreign oil companies[3] and state (Indonesian) owned enterprises descended on Aceh, bringing with them "foreigners" as employees.[4] Aceh contributes to a sizeable portion of Indonesia's gross domestic product, but the Acehnese have seen only a small portion of the revenues generated by these resources. This discontent over the sharing of revenues from oil and gas operations between the "center" in Indonesia and the "peripheral" province was one of the prime reasons for the rise of GAM. Hasan di Tiro (the last scion of the pre-colonial sultanate and in exile in Sweden) founded GAM (often called the Free Aceh movement) in 1976 to contest political, religious, and economic issues with the Indonesian government.[5]

The Indonesian government responded to the armed struggle with force. State repression against separatist movements is perhaps inevitable, but this was particularly so in Aceh during the long years from 1968 to 1998, when the country was under President Suharto's military rule. GAM remained small in size (it has several hundred full-time "soldiers") with few weapons, making it vulnerable to the strong and well-equipped Indonesian army—the Tentara Nasional Indonesia (TNI). GAM therefore indulged in guerrilla warfare, choosing its place and time to fight. The movement enjoys the support of many Acehnese, especially the rural folk, most of whose discontent with the Indonesian government is over their economic and social conditions.[6] The TNI and the BRIMOB (Police Mobile Brigade) have responded with brutal force and repression.

GAM intensified its struggles between 1989 and 1998. In 1998 Suharto's military regime came to an end. While violence did not really abate after 1998, at least negotiations accompanied it in the post-military-rule period.

Background to the Early Peace Efforts

In 1999, after the fall of the Suharto regime, Abdurrahman Wahid became Indonesia's first democratically elected president.[7] From that time until May 2003, there were serious efforts to bring about a negotiated end to this protracted conflict. Talks between the Indonesian government and GAM continued over these years, in spite of many breakdowns and serious setbacks. Roughly, there were three main periods in the peace talks. The first period was between 1999 and July 2001; the second from July 2001 to March 2003; and the third, characterized by rapid breakdown, took place between March and May 2003.

Two peace agreements resulted from negotiations between 1999 and March 2003, after which the whole peace process unraveled. One was concluded in the first period but obviously failed, leading to another, more promising agreement in the second period. Both these agreements, arising from a series of talks, came about largely as a result of the third-party intervention by the Henri Dunant Centre (HDC) of Switzerland. The HDC was launched officially in 1999 with the financial backing of the United States and a number of European countries, including the Netherlands (which had originally colonized Indonesia).[8] The HDC attributed the failure of the first negotiations in part to its own low-key involvement as a third party. Learning from this, the agreement concluded in the second period had a strong role for the HDC.[9] The next two sections describe the periods of negotiation in greater detail, leaving the period of breakdown to be discussed later.

First Period (1999 to 2001)

President Wahid brought a breath of fresh air to the war-torn region. He apologized publicly for human rights abuses by the Indonesian military in Aceh and took a softer approach with GAM. Following a massive demonstration by the people of Aceh for a referendum on independence, it seems the president began considering that idea seriously, but the military quickly opposed it and he was forced to drop the thought. He subsequently made the statement that while "autonomy" might be considered, "independence" was out of the question.

The president was, however, prepared to sit down and negotiate with GAM. An agreement entitled "The Joint Understanding on Humanitarian Pause" came into effect on June 2, 2000, and would, it was hoped, ultimately lead to an end to all hostilities. In this agreement both sides (the Indonesian government and GAM) agreed to "reduce the violence" and also provide "security modalities" to support humanitarian assistance in Aceh. The "humanitarian pause" was reviewed by the parties in September 2000, as planned, and entered its second phase when the cease fire was extended to January 15, 2001.

In reality, the "humanitarian pause" (an informal truce) was far from being a real pause in the conflict. With both sides frequently violating the cease-fire agreement, clearly the "pause" was a failure. The final symbolic straw came when Exxon-Mobil closed down its operations because of security threats to its work and employees.[10] Indeed, from the time military rule came to an end, there had been a series of attacks on the plant facilities and personnel, partly because when many of the human rights abuses of the military period were brought to light, the involvement of Exxon-Mobil in these activities was also unearthed.[11] Moreover, strong feelings against Exxon-Mobil employee policies and discontent over sharing revenues with the central government made Exxon-Mobil the target of increasing GAM attacks. From mid-2000, attacks on the company and its employees escalated further and finally, in March 2001, the company shut down its operations, citing "security threats" as the reason. This resulted in a closure of the main Arun LNG plant and other fertilizer companies that depended on supplies from Exxon-Mobil. More TNI forces were dispatched to provide protection to Exxon-Mobil. This resulted in a heavy crackdown on GAM, and once again human rights abuses peaked.

The first set of peace talks had clearly failed. In May 2001 a state of emergency was declared, and more violence followed. One of the few international agencies working in Aceh, Doctors without Borders, pulled out because of the escalating violence. President Wahid was again under pressure from the military to use more force and to allow the military to take greater control, while the vice-president, Megawati Sukarnoputri, seen as a "hardliner," was also supportive of military action. At the end of June 2001 both sides met in Geneva (again through the efforts of the HDC) and agreed to work toward peace, but no immediate efforts were made to start negotiations.

Second Period (July 2001 to March 2003)

The pressures of the military worked, and President Megawati Sukarnoputri succeeded President Wahid. The new president presented a new autonomy package (July 2001) to the Acehnese, but she firmly refused to entertain demands for independence. Under the new autonomy package Aceh was renamed Nanggroe Aceh Darussalem (NAD). Ironically, this translates as "Aceh: Abode of Peace." Under what became known as "NAD law," Aceh was offered an increase in the share of oil and gas revenue—to 70 percent from the 5 percent under President Suharto. (Other provinces received 15 percent of oil and 30 percent of gas revenues). In addition, Aceh was to be allowed to implement Islamic Law (Sharia).[12]

GAM rejected this special autonomy package and began moving more steadily in the direction of working for a wholly independent Aceh. More violence followed, with GAM setting up a parallel government (Indonesian *civil* administration hardly functioned in Aceh), indulging heavily in extortion, and spreading what was described as a reign of terror.[13]

Efforts by the HDC to bring the parties together continued. In February 2002 the two sides met again in Geneva, agreeing on two important issues blocking formal negotiations: GAM would no longer reject the idea of special autonomy, and the Indonesian government would no longer insist that GAM initially give up its call for independence. In May 2002 further meetings produced a joint statement on further consultations, and finally, on December 9, 2002, the Indonesian government and GAM signed a "Cessation of Hostilities Agreement." This agreement, henceforth referred to as COHA/FAIM (Cessation of Hostilities/Framework Agreement with Interim Measures),[14] proposed an immediate cease fire followed by (1) a dialogue about the political future of the region, and (2) elections in 2004. The agreement avoided the issue of independence. The special autonomy law (adopted by the Indonesian Parliament in 2001) was accepted as merely an interim arrangement by GAM.

The basis of COHA/FAIM was the acceptance of "NAD law" as a starting point but many problems associated with that arose subsequently. Two that immediately presented themselves were:

1. Indonesian electoral law stated that parties had to have "nationwide representation" to be officially registered. This would have caused problems for GAM, a local Acehnese party, should it have come to contest the elections scheduled for 2004.
2. The special autonomy law stated that candidates in elections should never have been foreign citizens; most of GAM's senior leaders had lived in exile for many years.[15]

Peace Zones for Aceh

In the first two periods of the 2001–3 peace process in Aceh and as part of both "The Joint Understanding on Humanitarian Pause" and the COHA/FAIM, peace zones were an important feature, although with more details about their nature and functions in the second period compared to the first. COHA/FAIM actually defined peace zones and provided mechanisms to establish and monitor them. There is less to say about peace zones in the first period, for they hardly lasted a week. However, the experience has its own significance when evaluating strategies concerning the peace zones in the second period, especially in terms of what the adversaries learned from the first, failed experience.

Peace Zones in the First Period

Under the "Joint Understanding on Humanitarian Pause" the following three committees were set up to ensure the implementation of the agreement and the establishment of peace zones:

1. The Joint Forum: The highest body had representatives from the Indonesian government and GAM, with the HDC acting as facilitator. This forum was to oversee the implementation of the humanitarian pause and comment on the basic policies to be adopted.
2. The Joint Committee on Humanitarian Action: This group was to implement the policies laid out by the Joint Forum, provide humanitarian assistance, and work closely with the Joint Committee on Security Modalities. It was also responsible for fundraising for humanitarian assistance. It comprised ten members (maximum)—five from each side—and was to be facilitated by the HDC.
3. The Joint Committee on Security Modalities: This committee was to ensure that there was an actual reduction of tension and cessation of violence. Committee members were responsible for making all the practical and logistical arrangements regarding movement of troops, enforcement of law, and maintenance of public order. The committee comprised ten members—five from each side—and was also facilitated by the HDC. The committee was to be supported by a monitoring team consisting of five persons "of high integrity" agreed to by both parties.

There appears to have been no clause in the "Joint Understanding on Humanitarian Pause" that dealt directly with the problems of disarmament, but otherwise the HDC focused on ways to improve security as none of the previous cease-fire agreements had succeeded. In early 2001, six months after the first signing of the joint understanding, the two sides agreed to set up exploratory peace zones in two districts (one in Bireun and the other in North Aceh). The zones were seen as the first step toward demilitarization. However, the week after the peace zones were set up, the HDC staff, harassed by the military and the police, found itself involved in an "incident" with GAM. (The HDC claimed it was accidental.) The team withdrew from the zones at the end of the first week.

In retrospect, it remains unclear why it was decided to create peace zones at the time (presumably the HDC had a plan) and how this process was to be linked to the humanitarian pause. Creating some areas as peace zones within Aceh implied that there was to be some distinction between the zones and the other areas, but the difference was not specified. There are few details on the rules or purposes of these peace zones, except that they would "lead to" demilitarization. How exactly this would come about was not made clear.

It seems that these pilot peace zones were a result of the ongoing negotiations between the Indonesian government and GAM. They were not mentioned or planned in "The Joint Understanding on Humanitarian Pause" agreement, but the idea seems to have been developed as part of a continuing process. The Joint Committee on Humanitarian Action and the Joint Committee on Security Modalities were involved in both the selection of sites and the monitoring of the zones. However, the monitoring was clearly not robust enough to face realities in the field. In terms of overall context, it appears that these initial zones were established as part of the implementation of a partial agreement (but not a full or final peace agreement) but without a general cease fire taking effect in the field.

Peace Zones in the Second Period

Under the COHA of December 2002, two main bodies were established to be responsible for the implementation and monitoring of the agreement:

1. The Joint Council: The Joint Council comprised senior representatives of GAM, the Indonesian government, and the HDC. The council was intended to be the final authority and to resolve all disputes arising from the implementation of the agreement that other committees could not resolve. The council could also amend articles and provisions of the agreement.

2. The Joint Security Council: This council was composed of representatives of GAM, the Indonesian government, and a senior third party (envoy for the HDC). Its key task was to reactivate the Joint Committee on Security Modalities and the Joint Committee on Humanitarian Action. The council was responsible for the actual implementation of the COHA/FAIM, including establishing sanctions. It was supported by a monitoring team, with representatives of GAM, the Indonesian government, and third parties. The agreement provided for 150 monitors (50 international monitors from Thailand and the Philippines, together with 50 from GAM and 50 from the Indonesian government) to supervise a cease fire, the process of disarmament, and the setting up and maintenance of peace zones.[16]

While a cease fire and the disarming of GAM seem to have been the two key components of COHA/FAIM, setting up peace zones within which disarming would take place and which in turn would pave the way for humanitarian aid, reconstruction, and rehabilitation was also crucial. Peace zones were to be a prelude to the implementation of COHA/FAIM—in a very literal sense. The agreement elaborated the commitment to establish peace zones and the nature of these zones. It also made clear that the Joint Security Council would be responsible for selection, establishment, and implementation of this and any subsequent agreement on zones. It should be noted that a cease fire clearly was a separate issue from the establishment of peace zones, for it would be applicable to all regions of Aceh and not geographically limited. In contrast, the peace zones were intended to have clear geographical boundaries.

The Joint Security Council initially selected as peace zones areas that had been very violent in the past. Humanitarian assistance, rehabilitation, and reconstruction were to be of primary importance in these zones. Happily, international donors showed some willingness to fund projects within the peace zones, recognizing the economic importance of sustaining them. In a conference in Bali in January 2003 international donors pledged US$2.7 billion in aid for 2003 to Indonesia, a substantial portion of which would go to Aceh.[17] Donors specifically cited peace zones as targets for funding. Later, the European Commission promised a €2.3.million aid package.[18]

The peace zones were also intended to be the first step toward demilitarization. Through COHA/FAIM, GAM, and TNI/BRIMOB both agreed that

1. they would carry no weapons within the peace zones outside of their respective posts and bases;

2. if they were unarmed, they could move freely within the peace zones;

3. no political or clandestine activities would take place within the peace zones;

4. neither would engage in "provocative acts";

5. no military posts would be allowed within the ZoPs;

6. neither side could move more forces into any existing peace zones; and

7. POLRI (Polisi Republik Indonesia—Indonesian Police) were to investigate criminal activities in these areas, but in consultation with the Joint Security Council.

GAM agreed to a "phased disarmament" spread over five months and starting February 9, 2003 (two months after signing the peace agreement). In areas that had been declared peace zones, GAM members would place their weapons in secret, designated locations, known only to the HDC. The weapon sites would be subject to inspections without prior notice by HDC inspectors. GAM would need to trust the HDC not to reveal the placement locations, and the Indonesian government, in turn, would need to trust that the HDC was fully monitoring the placement. The Indonesian government agreed that BRIMOB paramilitary units would move from "offensive" to "defensive" positions.[19]

Violations and Sanctions

While the Joint Security Council was primarily responsible for setting up peace zones, it was also charged with administering sanctions to be imposed should either party break any of the provisions of the agreement. From the start, the Joint Security Council view was that sanctions needed to be thought out carefully, as liberal use would make them lose their effectiveness. Since the agreement did not state all the rules to be followed explicitly, conditions had to be established by the committee.

The Joint Security Council categorized violations into three types: a minor violation, a serious violation, and a very serious violation. For any accusation the Joint Security Council tripartite monitoring team (GAM and Indonesian government representatives plus a neutral international mediating team under the aegis of the HDC) was to investigate and determine whether a violation had, indeed, been committed. If the committee decided that a violation had taken place, the case would be passed on to the Joint Security Council's Information Management Committee, which would determine the severity of the violation and whether there was enough evidence to proceed with sanctions. In the case of a serious violation or a very serious violation, there was to be further independent investigation by a verification committee appointed by the Joint Security Council. If the verification committee confirmed the nature of the violation, the case would be passed to the Joint Security Council leadership for appropriate sanctions.[20]

Both parties were then to be asked to review the violations, discipline the violators, and report both the findings and disciplinary action taken to the Joint Security Council for publication. Violations and sanctions were to be made public locally through the Public Information Unit of the Joint Security Council, making the GAM and TNI/BRIMOB accountable to people, nationally and internationally. Top priority was to be given to publicizing any violations, especially through print and electronic media. Once these procedures had been agreed to, the crucial question became whether they would be implemented and whether they would work. The whole success of the peace zones seemed to be bound up with the need to prevent, deter, or sanction breaches of the COHA/FAIM, but as the early months of 2003 unfolded it became obvious that equal if not more importance had to be afforded to the process of further talks and negotiations for which COHA/FAIM was a preliminary. At this level, matters did not proceed smoothly.

The End of the Peace Process: March–May 2003

As we noted above, there were early indications that maintaining any fragile peace in Aceh and continuing the search for a long-term solution to the conflict were going to be difficult processes. However, there were some initial signs that both sides intended to give the COHA / FAIM a chance. Immediately after its signing Indonesia's military chief announced the army's withdrawal from GAM's stronghold in the marshes in northern Aceh. A GAM spokesman stated that GAM forces would "hold back" even if attacked. And the first of the planned fifty international monitors began to arrive in the province. In the early months overall violence declined markedly, and one month after the signing of the accord HDC spokesmen were able to announce that during that time period there had been a total of seventeen deaths in the province (compared with a monthly average of eighty-seven and an overall total of ten thousand since the war started in 1976) and that no armed clashes at all had occurred during the previous week. The Joint Security Committee was in place, and several peace-monitoring teams had been deployed throughout the countryside. Just over a week later, on January 28,

2003, the Joint Security Council declared the Indrapuri sub-zone of
Aceh Besar to be the first peace zone.

However, problems were starting to arise even at this early stage
of the implementation process, and as January turned to February
2003 armed clashes between the TNI and GAM continued, with each
side accusing the other of violating provisions of the COHA. February 9 had become a deadline for GAM to begin to stockpile its arms
in sites to be monitored by the HDC, but this increasingly began to
appear improbable, an impression that was confirmed when two
outside arms verification experts arrived in Indonesia on March 1,
ready to supervise GAM disarmament later that month. For their
part, GAM leaders increasingly began to claim that the TNI had not
relocated to adopt a "defensive position" but, on the contrary, was
indulging in aggressive sweeps and reinforcing its units stationed
in Aceh.

On the political level, both sides tried to use the terms of the agreement to their advantage. The Indonesian government insisted that
COHA/FAIM was simply a step toward a settlement whereby Aceh
was granted some form of autonomy, which preserved Indonesian
sovereignty. On the other side, GAM informed its followers and the
people at large that the agreement was a step on the road to independence, the next step being a referendum on that option. Not surprisingly, each side's claims infuriated the other and did little to build
trust for the next stage of the peace process. In addition, the Indonesian authorities complained that GAM was simply using the cease
fire to collect funding (often through intimidation) to organize, to recruit, and to train fighters. As early as mid-February the government's
minister for political and security affairs, General Susilo Bambang
Yudhonoyo, was talking about a contingency plan to anticipate the
breakdown of the peace process. Throughout March 2003 violence
continued, incidents multiplied, and each side accused the other of
violations of the December agreement. No disarmament seems to have
taken place, monitored or otherwise, while Indonesian forces appear
to have become increasingly aggressive in their actions or reactions.
During the first week in April 2003 it was reported that three GAM
members had been shot dead by Indonesian police while extorting
money from local residents, while two others were killed in the capital of the province, Banda Aceh. In the same week an Indonesian sol-
dier was killed in a shootout in East Aceh, and an Indonesian Air
Force officer was kidnapped in Banda Aceh. Most relevant for the
establishment and maintenance of peace zones, some of the frustra-
tion and violence were being directed toward the peace monitors
themselves (described in the next section of the chapter).

Meanwhile, at the official level, efforts continued to move the peace process forward, but by the end of April it seemed as though the negotiations had broken down completely with the failure of both sides to agree on a venue or a date for a meeting of the Joint Security Committee in order to consider the increasing number of problems that were arising in Aceh itself. With the Indonesian government insisting that talks begin on April 25 and GAM representatives declining to meet this deadline, the situation at the start of May looked distinctly unpromising, especially as the Indonesians had announced plans for major military operations in Aceh on the day following the failure to meet at Geneva. At an emergency cabinet meeting on May 1 the government announced that it was prepared to resume the peace process, but it added that first GAM had to make a formal statement explicitly abjuring the aim of independence as well as laying down its arms. It was also made clear that failing these conditions would mean the initiation of an all-out military assault. Government spokesmen gave GAM a two-week deadline to accept these conditions. For its part, GAM indicated that it was prepared to participate in talks about peace with the government, but it would neither abandon its aim of independence nor lay down its arms until government troops and special security forces had returned to their barracks.

From this point on, in spite of continuous efforts by the HDC and by friendly governments such as Japan and the United States, relations deteriorated rapidly, with both sides making conditional offers to resume talks that they probably realized the other side was bound to reject. Leaders of GAM accused the government of "beefing up" the twenty-six thousand troops already in the province. Government spokesmen accused GAM of having used the cessation of hostilities to stockpile weapons, to recruit, and to redeploy. On May 6 the government began openly to prepare for operations to "restore security" in Aceh, and the number of shooting incidents and deaths increased as the May 12 deadline approached. A last-ditch effort to save the peace process involving US envoy General Anthony Zinni, the Swedish and Japanese governments, and EU ambassadors came to nothing after five GAM delegates were arrested en route to a last minute Joint Security Council meeting in Tokyo. The Tokyo meeting adjourned on May 18 with no progress to report. The same day the Indonesian president, Megawati Sukarnoputri, signed a decree imposing six months of martial law in Aceh while Indonesian paratroopers made a televised jump into selected landing zones to join troops already there. Massive violence began once more in the province.

The Peace Zones during the Period of Collapse

Against this background of deteriorating relationships at the national level it was hardly surprising that the establishment and operation of the peace zones proved to be an initially difficult and eventually an impossible process. Events at the two levels, local and national, interacted and contributed to a malign spiral of mistrust and violence, eventually wrecking the peace process and returning Aceh to open warfare. Particularly between March and May 2002, at the provincial level, the whole implementation of the planned peace zones ground to a halt, peace monitors were withdrawn, and the initially promising moves toward local peace were reversed.

As we noted above, initial events "on the ground" seemed positive. An interim team of peace monitors began work in Aceh immediately after the signing of COHA/FAIM. A major contingent of the planned fifty international monitors (forty-two from Thailand, nine from the Philippines and one from Norway) began to arrive in the province within a week, so that the whole 150 were available for monitoring activities by mid-December. Both sides undertook initial confidence-building moves to implement the peace accord's provisions on disengagement, with some GAM units returning to their base camps and the Indonesian army withdrawing from an ongoing siege at Cot Trieng in North Aceh. The army also released nine GAM members from detention and handed them over to GAM.

By January 2003 members of the tripartite Joint Security Council had agreed on procedures for sanctioning breaches of the cease fire by either side, including investigation by monitoring teams from the Joint Security Council, disciplinary action on the perpetrators by their own superiors, and publication of the details of the infringement locally, nationally, and internationally by the Joint Security Council.

By mid January the Joint Security Council felt it appropriate to announce the establishment of the first peace zone at Indrapuri subdistrict, in Aceh Besar, twenty-four kilometers south of Banda Aceh, the region's capital. The zone was to become effective on January 25. Indrapuri had seen a great deal of violence and, in January 2003, required immediate humanitarian assistance. In a thirty-minute ceremony Major General Tuvinum of Thailand, the head of the Joint Security Council, made a public announcement of the peace zone to a crowd of about two thousand local people, although there seems to have been no dialogue between the Joint Security Council and the local population. Pamphlets containing peace messages had been displayed near the venue of the ceremony, together with a small poster detailing fifteen "prohibited acts."[21] One of these was rape and sexual harassment by the military and the police force. While local people seemed happy with the setting up of the peace zone, they remained suspicious of the Indonesians, and there was little or no interaction between them, language remaining a major barrier.

On February 11 the establishment of six more peace zones was announced by the Thai chairman of the Joint Security Council. (We should note that the announcement was made two days after the February 9 deadline for the start of GAM's planned stockpiling of weapons, although there had been no signs that arrangements for such a process were in hand.) The new peace zones were spread throughout the province, but all were in parts of Aceh that had seen major violence: Kawai XVI sub-district, West Aceh;[22] Peusangan sub-district, Birueun; Sawang sub-district, South Aceh; Tior sub-district, Pidie; Simpang Keremat sub-district, North Aceh; and Idi Tunong sub-district, East Aceh. The peace zones in the Tiro (Pidie) and Peusangan (Birueun) sub-districts officially went into effect on March 8. Brigadier General Lomodage Nagamura of the Joint Security Council accompanied by other Joint Security Council members (Brigadier General S. Noerdin Savjen of the TNI and Teungu Nasraddin Ahmad from GAM) officiated at the formal inauguration. Two other zones officially came into effect on March 9—Simpang Kramar sub-district in North Aceh and Idi Tunong in East Aceh.

Initial progress on the establishment of peace zones appeared to be meeting with some success, and it also seemed to be the case that, overall, the level of violence in the province was declining markedly with the coming into force of the peace agreement and the establishment of the Joint Security Council. Certainly the number of reported deaths and armed clashes declined markedly in the first month following the signing of the agreement. On January 11 a spokesman for the HDC noted that there had been no armed clashes between GAM and TNI for over a week.

Even at this early stage, however, there were signs that the peace process would face major problems at the local level. While armed confrontations and clashes had diminished in number, as had indiscriminate killings, they still occurred and increasingly began to demand the attention of Joint Security Council monitoring teams. By mid-January the Joint Security Council was investigating charges leveled by both sides at one another regarding violations of the COHA. The Indonesian government had been particularly vocal in denouncing two separate attacks by GAM fighters on units of the Indonesia military at Lokop and Lamno in West Aceh, although GAM spokesmen claimed that the units had been acting in self-defense. One of the GAM spokesmen also claimed that the Indonesian army had been conducting search operations for GAM members and making raids on people's homes. Bullet-riddled bodies were also being washed ashore in North Aceh. The Joint Security Council investigated and reported these and other incidents as violations of the agreement, but no action seems to have been taken either by the government or by GAM. They simply did not discipline the violators and, meanwhile, the Joint Security Council was accused of failing to bring many violations to book.

By mid-February the situation in the province had grown more tense, and the Joint Security Council issued a report on previous violations of the cease fire, blaming both sides for "serious violations" and emphasizing that reports on those violations had been signed by all members of the monitoring teams. According to the procedures agreed to between GAM and the TNI, both organizations were responsible for disciplining those involved in the cease-fire violations, but little seems to have been done on either side. With the failure of national leaders to agree on proceeding with further talks, the survival of the peace zones became largely dependent on their own success in dealing with local violations, but this increasingly began to look like a task well beyond the powers of the Joint Security Council and the peace monitors.

The violence spread during late February and early March 2003. On February 21 a homemade bomb exploded in a school in Nissam in North Aceh, killing three children. GAM denied responsibility. The TNI continued to hunt for, arrest, and kill GAM leaders, and there were no signs either that GAM was preparing to stockpile its arms or that Indonesian security forces were no longer engaging in sweeps, searches, and other forms of standard counterinsurgency operations.

More seriously, from the viewpoint of firmly establishing the ZoPs in the province, members of the Joint Security Council monitoring teams were themselves coming under more than verbal attack. At the beginning of March a mob of protesters numbering (according to some estimates) three thousand people attacked the offices of the Joint Security Council monitors in Takengon, in Central Aceh. Naturally, reports on the event vary. Indonesian officers and officials claimed that the vandalizing of the office, the torching of vehicles belonging to the Joint Security Council, and the injuries to two monitors (one belonging to GAM) were the result of (1) GAM continuing to extort money from and threaten major oil companies and (2) the local population and the companies' anger with the monitors for being unable to do anything about this. There were also accusations that the Joint Security Council was not maintaining impartiality. On the other hand, GAM itself and the Indonesian human rights organization Kontras claimed that at least part of the mob consisted of army-trained Javanese militia, specially transported to Takengon from surrounding villages as part of a sustained effort to disrupt the peace process—a claim vehemently denied by army spokesmen.[23] (Later there was an attack on the Jakarta office of Kontras by Pemuda Panca Matya, a group Kontras had reported in the past for pro-government violence.) The TNI then suggested that Indonesian police should escort Joint Security Council officials when they went into conflict areas, an offer that, if accepted, would undoubtedly have made the HDC and Joint Security Council monitors look less than impartial. The whole incident raised serious concerns, because similar incidents in 2001 had forced the HDC out of its role in establishing and monitoring peace zones and contributed to the collapse of the first agreement.

Whatever the truth about the underlying motives of all or part of the mob, the implications of the attack for the peace monitors and the Joint Security Council were serious. The situation became even more worrying ten days later when another large group of local people surrounded the Joint Security Council's office in Langsa, East Aceh, and demanded the release of a civilian who, they claimed, had been kidnapped by GAM. On this occasion six peace monitors from GAM were forced to flee and were unwilling to return to the Joint Security Council's offices following the incident. The Langsa office was left empty thereafter, while the TNI commander in Aceh warned that neither army nor police would be able to ensure the safety of GAM members of peace-monitoring teams.

As March moved into April 2003, violence in the province continued to increase, with each side accusing the other of killings, ambushes, and kidnappings. On April 6 a mob of over one thousand protesters returned to the Joint Security Council peace monitors' office in Langsa, destroying equipment and records and finally setting fire to the building. Again, protesters' demands were for the release of hostages kidnapped by GAM, but on this occasion they also demanded the disbanding of the Joint Security Council itself. The HDC's initial recourse was to call upon the Indonesian government to provide security for members of the monitoring teams, but two days later David Gorman, the spokesman for HDC, announced that the peace-monitoring teams were being taken out of the field and were withdrawing to Banda Aceh, pending talks with leaders from GAM and the government regarding ways of improving security for the teams.

As both the situation in Aceh and relations among the Indonesian government, GAM, and the mediators of the HDC deteriorated during April and early May 2003, it began to seem increasingly improbable that the security problem would be resolved, even for the peace monitors. A symbol of the failure of the efforts to set up peace zones involved two explosions that took place in the peace zone of Simpang Keremat village in early May. For the first time in twenty-two years the people of the village had seen peace and could enjoy something approaching a "normal" life. Their response to the explosions was to flee the village.

With the approach of resumption of full-scale hostilities, on Monday May 12 the international peace monitors were flown out of Banda Aceh to Medan, en route to Jakarta. The following day the Thai head of the Joint Security Council, Major General Thanungsak Tuvinan, told the press that the peace process had not been terminated and he hoped that the monitors would be able to return. However, full-scale military operations resumed in Aceh on May 19. Martial law was declared on May 16. By September 2003 all international NGOs had left the province, applications for visas allowing work to continue in Aceh having been refused by the Indonesian government.

Reasons for the Collapse

What were some of the factors accounting for the collapse of the ZoPs in Aceh, and could it be said that they enjoyed—however briefly— any measure of success? Clearly, the original plan envisaged that the zones' establishment was to proceed through a number of stages:

1. Selection by the Joint Security Council and public announcement of this designation.
2. Formal inauguration.
3. Organization of peace-monitoring teams and Joint Security Council offices in the zone.
4. Demobilization (weapons stockpiling and return to bases and barracks).
5. Humanitarian relief work.
6. Development projects.

Given the general failure of the peace process and the continuation and gradual escalation of the violence even before May 19, 2003, it is difficult to see that even those peace zones that were established in January or early February enjoyed any real success, apart from the overall diminution of violence noted for the whole of Aceh during the period from December 2002 to February 2003. Paradoxically, the actual establishment of the first peace zones seems to have been paralleled by an increase rather than a decrease in violence, although it is difficult to discern whether the increasing number of military clashes, killings, kidnappings, and other manifestations of violence occurred within, around, or apart from the zones themselves. It is true that most of the zones passed through the stages of selection, declaration, and formal establishment, perhaps together with the assignment of a team of peace monitors to a headquarters within the zones—even though a subsequent GAM report speaks of there only being three active ZoPs by the time the TNI resumed its military campaigns in mid-May.[24] However, for most of the zones mentioned in our last section, there was only a short period of time between their formal establishment in early March and the assaults on some of the Joint Security Council monitoring teams launched by mobs either angered by the peace monitors' incapacity (or lack of impartiality) or deliberately encouraged and organized by those wishing to sabotage the overall peace process. In short, none of the peace zones really "got off the ground" before the peace monitors were forced to withdraw to Banda Aceh and thence (for the international personnel) to Jakarta and home.

Why this rapid failure? The most obvious explanation is that the failure of the peace zones was the result of the breakdown of the peace process itself and the unwillingness of the parties' decision-makers—or some of them—to eschew the tactics of making further negotiations dependent on the other's public abandonment of key objectives prior to further talks. This may have been a simple application of standard tough negotiating tactics—getting the adversary to the negotiating table able to talk only about a range of solutions that excludes those deemed wholly unacceptable by "our" side. Thus the Indonesian government's demand that GAM permanently abandon the idea of independence and GAM's insistence that Indonesia acknowledge that some form of autonomy should be accepted merely as a step toward eventual full independence. On the other hand, it could have been a means of ensuring that meaningful negotiations would not take place at all—a variation on the so-called joker tactic of negotiating theory (see Spanier and Nogee 1962[25]). Whatever the reason, the negotiating processes between GAM and the Indonesian government clearly doomed the peace zones, once the government had decided that further investment in a negotiation process was valueless. However, we should not forget that there was clearly influence in the other direction. Had violence stayed at a low level within Aceh and had the peace zones prospered more than they did, this might have encouraged the Indonesian political leaders (if not the army leaders) to persist in a negotiation "track," exasperating though this might have been. It was undoubtedly the failures of the processes at both levels, national and local, that led to the final rupture and the resumption of violence.

Apart from the mutual causality between escalating violence locally and negotiating failure nationally, there remains the question of why the peace-zone strategy failed *at the local level*. We can make a number of suggestions, some alternatives, some mutually reinforcing.

Clearly, one problem for the peace zones and their monitors was the level of unrealistic expectations aroused among the local populations. Violence declined, but it did not vanish completely. Harassment, kidnappings, and extortion continued. Recruitment and rearmament were perceived as continuing—and probably were. General Ryamizard Ryacudu claimed that "before signing the peace agreement GAM had three thousand members and eighteen hundred weapons. It now has reinforced itself to five thousand personnel and twenty-three hundred weapons." On the other side, the activities of the security forces appear to have continued much as before, without any sign of TNI and BRIMOB becoming passive and leaving crime and security matters to the Indonesian police. To some degree this continuation of "conflict as usual" may have reflected the inability of both the government and GAM to control its local agents, but the results were unambiguous. No matter how pragmatic the expectations of local people in Aceh might have been regarding the peace process and life in the peace zones, the fact that, as time went on, nothing seemed to have changed very much may account, at least partially, for their disillusionment with the Joint Security Council and the peace zones, as well as their tendency to protest vigorously about what they saw as failures to act or to act effectively.

Add to this the fact that the combatants were engaged in a guerrilla war both in the countryside and in the towns, and then it is also possible to argue that, with the best will in the world, it would be difficult to avoid confrontations at some time and in some places between guerrillas and security forces. Confrontations can easily turn into clashes and thence into major fire fights that reinforce the perceptions that the other side has not abandoned previous military strategies and should be fought rather than trusted not to seize a tactical or strategic advantage. Withdrawal, disentanglement, and avoidance were indeed built into COHA/FAIM but such actions need much skill and determination to carry out successfully. Evidence indicates that, in Aceh, such skill and determination were lacking.

This last comment brings us to the issue of "spoilers." It seems clearly to have been the case in Aceh that while some people on both sides were serious about and committed to the idea of a negotiated peace, others were not. On the Indonesian government side, the overly simple division seems to be between those figures—mainly political—who wished to bring about an end to the violence in Aceh and those figures—mainly military—who rejected this option and felt that it was possible to achieve a military victory that might restore both the army's reputation and its strong political influence, which had, to some extent, recently been damaged by revelations in East Timor and the fall of Suharto. In the case of GAM, there are indications that splits between "doves" and "hawks" certainly existed, even though they are more difficult to delineate. However, it seems likely that the question of who were for and who were against a successful peace process in Aceh is more complicated than this. So, who were the spoilers who contributed to the end of the peace process and the collapse of the peace zones?

Writing on the subject of spoilers, Stephen Stedman has defined those taking up this role as "leaders and parties who believe that peace emerging from negotiations threatens their power, worldview and interests and use violence to undermine attempts to achieve it" (Stedman 1997, 5). He goes on to suggest that there are three broad types to be found in many conflicts:

1. *Total* spoilers, whose goals are immutable and who see the world and the conflict in all or nothing terms.
2. *Limited* spoilers, whose goals may or may not be negotiable.
3. *Greedy* spoilers, whose goals expand or contract according to estimates of cost and risk.[26]

In another formulation John Darby (2001) writes about spoilers in the five peace processes analyzed in his own work as falling into four types, three of which overlap with Stedman's categories: dealers, opportunists, mavericks, or zealots.[27] In Darby's scheme mavericks are those whose violence is motivated by personal rather than political objectives. This is an interesting additional category—although it seems likely that most spoilers operate from a mixture of political and personal motivations anyway.

There is no harm in assuming, absent evidence to the contrary, that all four of Darby's types of spoiler are likely to be present on both sides in any protracted intrastate conflict, including that in Aceh. There is some evidence that points to the fact that at least two kinds of spoilers clearly did help to undermine the Aceh process and contribute to the collapse of the peace zones. The first type of spoiler involved seems to have resembled Stedman's total spoilers and Darby's zealots, but it might be more appropriate to use less disapproving terms and point to those on both sides, GAM and TNI, who continued to believe both in the aims for which they had been fighting and the methods by which a victory in the conflict had previously been sought. In other words, on both sides there were those who regarded any compromise settlement as betrayal, who felt that victory was still possible, who therefore did not scruple to act in such a way as to undermine the peace process and the peace zones, and who gave rise to such post hoc judgment that neither the rebels nor the powerful military displayed any real interest in making the peace agreement work. There is also some evidence that a second category of spoilers was active in seeking to undermine the national peace process as well as the local peace zones; this included those who derived benefits from the sheer continuation of the conflict, regardless of its outcome. In theoretical terms, there seem to have been many on both sides for whom the conflict was "functional" (see Mitchell 1981, 61–75) and for whom a negotiated peace—or, perhaps, any kind of peace—and even the establishment of any ZoPs would have been detrimental. While the first type of spoiler would have wanted to keep the conflict going because of the anticipated outcome, the second type would have wanted to keep it going because of benefits derived from its continuation. Again, these individuals and groups are difficult to identify from a distance, but it is significant that many commentators on the Aceh struggle (and on efforts to make peace) have noted the benefits that accrue to some from its continuation. One characterization of the war is that it is about access to natural resources, especially oil and gas. More immediately, as one Western observer of the situation argued, the war was fueled by interests in logging (run by the army and police), marijuana (in which both the army and GAM have a shared interest), prostitution (run by the army), and extortion (conducted by both sides). Extortion includes both sides' collection of "tolls" at checkpoints along major roads, "taxes" from businesses and externally funded organizations, "protection" schemes, and straightforward kidnappings and ransom money (Bonner 2003). On the insurgent side, some of the money from such activities goes to purchase weapons. For the military and police, the income is presumably diverted to more personal uses. As the Indonesian army commander in Aceh pointed out on one occasion, his soldiers in the field are paid at a rate of US$1.95 a day (Donnan and Hidayat 2003). Clearly, the coming of a negotiated peace and a devolution of even some power to the local Acehnese population would be highly detrimental to the continuation of such activities.

Furthermore, there is the "settler factor." Again, the precise effect of there being a substantial Javanese population in Aceh on the overall peace process (but especially the setting up of local ZoPs) remains unclear. However, it seems reasonable to suppose, given the unpopularity of the Javanese settler population among native Acehnese, that this population would be a major target for GAM and would be those most likely to demand vigorous protection from Indonesian military and police forces as well as from the Joint Security Council's peace monitors. Mistrust and outright hostilities between the settlers and the indigenous population would undoubtedly be one of the problems that would exist for peace monitors within (and outside) the peace zones. And these divisions seem likely to threaten both the evaluation of the performance of peace monitors as well as any fragile peace that might be developed. The settler population, like any settler population, would be the first to go back to calling on its previous protectors for security and protection and also be likely participants in any anti-GAM or anti–Joint Security Council protests, provoked, planned, or spontaneous.

Our research into other examples of ZoPs suggests further possibilities that might help to explain the short duration and ultimate collapse of the zones in Aceh. One of ·the crucial features in understanding the relative durability of peace zones is to identify who set up the zone in question. In Colombia, the Philippines, and El Salvador the peace zones were largely set up by the local community or by third parties with the active involvement of the community. By contrast, the UNSZs in former Yugoslavia were set up by an outside third party and were literally enforced for a short period of time. However, as detailed in Chapter 7, these safety zones could not be sustained and ultimately collapsed. With these varied experiences in mind, it seem possible to hazard two further arguments about the zones in Aceh.

The first of these concerns the relevant third party, the HDC, which involved itself in the conflict as a third party with low power. The HDC attempted to play two difficult roles—peacemaker and peacebuilder—a position from which it is hard to create and sustain local, grassroots peace zones. The HDC is a small NGO, and in Aceh it attempted to increase its potential influence by involving three prominent figures in its team of intermediaries. However, none of these individuals officially represented the interests or positions of his own country. Anthony Zinni, the *retired* Marine Corps general, was urged by the State Department to take part in the HDC project but did so in a personal capacity. Dr. Surin Pitsiwan was the *former* foreign minister of Thailand. And Budimir Loncar, the *former* Yugoslav foreign minister, had been the Yugoslav ambassador to Indonesia during the rule of President Sukarno and was a close friend of President Megawati. However, none of these undoubtedly skilled and prominent individuals enjoyed the official backing—and hence the potential influence—of his respective government.

Moreover, drawing on the Yugoslav experience, it appears that it is not even enough that the third party initiating a peace zone wields considerable potential power, as the United Nations did in Yugoslavia, but that it needs to enjoy the support of all parties. This leads us to a second suggestion, namely, that it is important to obtain the support and involvement of the local community in the establishment and maintenance of any peace zone. Some of our more successful and durable examples of local ZoPs come from places in Colombia and the Philippines. In each of these cases the local community was very much included in or actually initiated the peace zone. In Aceh, as in the former Yugoslavia, outsiders (the Joint Security Council from the HDC) came in to create a peace zone. There seems to have been no sustained attempt to involve the local people—to give them space to express their own needs or suggest appropriate arrangements. From being mute spectators of war they were asked to remain mute specta-tors of peace. Other cases suggest that if some direct involvement had occurred and the local community had the opportunity to com-municate with the warring parties, there might have been a greater chance of the zones surviving.

Be that as it may, those creating the peace zones faced no easy task, and the factors discussed above may help both to detail some of the difficulties facing the Joint Security Council and the peace monitors within Aceh itself and to indicate what might need to be considered and planned for in any future efforts to establish and expand peace zones in Aceh as part of a future peace process. However, we end with some broader consideration of the place of local ZoPs as a part of peace processes in general, and how their inclusion might best con-tribute to a durable peace.

Peace Zones as Prelude

The peace zones established following the December 9 agreement were clearly intended to be disarmament zones. Moreover, it was hoped that successful disarmament would pave the way for humanitarian aid, reconstruction, and rebuilding. The zones were a prelude to de-militarization, but they were also a prelude to future negotiations. This arose from the fact that the process adopted to establish and keep the zones going was intended to be a confidence-building measure (the dialogue among members of the Joint Security Council) that would lead the parties toward a negotiated peace agreement. Ex-amples from similar conflicts indicate that peace zones that have de-militarization as their main goal can be established during the pre-negotiation stage (sometimes even imposed by an outside third party), in the negotiations stage, or in the post-agreement stage. The zones in Aceh were established as part of the negotiations that would lead to a final peace agreement. However, a cease fire is always an integral part of, or a background to, the success of such peace zones. This process is represented in Figure 8–1.

FIGURE 8–1. THE ACEH PEACE PROCESS

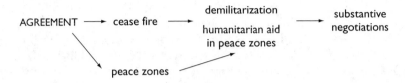

While it is often argued that a cease fire actually needs to precede the establishment of peace zones, in the Aceh case the two were intended to go hand in hand. Conceptually, then, one of the most interesting features of the peace zones that were established (however briefly) in Aceh was that, unlike other types of zones we have studied, they appear to have been set up as an integral part of an ongoing peace process, that is, as a *means* of moving the process forward and as a preparation for subsequent stages. This makes them unlike the zones in, for example, the Philippines or Colombia, most of which were established while those conflicts were "in full swing" and (at least partly) as a means of minimizing local violence resulting from the overall struggle. Nor were the Aceh zones set up following an already negotiated agreement, as part of an implementation process that involved safe assembly areas for combatants, secure zones for return of IDPs or refugees, or safe areas within which humanitarian relief could be distributed.

The peace zones in Aceh, then, were intended to be a *prelude* to disarming, demilitarization, and the provision of humanitarian aid, for it appears that all of these activities were to take place *after* the actual establishment of the peace zones but within those zones *before* they were to occur elsewhere in the province. The zones in Aceh thus seem to have been part of an incremental way of arriving at a final peace agreement rather than a way of implementing an already worked out and agreed upon arrangement for a substantive peace. Should they be regarded mainly as confidence-building measures? Were they planned as part of an incremental process of arriving at a final peace settlement? Was the plan to establish peace, security, and demilitarization in some of the most violent areas and then to extend these conditions outward to other parts of Aceh?

The collapse of the peace zones in Aceh and the abandonment of the search for a negotiated settlement raise some fundamental questions about the use of peace zones as confidence-building measures and as part of a prelude to substantive negotiations—especially when their establishment takes place before a general, and generally successful, cease fire is in place. If further substantive negotiations are partly conditional on the success of local ZoPs in contributing to and indexing an end to violence, this would seem to make those negotiations hostage to a fragile local process, one easily overturned by those in the locality who have an interest in the violence continuing. One possible lesson might be to alter the sequence diagrammed above and ensure that a general cease fire is in place *before* establishing local ZoPs and *then* proceeding to the next step of disarmament (or decommissioning) by the guerrillas and a return to barracks (or withdrawal from the region) by the security forces.

Notes

[1] Only after military rule was lifted in 1998 and freedom of information was restored did the rest of the world begin to hear the details of the conflict in Aceh. Yet, even today, news coverage of the current happenings in Aceh leaves much to be desired. This did prove to be a limiting factor in writing this essay.

The authors are grateful to Radhi Darmansyah of ICAR for helping them better to understand the conflict in Aceh and providing valuable insights in writing this chapter. Much was also learned from Mr. Muhammad Taufik, general secretary of Action Coalition for Reform in Aceh and a team of youth leaders from Aceh.

Newspaper articles used include the following: "Aceh Joint Security Council Announces Truce Violations," *The Jakarta Post* (February 17, 2003); "Clashes Said Down in Aceh One Month after Deal," *AFP Hong Kong* (January 11, 2003); "Force Will Not Solve the Aceh Conflict," *Agence France Presse* (May 11, 2003); "Peace Accord Raises Hopes of Ending Twenty-Six Year War in Aceh, *The Independent* (December 10, 12, 2002).

[2] Aceh was granted more autonomy (the Acehnese supposedly had control over education, religion, and customary law), although in reality none was realized, than other provinces of Indonesia, but its people were extremely frustrated at not being regarded as an independent state. They had never accepted being a Dutch colony, and the indignity of being included as part of Indonesia was more than they could take.

[3] Mobil (today Exxon-Mobil) was one of the first to enter the region. The company jointly owns the Arun NGL Co. with Pertamina (a state-owned enterprise) and JILCO (a Japanese liquid natural gas company). At one point the fields in Aceh proved so rich that they supplied more than a quarter of Mobil's worldwide revenue. Other oil companies like Gulf Canada Resources Ltd. and Caltex, owned by Chevron Texaco, operate in regions close to Aceh.

[4] Most of the top-level employees of Mobil and other plants are foreigners. They are housed in a luxurious walled compound in Lhokseumawe, while bars and brothels have established themselves right outside the gas plant. Also outside the plant live Acehnese in very poor living conditions. Most of them have the low-paid, labor-intensive jobs in the plant. The rest of the top jobs and contracts went to ethnic Javanese.

⁵ Political and economic reasons make up most of the explanations on the sources of the conflict; religious issues were less in the forefront. However, in recent times the religious aspect in the conflict (that is, the Acehnese being far more Islamic than most Indonesians and demanding that Aceh be an Islamic state) has assumed greater prominence.

⁶ GAM was able to mobilize the rural people in Aceh mainly because they were the ones who witnessed the setting up of Mobil's plants from very close quarters and saw how the benefits of the company (employment being one of them) went to outsiders and did nothing to improve their socioeconomic conditions.

⁷ After Suharto, B. J. Habibie was the president for one year, during which time he allowed East Timor to have its referendum, by which it chose independence. The military cracked down hard on East Timor, and Habibie was forced to quit.

⁸ The Henri Dunant Centre for Humanitarian Dialogue was reorganized in 1999. Formerly known as the Henri Dunant Institute, it was set up in 1965 by the International Committee of the Red Cross, the League of the Red Cross and Red Crescent Societies, and the Swiss Red Cross. Its main objective is to make available ways and means of carrying out studies, research, and training in all branches of the Red Cross, thus contributing to the strengthening of the universality of the Red Cross. In 1995 its general assembly began a discussion on the future of the organization with a view to redefining its role and activities. The study was concluded in 1998, and in 1999 the organization was launched with a new name and a mission to strengthen intercultural and multidisciplinary dialogue and to promote sustainable solutions to humanitarian problems. The HDC is currently involved in Aceh and Myanmar/Burma. For more information on past projects, see the hdcentre.org website.

⁹ There is a lot to be said about the role of the HDC as a third party. As a relatively new venture for the organization, there was no history to fall back on and to evaluate its position, stand, or strategy. Naturally, the HDC did not have the experience (knowing what works and what does not) in suggesting ground rules to the two parties or in framing the first agreement—and definitely not in implementing it. The HDC took a more visible, vocal, and strong approach in the second period.

¹⁰ Earlier, in May 2000, Exxon-Mobil had halted its exploration and administrative activities for a very brief period.

¹¹ It was discovered that the military had made use of the heavy drilling equipment of Exxon-Mobil to dig mass graves, torture victims, and had "taken away" many of its employees whom they thought had any connections to GAM. It was impossible for Exxon-Mobil not to have known what the military was doing.

¹² While the setting up of the Sharia court was described as a big concession made by the Indonesian government, many Acehnese believed that it was an attempt made by the Indonesian government to give a religious tint to the conflict. Besides, the Acehnese accuse the Indonesian government of making Aceh a target of the post-9/11 anti-Islamic sentiments of many. They claim the Sharia court had not been one of their demands.

[13] While GAM was said to target ethnic Javanese (whom they saw as the new colonialists) and the military, all people of Aceh end up being targeted when caught in the crossfire and, at other times, when GAM uses terror tactics to mobilize support.

[14] A report from the International Crisis Group (2003) argued that the December 9 agreement was not really a peace agreement but an agreed framework for future negotiations. This seems an acceptable argument, because the COHA was never an agreement to end (resolve) the conflict and build peace in Aceh; it only provided for mechanisms that would help parties work toward peace. It proved to be more than just an agreement for cessation of hostilities, and thus COHA/FAIM seems to be a more acceptable way to label the agreement, which contained initial points of agreement as well as mechanisms for implementing other potential agreements including the move toward a dialogue for elections and peace.

[15] There was no clear information that those in exile had taken citizenship of their host countries, but this was how the problem was represented in many contemporary reports.

It is also important to note that the global environment contributed to COHA/FAIM being concluded. For example, following the 9/11 crisis and the subsequent implications for oil supplies, the United States and the global market seem to have suddenly "felt the pain" of the Aceh conflict. The Bush administration put much pressure on both sides to resolve the conflict and pressured GAM to accept autonomy. A US envoy—Anthony Zinni, former envoy to the Middle East—was present in negotiating sessions. It could also be argued that the COHA/FAIM was expected to boost Indonesia's profile as a liquid natural gas producer, and that buyers could be secure and confident of receiving their supplies, and this was motivation enough for all involved to participate in the peace process. Without any attempt to underplay the genuine efforts of both sides to end the conflict, it seems that the global environment contributed to the COHA/FAIM coming into existence.

[16] Learning from the past, the HDC insisted that other third parties would be involved in monitoring the cease fire and the peace zones in Aceh. The governments of Thailand and the Philippines offered to help in the monitoring. It was decided that the international monitors would work under the aegis of the HDC and not as separate third parties. Hence they were called envoys.

[17] On December 3, 2002, Japan hosted the Preparatory Conference for Reconstruction in Aceh, in which twenty-four countries participated. This conference was jointly organized by Japan (the largest international investor in Indonesia), the United States, the European Union, and the World Bank. While the different countries did not pledge specific amounts of aid, they did voice their commitment to the reconstruction and redevelopment of Aceh. They also backed the forthcoming COHA.

[18] This was granted under the EU's Rapid Reaction Mechanism and was intended to cover the cost of fifty monitors for a period of six months.

[19] The general understanding of the term "defensive position" was that unofficial posts would be removed. The objective was also to designate posts in such a way that there existed "sufficient distance" between the two sides.

[20] In fact, by mid-January 2003 the Indonesian government had been accused of two very serious violations and one serious violation; the GAM was accused of one very serious violation.

[21] The pamphlets also gave a Joint Security Committee hotline that people were asked to use to report any violations.

[22] The peace zone in Kawai XVI was declared in February but its implementation was delayed and it failed to come into effect, even briefly.

[23] In Aceh there is strong resentment against the Javanese, who are seen as the colonialists who took over from the Dutch. Since independence, political power has been concentrated in Java. In addition, the Indonesian government has followed a strong policy of transmigration, resettling people from overcrowded Java in Aceh. As noted earlier, the better jobs at Exxon-Mobil have gone to Javanese.

[24] The Free Aceh movement issued its own account of the failure of the peace process and published it in Stockholm on May 26, 2003.

[25] Spanier and Nogee's *The Politics of Disarmament* describes the tactic of ensuring that a wholly unacceptable provision is included in a negotiating package, thus ensuring its rejection.

[26] Stedman also distinguishes between spoilers who are part of the peace negotiations and complete "outsiders" who have no stake in the peace process and no incentive to abandon violence.

[27] The labeling here is somewhat loaded. To those who continue to believe in the party's original goals and in the justice of the struggle, those Darby labels zealots would appear as the consistent, the steadfast, or the faithful.

Works Cited

Bonner, Raymond. 2003. Indonesia agrees to Aceh Peace Talks. *The New York Times*, May 1.

Darby, John. 2001. *The effects of violence on peace processes*. Washington, DC: United States Institute of Peace Press.

Donnan, Shawn, and Taufan Hidayat. 2003. Aceh people greet peace with cynicism and doubt. *The Financial Times*, December 10.

Mitchell, C. R. 1981. *The structure of international conflict*. New York: St. Martin's Press.

Spanier, John W., and Joseph L. Nogee. 1962. *The politics of disarmament: A study in Soviet-American gamesmanship*. New York: Praeger.

Stedman, Stephen John. 1997. Spoiler problems in peace processes. *International Security* 22 (2): 5–53.

9

OPERATION LIFELINE SUDAN

KRISTA RIGALO AND NANCY MORRISON

Introduction

A traditional Sudanese saying proclaims that when there is fire in the house, everyone gets burned. This proverb is no better exemplified than by the two-decade-long conflict in Sudan. Often described as a power struggle between two forces and their leaders—President Omar Hassan Ahmad al-Bashir of the government of Sudan, and the former leader of the Sudanese People's Liberation Movement (SPLM) and its military wing, the Sudanese People's Liberation Army (SPLA), the late Colonel John Garang—the twenty-one-year-old civil war has cost an estimated two million lives and consumed incalculable resources. War has become a way of life, creating a culture of violence that contributes further to the complexity of the conflict.

In the face of a devastating war-induced famine in 1988, the international community felt compelled to intervene to alleviate the massive suffering in Sudan. Given the nature of the ongoing war and the relative lack of access by aid agencies to the most vulnerable populations, Operation Lifeline Sudan (OLS), an umbrella organization of over forty aid organizations, was created to negotiate access and to facilitate combined logistics. "Since 1989, OLS made possible the distribution of tens of thousands of tons of relief food to the south, negotiating 'corridors of tranquility' to deliver food to the hungriest" (Peterson 2000, 232). In many ways OLS was an innovation, "the first UN Program to rely on negotiated access with primary warring parties to provide relief assistance to war-affected populations within a sovereign country" (ICG 2003, 8).

This chapter explores the experience of OLS as a possible ZoP. In order to do so, one must first give a brief history of the conflict and its

167

major players. The history of OLS will then be delineated, culminating in a discussion of whether OLS constituted a ZoP and the possible lessons learned.

The Conflict in Sudan

The history of Sudan as a nation is characterized by an almost perpetual state of competition for political control; indeed, this dynamic has remained constant, though the actors have changed over time.

Civil Wars

Sudan first achieved independence from British colonial rule in 1956. In 1962 the first civil war between the "Arabized" north and the partially "Christian-missionized" south broke out. During its period of colonial rule Britain had—as a matter of course—encouraged the presence of Christian missionaries in the south of the country. These evangelists played a role beneficial to Britain's political schemes, bringing with them Western education along with the potential to weaken future generations of tribal leadership (Johnson 2003).

In the 1962 civil war the southern separatist movement—the Anya Nya—comprising survivors of the 1955 mutiny in Torit of the southern Equatoria Army Corps together with disgruntled southern students, instigated the southern revolt. By 1964 the military junta in power in Khartoum fell, due to a general strike by teachers, lawyers, and union organizers. The next year Sayyid Sadiq al-Mahdi took office as civilian president over a national government. But the conflict between the north and south continued. In 1969 Colonel Jafar Numieri led yet another military coup, supported by the communist Sudan Socialist Union, which was then declared to be the only legally recognized political party in the country. In 1971, however, Numieri executed alleged insurgent leaders within the Sudan Socialist Union and banned the party completely.

In 1972 the landmark Addis Ababa peace agreement with Anya Nya was signed, and in southern Sudan hope flourished for self-governance under secular law. Sudan then experienced a time of relatively peaceful coexistence, but in 1978 it faced a new challenge—the discovery of oil in the south. The presence of oil meant a broadening of focus from rule to resources. Religion, sovereignty, and oil became points of contention that defined the renewed conflict. Attention and interference from foreign interests added to the fray.

Sharia Law, and the Formation of the Sudanese People's Liberation Movement

President Numieri introduced Sharia law in 1983, in defiance of the 1972 Addis Ababa peace agreement. In that year a fresh lieutenant colonel in the Sudan People's Armed Forces by the name of John Garang was sent to crush a mutiny in Bor. Instead, he started a rebel movement, the SPLM, determined to oppose military rule and Islamic dominance by the northern government. The SPLM consisted mainly of integrated former Anya Nya soldiers as well as fighters from Anya Nya II who had resisted integration into the government's army. As the second phase of Sudan's civil war commenced, the SPLA had little initial effect on Khartoum's hold over the south. Numieri actually succeeded in dividing the south, establishing three distinct regions. In 1985 he was overthrown in the third military coup in Sudan since 1958. The SPLA began to make substantial military gains, beginning in 1986 with the capture of the town of Wau and the liberation of Rumbek. In 1988 a cease fire was negotiated between Garang and Muhammad Uthman al Mirghani, a member of al Madhi's coalition government and the leader of Sudan's Democratic Unionist Party (Metz and Library of Congress 1992). This agreement, like many others, was not respected. A civilian government was in power in Khartoum until 1989, when Sudan's most recent military coup placed Brigadier General Omar Hassan Ahmad al-Bashir in the presidency. Al-Bashir brought into power with him the Islamic Front, now known as the National Islamic Congress (NIC). His adamant enforcement of Sharia law quelled any hope of successful peace talks, while in the south Garang rejected the government's attempt to negotiate peace through a federal system of government in 1991 (IRINews.org 2004). In 1990, an attempted coup intended to abolish Sharia law failed, resulting in the execution of twenty-eight army officers.

From this point on the NIC-dominated government controlled the northern regions, covering approximately two-thirds of Sudan. Al-Bashir's aggressive strategy was designed to neutralize ongoing peace talks and abrogate all previous agreements, which included key access agreements he negotiated with OLS. Al-Bashir's primary concern was the establishment of a purely Islamist state. From its inception the NIC consisted of a tight, organized core group, prepared for years to take power at the most opportune time. Founded originally by Hassan al-Turabi, an inner cadre was established by the recruitment of young men from universities, the civil service, and the military, including al-Bashir (IRINews.org 2004). The overwhelming success on the part of the NIC to achieve and maintain power can be attributed largely to al-Bashir's desire to retain control over the Sudanese government. Perhaps the most crippling tactic employed by the NIC was the dissolution of any form of alternative democratic institutions. The elected government was essentially overthrown from within. Ironically, al-Turabi himself would also be overthrown from within when, in 1999, rivalry between the two headstrong leaders resulted in al-Turabi's expulsion.

Hope for a New Sudan

After the SPLM's rejection of the federal proposal in 1991, other efforts at peacemaking followed. In 1992 the Nigerian government convened two peace conferences, Abuja I and II, neither of which resulted in any significant progress toward peace. However, the regional intergovernmental body concerned with the "Greater" Horn of Africa, the Intergovernmental Authority on Development, began its own Sudanese peace initiative and managed to obtain agreement to a Declaration of Principles, although scandal erupted when Egyptian President Husni Mubarak accused Sudan of attempting to assassinate him in Addis Ababa. In 1995, the National Democratic Alliance, a coalition of banned northern and southern political actors united in the search for change within Sudan, circulated its Asmara Declaration, which stated its objectives of overthrowing the NIC and calling for a separation of church and state. By 1997 the Khartoum government had accepted the Intergovernmental Authority on Development's Declaration of Principles and had signed the Khartoum Peace Agreement with Dr. Riek Machar, leader of the breakaway Sudan People's Democratic Front.

During this time, the SPLA and its political wing, the SPLM, had achieved preeminence as southern Sudan's hope for a "new Sudan." The organization suffered splits (including the Sudan People's Democratic Front), abandonment by external backers (Ethiopia, Eritrea, and Uganda), and criticism from the international community over a host of human rights abuses, all in the face of overwhelming odds against it with regard to any kind of military success. Until his untimely death in August 2005, the SPLA had been headed by the controversial John Garang, who dominated the southern presence at the negotiating table, although not without problems. Although lacking a certain degree of popular support, Garang continued to lead the party, finally becoming enamored of the prospect of holding the position of the country's "first vice president" as stipulated in the most recent accord, the Comprehensive Peace Agreement. His unexpected death left the SPLA with internal divisions that still threaten the movement, as clashes of opinions with regard to self-determination versus a fully independent state still persist.

The "Last" Civil War

The current civil war in Sudan has been raging since 1983. Death tolls estimated by the 107th US Congress in the Sudan Peace Act (US 2002) as well as by the Center for Strategic and International Studies' report (Deng and Morrison 2001) suggest that in excess of two million lives have been lost during that time. Humanitarian aid expert John Prendergast points out how difficult conducting assessments can be, owing to government interference. He adds that the post–Cold War policy employed by the United States with regard to Sudan has historically been one of neglect (Prendergast 1992).

As is typical of many post–Cold War examples, the war in Sudan resembles in every way a protracted social conflict (Miall, Ramsbotham, and Woodhouse 1999). Multiple sources document the following atrocities: acts of genocide, forced famine, rape, conscription of children, civilian targeting, population displacement, unlawful imprisonment, torture, slavery, refusal to allow aid, unlawful seizure of property, religious persecution, resource exploitation and general violations of basic human rights (Deng and Morrison 2001; Prendergast and Rone 1994; US Congress 2002; US 2002).[1]

However, it would be a gross oversimplification to describe the conflict in Sudan as a war between the northern government and southern rebel forces. Ethnic and intertribal clashes in the south, as well as the north, have escalated into armed violence, creating further hostilities from within. A briefing issued by the International Crisis Group entitled "Sudan's Other Wars" clearly identifies the Three Areas regions (Abyei, the Nuba Mountains, and the Southern Blue Nile) as experiencing intensified conflict among the various ethnic groups (ICG 2003), while a case study on behalf of USAID discusses further ramifications of internal conflict and interventions (Nyang'oro 2001).

Sudan Today

Most recently, the Darfur regions have been experiencing violent conflict, described by then Secretary of State Colin Powell as involving genocide when he testified before the Senate Foreign Relations Committee on September 9, 2004. Sudan's progress toward peace seems to be an intricate dance of two steps forward, three steps back. The signing of the Naivasha Agreement (also known as the Comprehensive Peace Agreement) on January 9, 2005, has again raised hopes of resolution for Sudan's four-decades-long civil war. The agreement is without a doubt the most comprehensive agreement thus far. This most recent document is an aggregation of multiple agreements, all of which have been broken, and none of which encompasses exhaustively the underlying causes of conflict between the north and south. Hence, many difficulties remain, and foreseeable challenges to implementation are evident.

The Naivasha Agreement and the Uncertain Future

The risk that the Naivasha Agreement may wind up yet another "labor lost" is considerable. Security concerns, unclear definitions and expectations, failure to address specific structural issues, exclusion of relevant parties, and a somewhat disputable plan of execution characterize even this most recent agreement, making it in some ways little improved over what has collectively been described as a "literature of accord" (Morrison and de Waal 2005). Further, the unexpected death of SPLA leader John Garang leaves his replacement, Salva Kiir Mayardit, in a politically precarious position. Given all this, one can return to our earlier metaphor and note that in Sudan, as the fire is put out in one part of the house, another part becomes engulfed in flames.

Understanding the history of what has become Africa's longest-running civil war is an integral component in the process of analyzing the response of the global community and how external forces can potentially affect internal structures for the long term. Thus, one can see that the Sudanese civil war, commonly referred to simplistically as a war of religions and tribalism, is in fact much more complicated and multilayered. It has both endogenous and exogenous factors, which equally enable and constrain the pursuit of war and the search for peace. It is into this mix of conflictual history, convoluted alliances, and patterns of begun yet aborted peace efforts that the international community has felt compelled to intervene.

Operation Lifeline Sudan: A History

In 1988 the International Committee of the Red Cross and several other NGOs attempted to undertake a major humanitarian initiative in Sudan but were blocked by the Khartoum government and the SPLA, both of which opposed the presence of international humanitarian personnel in operational war zones. A war-induced famine progressed with tragic implications. "During that year [1988] alone, some 250,000 Sudanese died of war and famine" (Minear 2002, 89). In response to this tragedy, James Grant, then executive director of UNICEF, was mandated by the United Nations to negotiate the establishment of Operation Lifeline Sudan, an umbrella organization facilitating the programs of forty-four NGOs seeking to obtain and secure access to war-vulnerable populations (Erasmus 2001; Peterson 2000; Minear 2002). This access, negotiated in a tripartite manner by the United Nations, the Sudanese government, and the SPLA, was to be guaranteed through pre-agreed "corridors of tranquility" in both the north and south (Minear 2002, 89).

These corridors were a result of negotiation and compromise. Initially the United Nations had sought a six-month cease fire, but this was rejected by both protagonists. "The UN countered by proposing a single month of tranquility throughout the south that the SPLA found too all-embracing. Both sides finally agreed on certain 'corridors of tranquility' through which, during an initial month, clearly identified relief supplies would be granted safe passage" (Minear 2002, 128). This pattern of negotiating access and safe passage would become institutionalized into the framework and functioning of OLS, the periods of tranquil passage needing to be negotiated and renegotiated on a month-by-month basis until the process faltered and war broke out again in October 1989 (Minear 2002, 128).

Both the government and the SPLA agreed to this month-by-month cease fire for predominantly strategic and tactical reasons. At this point in the civil war the SPLA had been making significant gains on the ground, capturing a number of important market towns and launching an assault on the southern, government-controlled garrison town of Juba. In need of food, the SPLA was ready to agree to a temporary cease fire. The government likewise welcomed the cease fire, which halted the SPLA advance and allowed the government the opportunity to regroup (Cohen 2000, 61).

As David Keen notes, the new relief corridors created through the OLS negotiations were declared off-limits to military operations. The SPLA announced a cease fire that lasted from May to mid-June 1989, and the government proclaimed a unilateral truce for July, which it then extended through August, then September. These complementary actions allowed a substantial number of relief deliveries to be made to both government-held and SPLA-held areas. "Zones of peace became established around the corridors." During these months OLS helped to reduce the conflict in the south, reducing economic exploitation and producing "a more normal pattern of trade and production." Throughout the first months of OLS's existence, it is credited with helping to maintain communication between the SPLA and the government, concurrently engaged in a peace process, when other issues were deeply polarizing (Keen 1994, 204).

OLS was a clear expression of a humanitarian imperative and "was based on the premise that humanitarian assistance must be provided to all affected civilians, irrespective of who exercised factual control over the area they lived in, and that humanitarian assistance can promote peace" (Erasmus 2001, 248). To operationalize this premise, the following OLS-brokered ground rules were negotiated: "The protection of civilians is fundamental to aid delivery; civilians have a right to live in safety and dignity; aid can not be denied even if it crosses lines of battle; responding proportionately to need does not represent an abandonment of neutrality; and the transparency of operations will be allowed at all times" (Prendergast and Center of Concern 1996, 50).

Consistent with the process of humanitarian assistance negotiations in Sudan at this time, both protagonists were engaged in 1994 in dialogue regarding OLS ground rules independently of each other. "The southern Sudan ground rules have been signed by OLS and the two major rebel factions in the south. It is the first time anywhere in the world that rebel organizations have recognized and signed the Conventions of the Rights of the Child" (Prendergast and Center of Concern 1996, 50). Unfortunately, the ground rules differed in text and in application between the north and south. "A major shortcoming of the southern Sudan ground rules is that they have been offered to and signed by the rebel factions. A corresponding interest on the part of the leaders of OLS in Khartoum is not there. This problem leaves agencies open to charges of double standards because they appear to be placing higher demands and expectations on rebels than on the government" (Prendergast and Center of Concern 1996, 51).

The functioning of OLS remained inextricably tied to the vagaries of the larger civil war and various peace processes. The Sudanese government of Sadiq al-Mahdi, in power when OLS was first negotiated during 1988–89, "was willing to compromise in seeking an end to the conflict with its opponents in Southern Sudan" (Ingram 1993, 186). This government was replaced in a military coup in June 1989 by the hardline fundamentalist regime of Omar al-Bashir. After initially espousing support for the arrangement, a different governmental approach gradually emerged, one much more willing to manipulate OLS for its advantage. "Ever since then, OLS has been very uncertain, falling short of the achievements of its first year" (Ingram 1993, 186). Keen more bluntly cites an obvious hindrance to aid after mid-1989, stating that al-Bashir "reinstated the blatant obstruction of relief" (Keen 1994, 204).

As the protagonists returned to war, access through the corridors of tranquility became less than functional; indeed, only five of the eight corridors saw regular use in the best of times. Late starts required air transport, rather than trucks or barges, with a corresponding increase in operational costs. "In OLS, the cost of transporting relief supplies, normally $300/ton, climbed to as much as $2000/ton" (Minear and Weiss 1995, 79). These same authors note that "operations in active war zones raised not only the transportation costs but also items such as insurance for equipment and personnel… small wonder that assistance in active war zones is often 10–20 times more costly than elsewhere" (Minear and Weiss 1995, 80).

The al-Bashir government negotiated a new program for 1990, Operation Lifeline Sudan II, which was clearly in jeopardy from the start. The regime in Khartoum began impeding its work, complicating and hassling relief flights, delaying rail and barge shipments, and commencing to bomb southern towns once again (Cohen 2000). The Sudanese government was, however, susceptible to pressure from the outside. It observed the US intervention in neighboring Somalia and feared a similar incursion on imperative humanitarian grounds. Journalist Scott Peterson noted that "Khartoum's policy changed overnight," with the number of permitted UN flights to rebel areas jumping from seven to forty-one (Peterson 2000, 237). Unfortunately, when the US intervention in Somalia soured, Khartoum again became intransigent. It again began to withhold approval for access to some rebel-held towns and resumed bombing. "With barely a whimper of complaint, the UN, relief agencies, and donors again scaled back their minimum expectations" (Peterson 2000, 238).

In 1996 the al-Bashir government instigated a pacification campaign, called Peace from Within, hoping to capitalize on the growing splits within the various rebel groups in southern Sudan. The Sudanese government worked to bring OLS more tightly under its control, seeking to link "the provision of aid, civil works, patronage, and other benefits of humanitarianism to itself in an integral part of the government's pacification campaign" (Prendergast and Center of Concern 1996, 33). "By 1996, the initial access agreement [of OLS] had been renegotiated six times and aid had become deeply implicated in the strife. Despite fifteen diplomatic missions, the pattern established in 1989—generous aid but secondary priority for conflict resolution—became entrenched over time" (Minear 2002, 156).

Operationally, OLS had to adjust its administrative structures in order to function and endure. During the first few months of its existence OLS headquarters were in New York, but it moved to Khartoum in late 1989. With this move came a perceived loss of impartiality and the danger of increased influence by the government of Sudan. In order to operate in both the government-held north and rebel-controlled south, OLS had to devise creative and appropriate mechanisms for operating. "OLS is officially one unit managed by the UN from

Khartoum, but in practice is divided into two sectors," notes Fr. Bill Turnbull (2000).

OLS Northern Sector functioned in close collaboration with the Humanitarian Aid Forum of the Sudanese government and with UN agencies, international NGOs, and donor organizations. It was concerned primarily with the delivery of aid to IDPs in Khartoum. Its activities in the north were not based exclusively on need but rather on serving the negotiated sites delimited by the government of Sudan and its Relief and Rehabilitation Commission. The Sudanese government established strict guidelines as to the status (and thus aid eligibility) of IDPs in Khartoum, using 1984 as its watershed date (Turnbull 2000). "Squatters" were those people arriving in Khartoum before 1984; they were granted the right to settle in Khartoum in "peace villages" created by the government. Seventy-two villages have been created since 1991 and played a crucial part in the government's Peace from Within strategy (Turnbull 2000). "Displaced" persons were those individuals who arrived in Khartoum after 1984 and who had no right to residence. They were to be located in temporary "peace camps" until they were able to return to their villages of origin (Turnbull 2000). Overall, the government of Sudan consistently insisted on ever greater control over OLS activities, perceiving them as threats to its sovereignty and as benefiting its armed opponents in the south.

OLS Southern Sector operated programs and aid initiatives in the rebel-held south of Sudan, with its operational headquarters in Nairobi and Lokichoggio, Kenya. UNICEF acted as the lead agency, providing humanitarian services coordination and seeking to ensure that all participating NGOs followed compatible guidelines and minimum standards of operations. OLS Southern Sector worked in operational partnership with the humanitarian wings of the various armed opposition groups in the south, negotiating agreements on ground rules that bound the parties to the principle and practice of unimpeded, safe access. In contrast to the government's concerns about sovereignty, the rebel groups consistently tended to seek larger proportions of the aid delivered and resisted calls for accountability. Further, at least one source indicates that SPLA and government forces were both responsible for ambushing deliveries (Human Rights Watch 1998).

While perhaps the best operational design given the context, critics have noted that the disparate programs in the north and south contributed little to longer-term peacebuilding. As Minear (2002) writes, OLS Northern Sector and OLS Southern Sector became two disjointed programs without consistent or uniform objectives or systems of accountability.

Operation Lifeline Sudan: A Zone of Peace?

Given this overview of the history of OLS, did OLS operate as a ZoP? In order to answer this, one must first return to its original mandate: to negotiate safe access to war-vulnerable populations in Sudan. OLS was created as an expression of the humanitarian imperative, based on the "belief that all of humanity—regardless of race, religion, age or gender—deserves protection from unnecessary suffering" (Weiss and Collins 2000, 7). Given the sacrosanct nature of this imperative at that moment in history, it would have appeared "problematic to assume that humanitarian aid goes beyond the direct alleviation of suffering" (Schloms 2003, 43). Inherent in this norm are the values of neutrality and independence of action for humanitarian-aid providers. This highlights a fundamental debate that dominated the field during the implementation of OLS: Should aid agencies seek to expand their mandate above and beyond the alleviation of human suffering? Would the goals of structural change found in peacebuilding threaten humanitarian aid's operational values of neutrality and independence? (Schloms 2003, 41).

Roger Winter, an assistant administrator in USAID's Bureau of Democracy, Conflict, and Humanitarian Assistance, has stressed that OLS was never consciously or broadly construed as a peacemaking mechanism.[2] By 2001 the connection between humanitarian access and peacemaking and peacebuilding had become much clearer. But at its inception OLS was conceived of as a humanitarian mission, a neutral provider of aid whose role was not to judge those who prosecuted the conflict or committed atrocities (Peterson 2000, 232).

The corridors of tranquility did foreshadow, however, an exploration of creating conflict-free zones. As Prendergast writes, "The corridors of tranquility agreed to in Sudan presaged an entirely new approach to humanitarian action in which the UN negotiates access and NGOs implement, in the context of elaborate access agreements" (Prendergast and NetLibrary Inc. 1997, 14). OLS is seen as having set an important, innovative precedent in gaining access to victims of civil conflict. "Indeed, some observers saw the process of persuading the warring parties to agree to UN access *as itself promoting peace*" (Ingram 1993, 172). The principle behind the actual physical corridors was important. "Rather than providing simply 'bubbles' of protection for individual relief vehicles passing through the stated areas, the protagonists declared the corridors themselves off-limits to all military operation" (Minear, Bread for the World, and Abuom 1991, 128). These same authors stress the overall importance of the corridors to the success of OLS: "The corridors of tranquility and their reinforcing political arrangements were critical to Lifeline's success." They continue: "In addition to their logistical benefits, the corridors had psychological value as well. People in the streets of Juba and throughout the rural south saw relief activities as a harbinger of peace" (ibid., 132). The calm associated with OLS-stimulated commerce and enhanced prospects for the future, some authors contend, facilitated the expansion of the corridors into genuine ZoPs. "With the perceptible decrease in tension and upswing in market activity, the enlarged corridors became, in effect, zones of peace" (ibid., 129).

The process of negotiating access is also credited with creating conditions for a more general peace. "Lifeline also stimulated dialogue on the issues underlying the conflict. . . . Lifeline, in short, could serve to generate momentum towards peace through relief" (Minear, Bread for the World, and Abuom 1991, 132). Importantly, the OLS negotiation process brought to the forefront some fundamental values underlying social peace. "One of Lifeline's signal accomplishments was to persuade the warring parties to commit themselves publicly to the principle that all civilians have a right to humanitarian assistance, wherever they happen to be located, and that access to them must be assured" (ibid., 28). Furthermore:

> The Sudan experience demonstrated a contribution by humanitarian actors in promoting legal norms. OLS imposed a certain discipline on both sets of belligerents. The initiative served as a means, at least in 1989, for bringing the practice of the Sudanese government, a signatory to the Geneva Conventions and Protocols, more nearly into conformity with international humanitarian law. While not a party to those agreements, the SPLA expressed its willingness to respect them, although the insurgents, too, fell short of agreed international standards. (Minear, Bread for the World, and Abuom 1991, 91)

This being said, OLS is not without its critics in terms of its actual contribution to peacemaking and peacebuilding. Though access occasionally resulted in humanitarian cease fires, often "after a few short months the warring parties were back at their bloody struggle, fortified by the reprieve Lifeline provided. Whatever short term tranquility Lifeline may have afforded, according to this view, it left untouched the roots of the long-standing conflict" (Minear, Bread for the World, and Abuom 1991, 125). Deng and Minear concur, stating that "the warring parties . . . used the tranquility associated with Lifeline to prepare for renewed combat" (Deng and Minear 1992, 100). Programmatically,

OLS was often manipulated by the belligerents to their own advantage:

> Aid may not directly prolong conflict unnaturally in Sudan, but it certainly has a major bearing on the course of the war. From 1989 to 1991, OLS boosted the rebel SPLA, from 1992 to 1995, the government army achieved some momentum through major aid programs in and through the north . . . and selective cut-off of humanitarian access for certain areas in the south, especially during the government's 1992 offensive, and its 1995 raiding campaign in the province of Northern Bahr al-Ghazal. (Prendergast and NetLibrary Inc. 1997, 140)

OLS was so tied to its initial vision of securing humanitarian access that it needlessly restricted its own mandate in terms of contributing toward general peacebuilding in Sudan. When asked whether a negotiated humanitarian access agreement between the warring parties might have contributed to a longer and more sustainable peace, James P. Grant, the UN official in charge of humanitarian efforts, said that there was nothing in his mandate regarding the resolution of the underlying conflict. By not tackling the war in its entirety, the United Nations undoubtedly missed opportunities to contribute to the creation and consolidation of peace in Sudan (Minear and Weiss 1995, 92).

Other critics are even more severe in their judgment. A 1993 Médicins Sans Frontières report states, "The opportunity [for peace] was squandered . . . [due to] the donors' preoccupation with sending food, in the absence of a broader strategy for achieving peace" (in Prendergast and NetLibrary Inc. 1997, 78). Philipe Borel, UN coordinator for Sudan relief operations, voiced disappointment at this self-imposed limitation, asserting that "it's unfortunate that OLS is only doing salvation work, but not finding a solution." He continued, stating that OLS was simply "giving serum to an agonizing problem. We are only treating the symptom, not the disease" (Peterson 2000, 235–36). Further, OLS has fallen under criticism for inadvertently contributing to the escalation of the conflict, especially when air drops were inconsistent:

> Before international pressure was brought to bear in 1998, a combination of government restrictions and weather meant that the airstrips were restricted to only one or two to serve a vast area of assessed need, and they became aid ghettoes, provoking new movements of population. The lack of planning on the part of

the agencies and the unpredictability of deliveries provoked small speculative population movements and exacerbated social disruption. (Human Rights Watch 1998)

Nor were these criticisms coming only from external observers. "Interestingly, the protagonists themselves expressed a certain disappointment with Lifeline." Sudan's Ambassador Abdallah observed, "We look at peace as a process. You start with a cease-fire and corridors of tranquility and then take another step . . . gradually getting to the point of resolving political differences" (Minear, Bread for the World, and Abuom 1991, 141). Unfortunately, "corridors of tranquility were founded on the belief that humanitarian aid could somehow end conflict by bringing warring parties together. In Sudan and Angola, such policies have failed" (Duffield, Macrae, and Zwi 1994, 228).

A key element to this failure might be in OLS's actual design. "The structure was flawed in many ways: important aspects in hindsight are that OLS gave an inordinate amount of control to the regime in Khartoum and limited itself to an emergency agenda." This "short-term emergency agenda dominated humanitarian assistance, with emphasis on the delivery of survival services and with little consideration for the community's intrinsic capacity to help itself" (Erasmus 2001, 248–49). OLS displayed enormously high operational costs, had a large expatriate staff, and had relatively little involvement of local counterparts. Roger Winter notes that due to manipulation of access by the government of Sudan, the corridors did not remain actual physical corridors and that delivery was often relegated to air transport.[3] Cohen concurs with the OLS critique, stating that "clearly the humanitarian problem could not be solved without ending the war and resuming normal political life. Programs like OLS provided only [a] temporary solution" (Cohen 2000, 63).

Was OLS then a ZoP in any sense of the term? When answering this question, one must bear in mind OLS's original mandate:

Contributions towards peace notwithstanding, Lifeline was not a peace initiative. . . . Lifeline cannot be faulted for not accomplishing what it was not explicitly charged with doing. At the same time, it fell short of its potential by not capitalizing on the possibilities for peace that it reflected and helped create. Lifeline's mandate seems unnecessarily narrow. (Minear, Bread for the World, and Abuom 1991, 131)

One must also consider more broadly the concept of ZoPs. Are they intended to create situations distinguished by the absence of violence and war (negative peace), or are they intended to create conditions for social justice, equality, and right relationships (positive peace)? Clearly OLS was designed with the first outcome in mind: the creation of negotiated conflict-free zones where civilians could access aid unimpeded and unmolested. That OLS could have had the potential to bring into being the second outcome, that of a sustainable just peace, is now, in hindsight, apparent. Hindsight is, of course, 20–20, and much reflection on better practices in humanitarian aid has been undertaken in the years following the creation of OLS.

Lessons Learned from Operation Lifeline Sudan

Humanitarian-aid expert John Prendergast has a number of clearly articulated recommendations gleaned from studying the OLS experience (Prendergast and NetLibrary 1997, 21). He comes out very strongly for supporting the conditionality of aid, tying aid programs to the compliance by groups in power to standards of good governance and respect of human rights. He stresses the need to build local capacity and support civil structures, advocating a rehabilitative approach to aid. Finally, and tellingly, he recommends that in future efforts, a multilevel *peacemaking* approach be supported: "A renewed, coordinated, multi-track effort is needed to encourage peacemakers within and outside Sudan to simultaneously work in formal and informal ways to bring peace to all levels of society" (ibid., 25).

A second lesson is that humanitarian aid is a double-edged sword; it can save lives, but also, "most insidiously, humanitarian aid influences the way people think; it makes them expect solutions from outside. International aid has *managed* Sudan's political decay rather than *halted* it" (Peterson 2000, 234). Aid must therefore have a strategic, intentional, planned component for halting political decay as it seeks to save lives.

Third, and paying attention to the discussion on the nature, structure, and variety of peace zones found in Chapter 2, one must also revisit the locus of power and agency in the designation and implementation of ZoPs. As Hancock and Iyer point out, ZoPs seem to operate best when created locally by indigenous actors. Minear concurs, examining this phenomenon from an aid perspective:

> To date, the most positive synergies between humanitarian action and peace appear to have come at the local rather than national level. The record suggests that "relatively small-scale and contextually sensitive efforts to adjust humanitarian programming in active conflict may have a positive effect in mitigating

the impacts of aid on war. Moreover, carefully delivered transitional assistance may assist in building sustainable peace." (Minear 2002, 158, quoting McFarlane 2000)

Schloms applies this understanding specifically to aid organizations and peacebuilding, stating that "it is in particular in the field of 'low-level peacebuilding' where humanitarian organizations 'have the resources necessary to carry out activities necessary for reintroducing a sense of security which may promote sustainable peace'" (Schloms 2003, 40, quoting Spencer 1998).

Fourth, and perhaps most important, we can refer to the seminal work *Do No Harm* by Mary Anderson (1999) and apply many of her concepts to our discussion of lessons learned from the OLS corridors of tranquility. Anderson's basic contention is that "when international assistance is given in the context of a violent conflict, it becomes part of that context and thus also of the conflict" (Anderson 1999, 145). Minear concurs, writing that "the issue, as we see it, is not whether humanitarian action influences conflicts, but to what extent and in what ways" (Minear 2002, 157). Anderson argues further that "the fact that aid inevitably does have an impact on warfare means aid workers cannot avoid the responsibility for trying to shape that impact" (Anderson 1999, 146).

The injection of international aid has been held to exacerbate certain conflict situations when it encourages intergroup tension and weakens intergroup connections. In attempting to mitigate these nefarious effects, Anderson proposes that aid workers seek to identify both the factors that can be labeled as "dividers, tensions, and war capacities," and those factors that constitute "local capacities for peace and connectors" (Anderson 1999, 69). When identifying dividers, one should differentiate between the root and proximate causes of the conflict, the degree of commitment of the parties and the local populations to the conflict, and the endogenous/exogenous components of the conflict. Paying attention to the "actual systems, actions and interaction" within the conflict setting, one can begin to identify local resources and structures for peacemaking and peacebuilding (Anderson 1999, 71).

Aid agencies should therefore reflectively identify and examine aspects of their programming that affect these dividing and uniting factors. Anderson's argument is that humanitarian aid can and must mitigate impacts that promote dissension and division, while at the same time strengthening and empowering local capacities for conflict transformation. If and when aid agencies can accept the principle that aid is political and not neutral, they will be better able to seek consciously to make aid work for peacemaking and building.

One must acknowledge that OLS did learn throughout its years of existence and did in fact engage in capacity building programs with the Sudan Relief and Rehabilitation Association in 1993. "The initial objective was to build the capacity of these organizations for delivering humanitarian aid" (Prendergast and Center of Concern 1996, 102). The results of this capacity building effort have been extensively debated. Some, such as African Rights, argue that the humanitarian space that this program engendered created an opportunity for badly needed dialogue among southerners, while others, such as donor agency personnel, argue that the capacity building workshops "only succeeded in bolstering the mafiosos" (Prendergast and Center of Concern 1996, 103). Prendergast argues that such capacity building initiatives would be more efficient if—rather than working at higher levels in the political structure—they were to address the local institutions, where the grassroots civil society in southern Sudan has traditionally been the healthiest (Prendergast and Center of Concern 1996, 104).

Applying Anderson's local capacities for peace framework to OLS, one could argue that from the inception there was sufficient reflection neither on the impact of aid on the conflict context nor on the potential of the aid to do more than just save lives in the immediate situation. Anderson rightly points out that the very programming of food and material aid, when conceived and implemented with a conflict-sensitive lens, has the potential to work toward the reinstallation of positive peace. Applying the local capacities for peace framework would suggest that the Corridors of Tranquility, if initiated and supported by indigenous communal organizations and infrastructures promoting peace, could have had the very necessary secondary effect of reempowering local parties to impose themselves on the war, laying the foundations for the involvement of Sudanese civil society in peacemaking and postwar reconstruction.

Instead, by introducing these corridors in a "top down" manner, as the result of exclusive negotiations between external aid agencies and the belligerent parties, OLS reduced the local populations to the passive status of victims and beneficiaries rather than active participants in the search for peace. Given the very real—and extremely dire—humanitarian situation in Sudan at that point in time and the difficulty of securing access to the most vulnerable populations, it is perhaps unfair to criticize OLS for not achieving an objective it never assigned itself. One should rather argue that the lessons learned from OLS and other complex humanitarian interventions, gleaned from the relatively peaceful tranquility of hindsight and retrospection, have educated us to the potential for aid to have adverse or beneficial impacts on peacemaking and peacebuilding.

Conclusion

OLS was an innovative and creative response by the humanitarian aid community to an extremely difficult and complex situation. In its first year it was credited with saving tens of thousands of Sudanese civilian lives. Yet in subsequent years the warring parties learned to manipulate OLS, correctly identifying its very weakness: "the organization has been restricted by its own cardinal rule: it must have the approval of both sides and so has been easily manipulated" (Peterson 2000, 175). "The principle [of negotiated humanitarian access] was the best part of OLS" (Minear, Bread for the World, and Abuom 1991). Perhaps its "best part" became its greatest weakness. Manipulated by the machinations of the parties to the conflict, OLS evolved from a creative, innovative approach for securing humanitarian access to a reactive pawn, increasingly preoccupied with the process of seeking to preserve this access at any price.

Ultimately, the OLS experience highlights the inherent paradox of any form of peace zone. Were these corridors of tranquility intended to be an end in themselves or a means to an end—that of stabilizing a positive general peace and fostering the reinstallment of civic life? From the statements of James Grant and others, one can infer that the corridors were intended to be safe havens through which humanitarian aid could be transported unmolested so that unarmed civilians could access food and health care with a degree of safety and security. In other words, the corridors were intended—in technical terms—to be limited and negative peace zones (places marked by a guaranteed absence of violence) that would provide safety for those civilians who could reach them, while a larger, unrelated peace process was pursued separately by other actors, not restricted by the defining principles of impartiality and neutrality of the humanitarian aid community.

This division of labor and the assumption of the possibility of impartial and neutral intervention have since been challenged both by researchers and practitioners in the field. Instead of the humanitarian imperative, practitioners are now speaking of "humanitarian negotiation" in which interveners can—and should—shuttle back and forth between peacemaking and ensuring humanitarian access. Slim argues that this involves a seamless movement between humanitarian and political ground, a "path-breaking role in engaging the parties and a fallback role in keeping them engaged at low points in any political talks" (Slim 2004, 824).

Able to see the bigger picture in hindsight, one can now argue that perhaps OLS squandered an opportunity to aim for a higher objective of positive peace as it conceived and created its corridors of tranquility.

The OLS experience also crystallizes the inherent paradox of peace zones: by settling for safe spaces of negative peace, do we preclude—or at least lessen—the possibility of achieving positive peace?

Notes

[1] Many more sources address issues specific to the condition of women. Among them are "Human Rights of Women in Sudan," UN Commission on Human Rights, UN Economic and Social Council (1998); "Special Report on Women in the South," UN Integrated Regional Information Networks (August 20, 2003); and "Women and Children in Prison," UN Integrated Regional Information Networks (August 20, 2003).

[2] Roger Winter, interview by Krista Rigalo and Nancy Morrison, April 18, 2005.

[3] Ibid.

Works Cited

Anderson, Mary B. 1999. *Do no harm: How aid can support peace—or war*. Boulder, CO: Lynne Rienner Publishers.

Cohen, Herman J. 2000. *Intervening in Africa: Superpower peacemaking in a troubled continent*. Studies in diplomacy. New York: St. Martin's Press.

Deng, Francis M., and J. Stephen Morrison. 2001. US policy to end war. In *Report of the Center for Strategic and International Studies Task Force on US-Sudan Policy*. Washington, DC: Center for Strategic and International Studies.

Duffield, Mark, Joanna Macrae, and Anthony Zwi. 1994. Conclusion. In *War and hunger: Rethinking international responses to complex emergencies*, ed. J. Macrae, A. Zwei, M. Duffield, and H. Slim. London: Zed Books.

Erasmus, Vivien. 2001. Community mobilization as a tool for peacebuilding. In *Peacebuilding: A field guide*, ed. L. Reychler and T. Paffenholz. London: Zed Books.

Human Rights Watch. 1998. Famine in Sudan, 1998: The human rights causes. Available online.

ICG (International Crisis Group). 2003. Sudan's other wars. In *Africa briefing*. Khartoum/Brussels: International Crisis Group.

Ingram, James. 1993. The future architecture for international humanitarian assistance. In *Humanitarianism across borders: Sustaining civilians in times of war*, ed. T. G. Weiss and L. Minear. Boulder, CO: Lynne Reinner Publishers.

IRINews.org. 2003. Two reports: (1) Special report on women in the South and (2) Women and children in prison. UN Integrated Regional Information Networks (August 20). Available online.

———. 2004. IRIN webspecial on the Sudan peace process. United Nations Office for the Coordination of Humanitarian Affairs (March). Available online.

Johnson, Douglas Hamilton. 2003. *The root causes of Sudan's civil wars, African issues*. Bloomington: Indiana University Press; Kampala: Fountain Publishers.

Keen, David. 1994. *The benefits of famine: A political economy of famine and relief in southwestern Sudan, 1983–1989*. Princeton, NJ: Princeton University Press.

McFarlane, S. Neil. 2000. Politics and humanitarian action. Providence, RI: Watson Institute for International Studies. Available online.

Metz, Helen Chapin, and Library of Congress. 1992. *Sudan: A country study*. 4th ed. Area handbook series. Washington, DC: US Government Printing Office.

Miall, Hugh, Oliver Ramsbotham, and Tom Woodhouse. 1999. *Contemporary conflict resolution: The prevention, management and transformation of deadly conflicts*. Cambridge, UK: Polity Press; Malden, MA: Blackwell.

Minear, Larry. 2002. *The humanitarian enterprise: Dilemmas and discoveries*. Bloomfield, CT: Kumarian Press.

Minear, Larry, Bread for the World, and Tabyiegen Agnes Abuom. 1991. *Humanitarianism under siege: A critical review of Operation Lifeline Sudan*. Trenton, NJ: Red Sea Press.

Minear, Larry, and Thomas George Weiss. 1995. *Mercy under fire: War and the global humanitarian community*. Boulder, CO: Westview Press.

Morrison, J. Stephen, and Alex de Waal. 2005. Can Sudan escape its intractability? In *Grasping the nettle: Analyzing cases of intractable conflict*, ed. C. A. Crocker, F. O. Hampson, and P. R. Aall. Washington, DC: United States Institute of Peace Press.

Nyang'oro, Julius E. 2001. Local level intergroup peace building in Southern Sudan: An assessment of effective practices. In *The effectiveness of civil society initiatives in controlling violent conflict and building peace*. Washington, DC: Management Systems International.

Peterson, Scott. 2000. *Me against my brother: At war in Somalia, Sudan, and Rwanda: A journalist reports from the battlefields of Africa*. New York: Routledge.

Prendergast, John. 1992. *Peace, development, and people in the Horn of Africa*. Washington, DC: Center of Concern.

Prendergast, John, and Center of Concern (Washington, DC). 1996. *Frontline diplomacy: Humanitarian aid and conflict in Africa*. Boulder, CO: Lynne Rienner Publishers.

Prendergast, John, and NetLibrary Inc. 1997. *Crisis response: Humanitarian band-aids in Sudan and Somalia*. London: Pluto Press; Washington, DC: Center of Concern.

Prendergast, John, and Jemera Rone. 1994. *Civilian devastation*. New York: Human Rights Watch.

Schloms, Michael. 2003. Humanitarian NGOs in peace processes. In *Mitigating conflict: The role of NGOs*, ed. H. F. Carey and O. P. Richmond. London: Frank Cass.

Slim, Hugo. 2004. Dithering over Darfur? A preliminary review of the international response. *International Affairs* 80 (5): 811–33.

Spencer, Tanya. 1998. A synthesis of evaluations and peacebuilding activities undertaken by humanitarian agencies and conflict resolution organisations. London: Overseas Development Institute. Available online.

Turnbull, Bill, Fr. 2000. Some notes on The Sudan. *White Fathers—White Sisters* 351 (April-May). Available online.

US (United States). 2002. *Sudan peace act.* Washington, DC: US Government Printing Office.

US Congress (House of Representatives, Committee on International Relations). 2002. Following the Danforth report: Defining the next step on the path to peace in Sudan. 107th Congress, 2nd session. Washington, DC.

Weiss, Thomas G., and Cindy Collins. 2000. *Humanitarian challenges and intervention.* Boulder, CO: Westview Press.

10

LOCAL ZONES OF PEACE AND A THEORY OF SANCTUARY

CHRISTOPHER MITCHELL
AND LANDON E. HANCOCK

Introduction

The foregoing analyses of historical and contemporary efforts to provide sanctuary for people threatened with violence hardly exhaust available evidence about such sanctuaries. Nonetheless, these accounts afford some guidelines for answering queries about the factors that increase the likelihood that certain kinds of sanctuary might remain inviolable over a long period of time and succeed in at least their basic function of offering security and protection to those within the boundaries of a space designated as safe from various forms of violence—assault, impressments, capture, or recapture. At the very least these practical examples of sanctuaries in operation offer a number of broad lessons that lead to some theories about factors that increase sanctuaries' inviolability and durability.

The accounts also raise a major problem about making any form of generalization about sanctuaries—or even ZoPs—as a category, given the wide variety of sociopolitical organizations and political practices to which these labels are attached. At the very least, sanctuaries can differ in four major respects:

1. The type of sanctuary.
2. The functions that the sanctuary is established to perform.
3. The environment within which the sanctuary operates.
4. The form of protection offered by the sanctuary.

Inevitably, all four of these features are interconnected and affect one another, but we argue that they all need to be understood and taken into account separately and distinctly whenever any analysis of successful durability and inviolability is being undertaken. This final chapter begins, therefore, with a consideration of these four "differentiations" before considering what might, in general, contribute to the likely success of any type of sanctuary.

Type of Sanctuary

As we argued in the opening chapter of this work, and as has been evident throughout subsequent chapters, there have been a large number of different social arrangements to which the title sanctuary could legitimately be applied. Disarmament zones in Rhodesia, peace corridors in the Sudan, church buildings in medieval England, indigenous communities in Colombia, and self-policing *rondas* in northern Peru are all examples of forms of sanctuary from external assault or depredation, as are refugee camps across international borders or extraterritorial embassies in the modern international system. Even the more specific term *zone of peace* permits some variation in the real-world organizations contained within that category, ranging from externally declared and protected safe zones in Croatia and Bosnia, through indigenous communities in Luzon, to Afro-Colombian communities returning to their villages on the River Cacarica in northwestern Colombia.

In our initial chapter we essayed a preliminary classification scheme to distinguish among the institutions and practices concerned with offering protection. There, we argued that one important distinction is that between protected categories of *persons*, wherever they might be physically located—doctors, ambassadors, priests, children, heralds—and geographical *spaces* within which all present are viewed as protected persons. Even having taken a decision to concentrate upon the second type, locational protection, it was clear that it would also be necessary to distinguish between

1. intra-societal sanctuaries, located within the geographical and jurisdictional boundaries of the society from which threats emanated to those in sanctuary; and
2. extra-societal sanctuaries, located at a distance, that is, outside the geographical and—perhaps more important—jurisdictional boundaries of the threat-producing society.[1]

Accounts of other historical and contemporary cases of sanctuaries and peace zones further complicated our efforts to develop a reasonably simple classification scheme. For example, with respect to intra-societal sanctuaries, there was clearly the question of longevity; that is, whether a sanctuary had existed for a long time as a sanctuary, independent of the contemporary conflict, traditionally offering protection to a wide range of persons seeking safety and security, or whether it had been recently constructed to meet specific threats arising from an immediate danger caused by some form of social or political upheaval, as with the LZPs in the Philippines or Colombia. Did this make a difference to the capability of a locational sanctuary to offer effective protection?

Again, further study of LZPs revealed more distinguishing characteristics likely to influence their durability one way or another. For example, as studies by Catalina Rojas and by Kevin Avruch and Roberto José showed, some peace zones in both Colombia and the Philippines had been established by the inhabitants of a local town, county, or village who saw themselves to be under some serious threat and had declared their home territory to be a peace zone or peace community. In such cases the terrain and boundaries of the zone must be completely familiar to those within the sanctuary. In contrast, other peace zones or communities were set up by groups of people "in exile" (often IDPs expelled from their original homes) as a means of carrying out a secure return to their region, but not necessarily precisely to their original home.

Some of these distinctions can be added to our original typology of types of sanctuary, which would then help to focus attention on important subcategories of intra-societal sanctuaries providing protection to those within spatial boundaries (see Figure 10–1).

Figure 10–1. Typology of Sanctuary

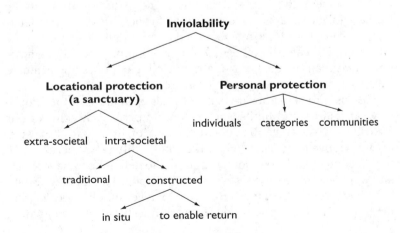

Functions of the Sanctuary

Our studies have revealed a second major means of distinguishing among different types of sanctuaries and peace zones. This is through an examination of the functions that particular sanctuaries have been set up to fulfill. At first, this may seem paradoxical. Sanctuaries are surely established largely to provide protection to those within, and this must also be true of peace zones and peace communities, which are subcategories of sanctuary. However, while it is undoubtedly the case that one of the primary functions of any sanctuary is to provide protection from outside violence of some description,[2] some peace zones or communities are also established to fulfill secondary functions—or develop these as part of or following the initial creation of the secure zone. Over time, these can become the main raison d'etre for a sanctuary or peace community continuing to survive and even to flourish.

Change and Multiple Functions

We noted above examples of communities in both the Philippines and Colombia that had declared themselves peace communities as a way of constructing sanctuaries and protecting themselves but at the same time as a way of leaving IDP camps (or other refuges) and returning to their own territory. This process can be seen as linking return and protection functions, and it raises in another form the issue of criteria for success. In this case success has to be seen—at least partially—as a matter of being able to go back. In other words, the peace community or zone has been established not only to ensure safety for its members but also to enable a safe return to their homes or at least their home territory. On occasion the two objectives can clash, as when return, reestablishment, and refusal to move invite further violence against the community. In such situations the determination of at least some members of the community to stay on, come what may, indicates that the goal of remaining has come to be more important than the goal of being protected. How does one evaluate success in such changing circumstances?

This last problem appears to be a lot easier in terms of the temporary sanctuaries and limited peace zones described by some of our contributors. As Krista Rigalo and Nancy Morrison note, at the start of OLS's move to develop corridors of tranquility in southern Sudan, the function of such corridors was simply to deliver food, medicines, and other essential supplies to the civilian population being fought over. It was only later, when the delivery of relief supplies became contentious and highly politicized, that critiques developed regarding missed opportunities for using the process of negotiating such corridors to fulfill much broader functions. These were held to include building contacts between the adversaries, expanding regions of nonviolence, and/or initiating conversations about a more general, nationwide peace process. We return to this last point below.

Similarly, the functions of protected and safe disarmament zones are normally clear, and while those of peace zones focused on DDR are more extensive and open ended, it still remains possible to make some evaluation of how well those functions were carried out and what contributed to their effectiveness. However, as Pushpa Iyer and Christopher Mitchell suggest in Chapter 8, in cases where local sanctuaries—such as the peace zones in Aceh—have unclear, multiple, or open-ended functions (local cease fires, disarmament, reintegration, confidence building, inputs to national-level negotiations), it becomes more difficult to fulfill all or even most of these functions and theoretically more difficult to account for any level of success in fulfilling such functions. Such difficulties seem less apparent in the case of limited and temporary peace zones that involve truces to enable vaccination programs to take place, religious festivals to be held, or goods to be taken to local markets.

Part of this problem of evaluation arises from our finding that sanctuaries and LZPs are highly dynamic phenomena, starting out with one function that can change into others by a process of accretion. Jennifer Langdon and Mery Rodriguez point out in Chapter 5 that the *rondas campesinas* in northern Peru started with a crime-control function that rapidly changed into the function of delivering "local justice" and eventually, over time and with the addition of some of the surviving southern *rondas*, became legally recognized organizations with representative, development, and investment functions. Langdon and Rodriguez correctly note that from starting as organizations whose main function involved seeking negative peace—protection from outside crime and violence—the *rondas*, north and south, ended as organizations with the multiple functions involved in seeking positive peace—justice, participation in decision-making, development projects, the reform of inequities, and recognition of identities and needs.[3]

Similar changes of function—broadly, from providing negative peace to providing positive peace—can be noted in many of the peace zones and communities in other countries, and in many cases these two broad functions seem to have been equally present from the start. Catalina Rojas makes clear that in the three Colombian peace experiences she has described, the functions of ridding the municipality of corruption, developing local democracy, reinvolving neglected sectors of the community in important decisions, planning and implementing community-wide development projects, resolving intra-community conflict peaceably, and finding alternatives to joining the armed actors for vulnerable members of the community were all important for members of the peace community as the goal of providing safety and security. Moreover, these were often important reasons for the initial creation of these peace communities rather than functions that developed later in their life span. The same can be said about many of Colombia's 100 Municipalities of Peace, which we have surveyed in areas as far apart as Cauca, Meta, Santander, Narino, and Antioquia. Both in Colombia and the Philippines efforts to achieve positive peace within the zone or community appear to be as important as efforts to create negative peace in the immediate environment containing the combatants.[4] The implications of all this for evaluating the success of a particular peace zone are clearly that an evaluation has to be both relative and multidimensional—relative in the sense that the degree of success or failure has to be measured in terms of the objectives the community had in mind when the zone was first established, and multidimensional in that these goals would very likely go beyond the single one of providing sanctuary from external violence. The argument also suggests that, analytically, it would be possible for particular ZoPs to be relatively unsuccessful at providing long-term safety for their denizens but highly successful at banishing corruption, improving living conditions, or developing a sense of unity, purpose, and shared identity. Practically, this might account for the fact that some peace communities survive in spite of an increase in violence directed at the people of the community, as seems to have been the case in Colombian peace communities such as San Jose de Apartado (where over 170 people have been killed since that peace community was established in 1997), Sonson, and indigenous communities in northern Cauca.

Linking Local and National Peace

If peace zones or peace communities are often set up with functions well beyond that of a traditionally conceived sanctuary—providing protection from an outside threat of violence—then the question arises as to whether these functions include having a positive impact on the search for a general peace in a conflict-torn society. This particular possibility has surfaced briefly at a number of places in the accounts of local peacemaking and peacebuilding provided by our contributors, where links—or potential links—between local and national peace efforts have been sketched out or implied. Hence, our discussion of the different functions of LZPs and peace communities has to end with some consideration of these questions: Can LZPs and peace

communities set up—at least partially—as sanctuaries from generalized violence in a war-torn society make some contribution to the
achievement of a general—as opposed to a local—peace? And, if so,
what might this contribution be?

As Peter Sales points out in his critique and evaluation of LZPs
peace in the Philippines, a connection between local and national
peacemaking is a central assumption of much writing about LZPs. It
is most clearly spelled out in official terms in the (Filipino) House of
Representatives' Peace Zones Policy Act of 2000, in which a peace
zone is defined as

> a people initiated, community-based arrangement in a local
> geographical area which residents themselves declare to be off
> limits to armed conflict, primarily to protect civilians there and
> *also to contribute to the more comprehensive peace process.* (Sales 2004,
> 2, emphasis added)

That this clear connection should be made in a formal, government
document emanating from the Philippines should be no surprise. As
Kevin Avruch and Roberto José note in their analysis of Filipino peace
zones, descriptions of such zones make regular references to each local zone's support for national peace efforts. Furthermore, such zones
are conceived partly with the idea of connecting their own efforts to a
larger, national peacebuilding process—without specifying in much
detail how this is to be accomplished.[5]

Other connections between the local and the national levels of
peacemaking—if only in the sense of achieving negative peace at the
national level—are implied by other contributors. Pushpa Iyer and
Christopher Mitchell note that the peace zones in Aceh were intended
to contribute to national-level negotiation by demonstrating that local (negative) peace, disarmament, and development could be
achieved in key areas in Aceh, thus building confidence among nego-
tiators that a satisfactory regional-level settlement could, with care
and good will, be constructed—possibly by expanding the number
of LZPs gradually. The zones were thus to serve both as models for
practical arrangements in other localities and, at a psychological level,
as confidence-building exercises that would enable trust to grow
among those involved in seeking an overall solution to the conflict.

A somewhat similar set of assumptions seems implicit in a number of critiques of the OLS project by Krista Rigalo and Nancy
Morrison. Some of these take the form of regretting the absence of
any serious efforts to expand the negotiations about safe corridors
for relief into talks concerning a more general cease fire or even to
focus on substantive negotiations about solutions to the civil war. Such

critiques clearly assume that, rather than being ends in themselves and concentrating upon relief efforts, the peace corridors—or at least the process of bringing them into being—could have become the means of achieving a wider peace in the Sudan.

But what, more explicitly, are the links between local processes for establishing local sanctuaries in the form of LZPs and national processes for ending the violence and negotiating a comprehensive settlement? One idea takes the form of what might be termed an emulation theory, or a "leopard spot" model, whereby the initial establishment of a few peace zones sets off a process of widespread and successful imitation. Whole areas of a country involved in a protracted and violent conflict become off-limits to violence, thus forcing the armed actors to realize that a negotiated solution is not simply feasible but actually—given the demonstrated and geographically widespread lack of support for solutions achieved through violence—the only realistic option. The Colombian experience over the last decade, with the growth of region-wide associations of peace communities and peace zones—indicates that at least the first part of this theory might well be valid. However, the reactions of the Colombian guerrillas and paramilitaries during the same period, and particularly of the national government since 2002, seem to show that even a major growth of LZPs and of regional associations of peace communities does not inevitably lead to national-level peace negotiations, even when accompanied by substantial pressure from civil society in support of such a process.

Many of the other ideas about links between local peacebuilding through the establishment of various types of sanctuary and national processes aimed at achieving a more general peace tend to be rather ambiguous and often take the form of aspirations rather than clear propositions about likely effects. Distinguishing between "top down" localized initiatives and genuine "bottom up" grassroots processes might help to clarify exactly what arguments are made about such local-national linkages as the two are often conflated. In other words, the indirect effects from processes initiated at the national level—safe corridors in the Sudan, peace zones in Aceh or Bosnia—seem likely to be very different from the effects apt to result from those initiated at the grassroots level, such as the peace zones in the Philippines, El Salvador, or Colombia.[6] To oversimplify somewhat, the first kind of process—national initiatives with local impacts—seems likely to produce indirect effects through expansion, while the second—local initiatives with local impact—is more likely to produce indirect effects through modeling. By this we mean that, under ideal circumstances,[7] the experience of having negotiated limited, temporary, or local peace initiatives may have the following direct effects on those involved in such processes at a national level:

- Expanding the range of issues that might be open to discussion or negotiation, from the delivery of medical supplies and the mutual recognition of safe zones to the release of kidnapped notables, the exchange of prisoners, and eventually to the substantive issues that underlie the conflict.
- Developing a recognition that negotiated outcomes can bring mutual benefits at low cost.
- Developing skills in negotiation rather than coercion.
- Establishing personal relationships with "the enemy."

In contrast, the impact of local or even regional initiatives on those responsible for national peace processes may operate indirectly, through example and precedent, or simply by opening up possibilities where none had seemed to exist:

- Discovering that a potential negotiating partner actually exists.
- Establishing hopeful precedents for talks.
- Confidence building, testing the other side, and reducing mistrust.
- Demonstrating "best methods" of dealing with the other side through dialogue.

All of the above, of course, assume that interaction between local-level and national-level peacebuilding will be positive and lessons can be learned or procedures transferred that lead toward an end to violence and eventually to positive peace at local, regional, and national levels. However, the examples of Aceh and the former Yugoslavia show clearly that the influence of the local on the national—and of the national on the local—can instead be baleful and destructive. Our question about whether LZPs and peace communities might have an impact (positive, it is to be hoped) on peacemaking at the national level has to remain unanswered at present. Our knowledge needs to be expanded considerably before moving away from an uncertain position between positive hopes, claims, and aspirations, on the one hand, and pessimism and warnings of interconnected failure, on the other.

Environments

The third major feature that differentiates types of sanctuary and ZoPs and makes generalization difficult has less to do with the actual zones themselves and more to do with the kind of environment in which they operate. Our contributors have indicated that there are two ways in which this issue of context or environment can be approached. One is the macro level issue raised most clearly in Hancock and Iyer's survey in Chapter 2, namely, the question of the stage of the conflict within which the peace zones or communities are called upon to survive. Originally our study had focused on peace zones that had been established at the height of a conflict and with the aim of providing security against ongoing and widespread violence. However, as many of the previous chapters remind us, conflicts are not simply a matter of coercion and violence, but go through some kind of life cycle, usually involving emergence or conflict formation, escalation, violence, pre-negotiation, cease fire, negotiation, agreement, implementation and post-violence, and long-term peacebuilding (see Mitchell 1981). Peace zones and peace communities are inevitably established largely as reactions to widespread violence and as a way of providing some form of sanctuary against this threat, but they often continue beyond that stage of the conflict into the post-violence period, particularly if, as with the Peruvian *rondas*, they have developed capacities for constructing components of positive peace in addition to providing protection against violence.

As Hancock and Iyer suggest, peace zones exist in a changing conflict environment and so need to be analyzed from a temporal point of view if their sustainability is to be understood clearly. While these authors suggest a useful classification based upon whether a peace zone or community is being analyzed before violence erupts, during ongoing violence, or after the violence has died down and some agreement is being implemented, we suggest a modification of this tripartite distinction to make allowance for variations in the environments of peace zones brought about by smaller but nonetheless important changes in the surrounding conflict. Thus, communities in peace zones would face somewhat different problems, depending on whether they were confronting

1. continuing high levels of coercion and violence;
2. ongoing pre-negotiations or negotiations carried out while violence continues;[8]
3. negotiations, accompanied by a general cease fire;
4. conditions after negotiations break down and violence resumes;
5. implementation of a substantive agreement; or
6. post-conflict peacebuilding.

Different Stages of Conflict with Different Challenges

Each of the above contexts presents rather different challenges with which peace communities will have to deal, and our various chapters have indicated some of the differences that such contexts bring to efforts both to provide sanctuary and to begin to build positive peace.

Our original assumption was, and remains, that the most testing environment for establishing and maintaining peace zones and communities is at the height of the violence. Periods of national-level negotiations somewhat ease the pressure on peace zones and communities, whether or not the negotiations are accompanied by a general cease fire, although obviously a general cessation of the overall violence should logically lead to a diminished need for protection at the local level.[9] Even if the negotiation process is undertaken without a general cease fire, the very fact that negotiations are being carried out should, one would assume, dampen the continuing level of violence. Nonetheless, the effects of a strategy of continuing to fight in order to gain an advantage to use at the negotiating table or even simply to demonstrate that one is not negotiating because of weakness should not be underestimated.[10]

It also seems likely that peace communities and others trying to maintain sanctuaries will face a somewhat different set of problems from the problems that preceded any negotiations should those national-level negotiations break down and violence be resumed. This is a set of circumstances much neglected in the literature on peace zones but is certainly a fairly common occurrence. In Colombia, negotiations between the government and the FARC came to an abrupt and abrasive halt in February 2002. Negotiations in the Philippines between the NPA and President Corazon Aquino's government suffered a similar fate, in spite of all the hopes raised by the EDSA revolution. Similar crises afflicted peace processes in Sri Lanka, Northern Ireland, and many other protracted conflicts. What are the effects on LZPs when fighting is renewed between frustrated and disillusioned adversaries? The end of the Colombian negotiations in 2002 was followed by the renewal of combat at new levels of ferocity; a greater unwillingness, particularly on the part of the Colombian government, to countenance the existence of zones or communities that had "withdrawn" from the struggle again the rebels; and a greater willingness to argue that the peace communities were—at least indirectly and in many cases directly—aiding the insurgency. Certainly in this case conditions for peace zones became even more difficult than they had been during previous stages of the conflict.

The environment surrounding peace zones and communities immediately following the conclusion of a general agreement and in its implementation stage will undoubtedly be very different from contexts in which violence continues. Empirical evidence on such situations is sparse. The only cases mentioned briefly in previous chapters involve the disarmament zones in Rhodesia, specially constructed as part of the peace agreement for concentration and disarmament, and the peace zones in Aceh, which were part of an interim agreement that left the conclusion of a fully negotiated settlement until some later time. The question remains open, then, about what might happen to established grassroots peace communities once violence has ceased, an agreement been negotiated, and its details—especially those involving disarmament and reinsertion of combatants—await implementation. Can LZPs expand their functions with a view to ensuring that a peace agreement does not break down and that the conditions of violence and mayhem that led to the establishment of the ZoP in the first place do not return?

Similar questions can be asked about the role of peace zones and communities in the stage of reconstruction, repair, and reconciliation that follows the conclusion and short-term implementation of a national-level peace agreement. What happens to *local* peace zones when *general* peace breaks out? The El Salvador case provides one answer, which is that peace zones can be created during this stage in order to fulfill a variety of peacebuilding functions at the local level, the first of which is to put in place effective processes for dealing with the conflicts that arise within the local community itself. Others include many of the positive peacebuilding activities that many peace communities have tried to implement in the more difficult context of widespread combat and violence: removing corruption, encouraging participatory local democracy, developing a culture of peace for local communities and local homes, and engaging in appropriate community-based development projects. The experience of the Peruvian *rondas* provides a similar answer, even in the case of peace communities that were established well before the conclusion of a general peace, at a stage in the conflict when the search for protection against violence predominated. Having survived the period of sustained violence and—in this case—the defeat of one of the adversaries, many of the Peruvian *rondas* that had developed aspects of positive peace appear to have made these the main focus of their efforts to develop an influential sense of unity and identity within Peruvian society.

However, at this "aftermath" stage of a conflict, local peace communities—together with almost all post-combat communities—seem also likely to face a range of new issues to do with the return of refugees and IDPs, and—more problematic—former combatants and their reinsertion into local life, as well as issues of truth, justice, and reconciliation between previous adversaries and between former combatants and their victims. While the post-agreement stage seems to have removed many of the difficulties in achieving negative peace locally, it also seems to present new and more difficult obstacles to achieving local positive peace in the long term.

Widespread Violence and Its Variations

It seems only common sense to argue, as we do above, that peace communities face different challenges and problems at very different stages of a protracted conflict. In addition, however, even during the stage of general and continuing violence, the specific nature of the surrounding, local violence will obviously present different challenges for local communities and for local sanctuaries, affecting their chances for survival. As Mitchell noted in his account of the fortunes of Christian missionary compounds in China during the early years of the last century, different problems were posed during the period when the Boxer Rebellion made the missions themselves targets from those arising in later periods when civil wars raged but the adversaries were usually careful not to involve mission compounds, clearly marked out as being under the protection of Christian missionary organizations and their governments. The nature of the problems changed again when the conflict involved an invading Japanese army and the protection of local Chinese communities against that army.

Hence, even within the same conflict that inflicts high levels of widespread violence on a society, there are likely to be variations in the nature and level of local violence and hence differences in the environments that challenge local peace communities. Put slightly differently, in any situation of protracted violent conflicts, different local environments will generate different needs for sanctuary and put different pressures on the local sanctuary providers. The problems confronted by the indigenous peace communities in the Luzon Corderilla region, the scene of major fighting between the AFP and the NPA, were very different from those facing the people in Naga City, whose major problems arose from the violence visited on local communities by armed vigilantes, ostensibly set up to provide local protection.

Our studies so far suggest that—hardly surprisingly—different stresses on peace zones and communities that arise from their environment depend mainly on the level and nature of local conflict and violence. A peace community that exists in a region that is firmly under the control of one side or the other in the conflict is likely to have different problems in its efforts to stay out of the conflict from one that is in a region where the adversaries are contending for control. In the former case, difficulties seem very likely to arise when local, grassroots decisions clash with the interests of the dominant combatants, whether these are the representatives of the state under attack or of the insurgents seeking to overthrow those incumbents. At the very least, the dominant actors in the locality will want local, grassroots activities to support their campaign to win the violent struggle and to conform to their own objectives, ideologies, and practices, viewing any deviation as evidence that local communities are acting in the interests of the adversary. "Weeding out" local individuals perceived to be a danger to "the cause" seems more than likely to occur, and this is likely to affect leaders of a peace community trying to maintain the non-involvement of their community in the struggle.

In the case of peace communities that exist in a region of major contention between the combatants, or where the zone or community itself may be a valuable resource to control, the problems facing sanctuary seekers and sanctuary providers seem likely to be different, more difficult, and even more stressful for local people. In such an environment it becomes much more difficult to opt out of the violent confrontation, to keep the zone physically inviolate by keeping combatants out, and to avoid giving "assistance" (usually coerced) to one side or the other as they move through local territory. If one of the objectives of local armed actors becomes actual physical control of the zone and the resources it contains—for example, land for growing illegal crops such as coca, or safe access between other key regions—then the problems become even more acute. We have found cases where the only solution for the local peace community has been to move out of its territory and establish the community elsewhere.[11]

Our analysis thus far leads to two tentative conclusions. The first is that the most difficult environment for peace zones and communities in their quest for safety and security—and a place to establish some form of positive peace—is one where the firm control of a previously unchallenged armed actor is being disrupted by an adversary seeking to take over that region and its valued resources. This, in turn, suggests that it is helpful to think about the durability of ZoPs as being affected by their creation and existence in five contrasting environments:

1. In a region stably and firmly under the control of agents of the state as one of the armed actors.
2. In a region stably and firmly under the control of one of the armed actors seeking to overthrow the existing incumbents.
3. In a region of contention where armed actors are confronting each other for strategic control of that region.
4. In a region of contention where local armed actors confront one another in order to control the actual ZoP, which itself contains valued resources that are the prize being fought over.
5. In a region that has just changed hands and moved from the firm control of one set of armed actors to another.

This last situation reminds us that some sanctuaries can be established to deal with issues of protection and security in one type of local environment and then called upon to provide sanctuary in quite different circumstances. The more stable that environment, the more likely it is that local sanctuary providers will be able to work out over time some kind of *modus vivendi* with the dominant local actors, although this is unlikely to be an easy matter or to engender a stress-free relationship. In volatile regions, especially where armed actors gain and lose ground or control, the task for leaders of ZoPs is likely to become far more difficult; chances of survival for the peace community are lowered.

All of this is to argue that it is important to take a changing environment into consideration when asking whether this or that sanctuary remained inviolate when the environment changed dramatically and the nature and intensity of threats to inhabitants increased. Even in such daunting circumstances, however, some sanctuaries have survived and remained effective under the worst of circumstances. How did this come about? We attempt some initial hypotheses about this conundrum in the final section.

Protection

One line of thought that might throw some light on the connection between types of sanctuary and their sustainability switches attention from types of external environment to classifying sanctuaries according to who is inside them and what they are seeking protection from. It seems a reasonable starting assumption that outsiders are more likely to respect the inviolability of a sanctuary if they do not perceive those inside as a major potential danger to them or their interests.[12] Absence of any compelling reason for outsiders to violate sanctuary is probably as important an influence on inviolability as are factors that deter such a violation. If the answer to the question of who is inside turns out to be that *all* the inhabitants can be seen as harmless, then why not respect sanctuary itself? Clearly, if the sanctuary is sheltering enemies or potential enemies, the temptation to violate is greater than if the sanctuary is sheltering neutrals or would-be neutrals—although sometimes the presence of would-be neutrals within a self-declared sanctuary is not tolerated in a life-or-death conflict. However, the major danger to a sanctuary's inviolability seems likely to arise when outside combatants perceive that enemies masquerading as neutrals are present in the sanctuary or—more likely—a mixture of enemies, their supporters, and neutrals. In such circumstances it seems likely that, once violated by one side seeking to "root out" adversaries pretending to be neutral, the process is likely to continue as members of the other side violate the sanctuary in search of those who surrendered or gave away their members or supporters. However, to some degree, the likelihood of violation depends not just on who is within the sanctuary but also on what they are doing while sheltered there—a topic to which we return below when discussing the nature of neutrality and how this concept ties in with the preservation of a sanctuary.

That aside, the inviolability of any sanctuary is obviously going to depend very greatly on who is inside and how valuable their capture might be to outsiders, irrespective of how active or quiescent they are. Historically, criminals seeking sanctuary pose a greater temptation than children seeking the same protection. Debtors and escaped slaves usually have invited violation more than religious refugees, although not if the protracted conflict involves religious beliefs and adversaries. Civilian noncombatants present less of a temptation than wounded soldiers from the opposing army, prominent opponents, or wealthy individuals, worthy of ransom. The effort of some mission compounds during the Chinese civil wars to exclude prominent or wealthy individuals and even in some cases anyone other than women and children represents a conscious effort to lower the temptation and hence the probability of the sanctuary being violated. From a strictly categorical point of view, however, this practice does suggest the value of making a clear distinction between those sanctuaries that are completely open (anyone can ask for and receive sanctuary) and those that are closed to certain categories of would-be supplicants.

The Key Role of Neutrality

Apart from the question of who is within the sanctuary and what such individuals are being protected from, there remains the issue of the obligations of those within a sanctuary, the strict observation of which is likely to increase that sanctuary's inviolability. What are inhabitants *not* to say or do while inside a sanctuary or a LZP so that threatening outsiders (combatants, revenge seekers, forces of law and order) will respect obligations of inviolability regarding that sanctuary, even though they may not have agreed to or even been consulted about such obligations?

Implications for a Neutral Space

The answer to the above question seems to revolve around two key principles. The first is of *abstention*—things that the inhabitants of sanctuaries or peace zones will not do to offend outsiders. The second is *impartiality*—the equal treatment of outsiders who are also adversaries. In the case of sanctuaries that offer protection to individuals or communities in the midst of a civil war, the most effective rule seems to be complete abstention from any participation in the struggle. Thus, on the one hand, *campesino* communities in Colombia refuse to the best extent they can to feed, supply, or interact with any of the combatant groups in their locality, whether guerrillas, paramilitaries, or units of the Colombian army (many of which are closely linked to the paramilitaries anyway). On the other hand, indigenous peace communities in the Philippines have offered equal treatment to the wounded of both sides, and even some recreational facilities to members of the AFP and the NPA, provided the latter come into the community unarmed and with a promise of nonviolent behavior. However, it is difficult for a sanctuary to withdraw completely from what is going on around it, so there needs to be some speculation about whether a strategy of complete inactivity—doing absolutely nothing to help or to hinder—is most effective in maintaining inviolability, rather than constructive engagement, which somehow offers benefits equally to outsiders, adversaries, and combatants.

The question of appropriate behavior on the part of those in sanctuary and the likely effect this might have on outsiders' respect for the inviolability of the sanctuary closely parallels the idea and practice of neutrality in interstate relations and the capability of countries to stand aside from an international war or for national leaders to refuse to align their state with one side or the other in a violent conflict (whether between states or among factions within a collapsed state). The whole idea of staying neutral has a long tradition, and its ramifications have developed over a considerable period of time. The ability to stand aside from an armed conflict was understood and recognized in classical Greece, but whatever the origins of the concept of neutrality in international law and interstate politics, at least by the start of the twentieth century the legal status of being neutral was universally understood and accepted. As Michael Walzer points out, there exist two aspects to the idea of being (and staying) neutral in any conflict, a *right* to remain disengaged and not to be attacked, on the one hand, and a set of *obligations* on the other (1977, 234–38).[13] This second aspect—the international equivalent of what inhabitants of a sanctuary or a peace zone might be required not to do—forms an increasingly elaborate set of obligations that make up accepted laws of neutrality and is aimed at not conferring any advantage on one warring side rather than the other. In a negative sense, neutrals must refrain from giving aid to one side in the conflict but, in a positive sense, may continue "such pacific intercourse with belligerents as will not consist of giving direct aid to either side in the prosecution of hostilities" (Bauslaugh 1991, 164).

The practical difficulties of implementing these principles and even the specific rules about neutral behavior remain considerable, however, even in conflicts that involve sovereign states as parties.[14] Walzer makes the point well by noting that while formal rules of neutrality allow the continuation of "normal" patterns of trade, such a trade pattern rarely involves equally beneficial effects on both adversaries, so that its continuation is inevitably one sided (1977, 232–35). And if the neutral decides to suspend all trade for the duration of the conflict, this is likely to harm the country normally traded with to the advantage of the other. Parallels with the neutrality sought by those establishing a sanctuary may be imperfect, but they do raise questions about what the impact of a refusal to align with one side might be for the fortunes of that party, and how its leaders are likely to react to a strategy of abstention from participation—especially in terms of respecting the inviolability of a peace community adopting such a position.

There are numerous ways in which the analogy between neutrality in interstate conflict and sanctuary in intra-societal conflict breaks down. Hence, trying to draw direct parallels and lessons from the reasons why neutrality is respected to reasons why sanctuaries remain inviolable may be misleading, save in the important sense that, as a general principle, the behavior of those within the sanctuary and the behavior of those seeking to remain neutral should logically help to contribute in some way to the maintenance both of the neutrals' stance and to the inviolability of the sanctuary. Obviously, one of the problems that make the drawing of parallels difficult lies in the fact that there are relatively clear standards in international law by which the behavior of both aspiring neutral and contending belligerent can be judged. Is country X acting in conformity with the laws of neutrality?[15]

In the case of an intra-societal sanctuary seeking to stand apart from an ongoing civil conflict, there are few if any agreed standards for evaluating whether the right to remain inviolable (whatever that might mean) should be respected simply because certain (often self-defined) obligations are being observed by those within the sanctuary. In some societies particular norms and rules regarding within-sanctuary behavior have been developed and helped to ensure the observance of sanctuary by outsiders. This pattern of sanctuaries operating within well established, well understood, and accepted norms may be more common than one suspects, but in many cases there seem to be no standards about acceptable within-sanctuary behavior that increase the chances that the sanctuary will survive and be effective. This leads to the issue of whether, even if there are domestically no clear rules about the rights and obligations of intrasocietal "neutrals" (as there are in international law), there can be developed a set of norms (local and probably temporary) about rights and obligations regarding sanctuaries that is recognized and respected by relevant parties, even by state agencies. If this seems a possibility, then three further queries become important:

1. What might such norms look like?
2. What situations and whose behaviors might these norms cover?
3. What else affects the likelihood that observation of such norms would significantly increase the inviolability and the durability of the sanctuary?

Some evidence about efforts to establish this type of intra-societal "regime" in the midst of violent and protracted conflict suggests that the process is possible and successful, if only in the short term and under very specific circumstances. The latter have to do with the stability of the local situation surrounding the sanctuary and of the structure of the combatants involved (both of which need much further study). There are many examples of local agreements and norms regarding ZoPs that seek to stand apart from ongoing violence. These have usually been established through one of three basic processes:

1. Unilateral declarations by those establishing the sanctuary in which the norms proclaimed are articulated specifically to local conditions and the position of local combatants.
2. Declarations made in conformity with some generally recognized and understood (if not necessarily accepted) principles and laws (such as international humanitarian law, human rights laws, and so on).
3. Specific agreements negotiated between those establishing the sanctuary and local combatants.

To date there is little conclusive evidence to assert that one of these processes is more effective than the others in ensuring the inviolability of ZoPs or in extending their life. Some evidence points to the likelihood that linking local declarations to general laws (to sections of the national constitution or to international human rights law, for example) can help to sustain inviolability. And there are cases that support the hypothesis that it is most effective to negotiate acceptable terms and agreements with local armed actors and, whenever possible, to obtain their (preferably public) endorsement of the zone and its continuation, however temporary this might prove.

Amid these competing viewpoints, what seems clear is that all three processes involve efforts to establish some kind of local "rules of the game" for intra-societal neutrality and for acceptable behavior on the part of those within sanctuaries. The search for wholly acceptable and neutral behavior within a sanctuary may ultimately turn out to be a chimera, both theoretically and practically, but perhaps giving up the idea of perfect neutrality makes it possible to approach the dilemma from the opposite direction. This could then elucidate a connection between what a sanctuary does and its success in protecting and surviving. Let us inquire, then, what behaviors within sanctuary are wholly unacceptable and clearly likely to result in the rapid collapse of the entire enterprise under the weight of negative outsider reactions.

Sanctuary and Continuing Involvement in Conflict

The concept of forbidden or at least unacceptable behavior within a sanctuary has at least two aspects. The first concerns behavior demanded as far as the sanctuary itself and its providers are concerned; that is, what supplicants or inhabitants are required to do or not to do within the boundaries of the sanctuary. Acceptable within-sanctuary behavior shows a vast range of practices, depending upon the type of sanctuary and the beliefs of the sanctuary providers. In Greek sanctuaries, for example, supplicants had to be open about their presence in the sanctuary (anonymity was not an option) and were expected to avoid behavior that interfered with the normal ceremonies and observances devoted to the god within the sacred precinct.[16] In some of the late-twentieth-century ZoPs in Colombia the local population developed elaborate rules for life there. These rules ranged from abstaining from alcohol and observing a self-imposed curfew to establishing new decision-making systems, schemes for sharing resources in short supply (tractors, training materials), and methods for resolving internal disputes.

The second aspect refers to the kind of behavior that would be unacceptable to outsiders who could threaten the sanctuary's inhabitants (or some of them) and hence the overall inviolability of the sanctuary itself. What sorts of things might sanctuary dwellers do that would increase the likelihood that they would be regarded as legitimate targets by outsiders and make the violation of the sanctuary seem justified? One general answer is enjoying sanctuary but carrying on the conflict in some way from within that sanctuary. In other words, any inhabitants who use the protection afforded by the sanctuary to continue the struggle are likely to invite a reaction from outside adversaries that will end the sanctuary's immunity from attack, either temporarily or permanently.

The likelihood that this behavior will evoke such a reaction depends on whether the behavior in question is perceived as a nuisance or as a major threat. The outsiders may put pressure on the sanctuary providers to act to stop the offending behavior, or the outsiders may deem it necessary to act themselves, either to put an end to the unacceptable behavior or an end to the sanctuary itself. At one extreme are numerous cases of individuals enjoying sanctuary in exile in another country and continuing to write and publish material criticizing the home government. At the other is the situation in which an exile group or community, or a large population of refugees, uses the protection afforded by being physically across a border in another country to organize sustained assaults on their country of origin with a view to undermining and eventually overthrowing those currently in power there. This almost inevitably invites retaliation from the current government, irrespective of international rules governing territorial inviolability and national sovereignty.

This is precisely the kind of situation described by Sarah Lischer in her study of the support offered by humanitarian organizations for refugee communities enjoying the sanctuary afforded by being across an international border and on the territory of a neighboring country. Such sanctuaries can be, as Lischer points out, highly "dangerous," as in many cases they contain people who are willing and able to use refugee camps as bases from which to continue the struggle unless deliberately prevented from doing so. They thus pose a major threat both to the country of origin and also to the country affording sanctuary because of the former's likely reactions, which can include retaliatory strikes across "inviolable" international borders (Lischer 2005).

Clearly, the "sanctuaries at a distance" afforded Rwandan refugees in Zaire, Afghan refugees in Pakistan, and Khmer refugees in Cambodia are extreme examples of protected places within which denizens could, did, and were permitted to engage in a range of behaviors that resulted eventually in the ending of that protection.[17] The most obvious forms of "conflict continuing" behavior exemplified in such situations involve developing support for a political organization dedicated to continuing the struggle; solidifying political support from and control over those within the sanctuary; recruiting for a military or quasi-military wing; training, equipping, and arming recruits; imposing taxes on those in exile within the sanctuary, or otherwise expanding the resource base for continuing to wage the conflict; and establishing a propaganda machine to garner support and further assistance for the refugees forced into exile. Less obviously, the protection and help supplied to the refugees can obviate the need for the militants among them to cope with the opportunity costs of "looking after their own" and frees them up to concentrate on continuing the conflict. Lischer notes that Burundian refugee camps in Tanzania "sustained the militants' dependents and followers, freeing the rebel parties from the responsibility of providing material support" (2005, 24).

There is no need to emphasize that intra-societal domestic sanctuaries hardly offer the same opportunities as extra-societal refuges for some of their denizens to carry on conflict-continuing behavior, giving outsiders affected by such activities more than enough reason to violate the sanctuary as a response. Moreover, domestic sanctuaries are much more likely to contain inhabitants that resemble Lischer's category of "situational refugees," who are simply seeking safety from war, chaos, and deprivation as opposed to either "persecuted" refugees or "state-in-exile" refugees, some of whom aim to continue the conflict to some final triumph.[18] However, there remains the problem of unintended effects. What if activities within the ZoP inadvertently have some important impact on the conflict continuing outside that sanctuary or are perceived as doing so by one or other of the combatants? What effect is this likely to have on the inviolability and durability of that type of sanctuary? If any self-declared sanctuary is perceived as giving aid and comfort to the enemy, even unintentionally (for example, by providing a refuge for combatants' dependents, denying needed information, or impeding a key supply route), the temptation to remove such an impediment to military success will be great.

Of course, in many cases it might not be actual behavior by sanctuary dwellers that brings about the breaking of sanctuary by outsiders determined to stop such "unacceptable" activity. Rather, the anticipation of such a danger occurring in the future might prompt breaking of sanctuary. In many cases it is the *anticipation* of adverse effects, *fears* of likely costs, and *perceptions* of potential dangers that lead outsiders to ignore even widely acknowledged and normally accepted limitations on entering sanctuaries and "dealing with" inhabitants. This particular situation can be illustrated by the reactions of outside combatants to the establishment of ZoPs in civil wars. These reactions are often based upon perceptions of potential dangers and costs arising from the existence of such communities and their inhabitants. They are also based on implicit worst-case analyses regarding what could happen if—for example—the relatives of known members of an adversary, or former members of the other side, or individuals potentially critical of "us" were to be left free and secure merely because they lived within some (often self-declared) sanctuary. From such perceptions it is but a step to consider that any community that is not clearly and positively "for" our side in the struggle must, by definition, be positively supporting or at least indirectly helping the enemy, irrespective of their protestations of neutrality. The obvious reaction is to take action to eliminate this potential danger. During recent years in the protracted conflict within Colombia, Colombian government ministers led by President Uribe have accused the peace communities in that country of deliberately offering support and protection to the FARC and the ELN and insisted that they cannot remain neutral in the struggle.[19] On the other side, the FARC has warned civilians in Meta that all or any who stayed in government (or paramilitary) controlled areas and were not either killed or driven out by these pro-state forces would be regarded by FARC as collaborators and become legitimate military targets. If the only way to prove to one side in a protracted conflict that particular individuals or communities are not supporting the other side is to be killed or expelled by the latter, then the prospects for constructing any form of viable ZoP seem slim, to say the least.

However, the Colombian situation does seem to be an extreme one. The general lesson from this and other cases is that the norm of not permitting any form of behavior within a sanctuary that might be taken to harm one adversary or bring advantage to another can and often does increase the likelihood that the sanctuary will be tolerated (at least for a time) by outsiders. The observance of this—and other—guidelines can never guarantee absolute inviolability, of course, given the many factors in a protracted conflict. This observation returns us to these questions: After examining a variety of different forms of sanctuary in different historical eras and in changing circumstances, what initial guidelines might be suggested to increase the likelihood that sanctuaries will remain inviolable and be able to offer safety and protection to those within their social and physical bounds? What factors make it more likely that sanctuaries will survive?

Ensuring Sanctuary amid Protracted Civil Violence

En route to answering these questions it is helpful to return to our original working definition of a sanctuary and amend it by adding some ideas about key sources of effective protection that, in the light of our investigations thus far, seem to crop up frequently:

> A sanctuary is a place where certain individuals, communities, or categories of people can go to be safe from others who would otherwise harm them, usually through the use of violence.

Protection is afforded through the existence of certain—usually accepted—norms or rules or through the anticipation of various forms of sanction that would result from a violation of those rules.

This expanded definition implies at least three basic reasons why sanctuaries are more or less liable to remain inviolate and durable and suggests characteristics that might contribute to increasing the chances that particular sanctuaries will succeed in offering protection to those living within their boundaries:

1. The existence of sure and costly sanctions that would inevitably be visited upon those violating the sanctuary. (This can be linked to the final suggestion below of sanctuary-strengthening factors.)
2. The existence of some accepted rules about outsiders' behavior toward the sanctuary and its occupants.
3. The existence of some accepted rules for the occupants regarding behavior within the sanctuary and behavior vis-à-vis the armed actors in the environment.

It seems more likely that these rules will be widely recognized and generally kept if they are negotiated with all the parties affected by the existence of the ZoP. Evidence suggests that, wherever possible, ZoPs or other types of sanctuary should be established through processes of dialogue, negotiation, and agreement among all stakeholders (or as many as possible), rather than by unilateral acts or even actions justified by reference to externally obtained rules or norms.

Beyond these two general guidelines, the examples of sanctuary reviewed in the previous chapters also suggest a number of other factors that play a role in making it more probable (but never certain) that sanctuaries will "work" and "last." The cases we have discussed suggest that the following are important:

1. The existence of a high level of internal unity of purpose within the sanctuary, plus a successful mechanism for dealing (promptly, effectively, and nonviolently) with divisions and conflicts that arise within the peace zone or community.
2. The development of a wide and varied range of generally approved activities and projects beyond those involved in safeguarding the community from external violence.
3. The existence of effective and accepted collective leadership, which arranges to ensure its future continuation in the event of the demise or disruption of the founding generation.

4. The clarity with which the boundaries of the sanctuary are defined and marked.
5. The geographical and sociopolitical remoteness of the sanctuary from the centers of influence or combat, in the case of civil strife.
6. The impartiality with which those conducting the sanctuary treat outside interests, rivalries, and conflicts.
7. The existence of some legal or ethical basis for the existence and functioning of the sanctuary. This can either arise from the existence of some intra-societal rules or norms (preferably long held and sanctified by tradition) or be based upon some extra-societal but generally accepted laws or norms, such as international human rights law.
8. The absence of any kind of threat posed by the sanctuary to any of the intra-societal combatants, to the central government, or to a host society in the case of sanctuaries at a distance.
9. The absence of any valued goods within the sanctuary that would be a sufficient reward for violation. In some cases valued goods include denizens whose seizure would be so worthwhile as to offset any material or symbolic costs incurred by the violation.
10. The existence of outside bodies that have an interest in acting as protectors, patrons, or supporters of the sanctuary and who are willing to take action on its behalf.

Several of these factors have already been discussed in connection with particular historical examples of sanctuary, but some further comments seem warranted on the influence of clear boundaries, on the question of sanctuaries posing a threat, and on the importance of particular forms of outside patronage in keeping sanctuaries in being.

Clear Boundaries

In the territorial sense the issue of drawing clear physical boundaries that indicate where the protection offered by sanctuary begins and ends seems straightforward and somewhat trivial. It is true that arguments about the extent of church-based protection in medieval Europe could be a matter for debate—the altar? the nave? the church building? church grounds? It is also true that there were difficulties with some of the peace zones in the Philippines over differing definitions of the zone. Who had the right to stay in or to enter with arms into particular areas viewed according to traditional, indigenous criteria as outside the zone but according to local government criteria as within it? Normally, however, the negotiating, drawing, and marking of physical boundaries around locational sanctuaries appears to present few problems, at least in principle.

In contrast, the question of boundaries is less clear when dealing with peace communities. The issue of who is a member and who is not—and therefore not under protection—becomes a matter for controversy. In cases where the peace community consists of people from a different culture or ethnicity—an indigenous people speaking a different language, having a different appearance, following traditional practices—the problem might be eased somewhat, but it never disappears completely. In many cases threats to the inviolability of peace communities arise from disputes over whether those communities are harboring combatants pretending to be members of the community but in reality are using the protection afforded for refuge, rest, and recuperation. In others, individuals and groups have claimed membership in a particular sanctuary in order to gain not merely protection but other kinds of advantage, as was noted in the case of Christian missions in China becoming inadvertently involved in lawsuits through litigants claiming membership in Christian congregations. In many cases peace communities and other forms of sanctuary have tried to issue "markers" that indicate where the boundary between members and nonmembers lies—certificates, armbands, T-shirts—which resemble efforts to mark out the territory of the peace zone by notices, flags, or fences. The boundary problem becomes less capable of simple solutions when questions of family relationships arise and members of peace communities enjoying the protection of a successful sanctuary have relatives who are members of rival combatant organizations. It becomes even more intractable when people who have previously been involved on one side or the other of a protracted and violent conflict wish to join the sanctuary and become new members of the peace community. What processes are available so that adding members does not decrease the sanctuary's inviolability? How can these be made transparent and convincing to the outsiders who are already suspicious about the neutrality and harmlessness of that site, zone, or community?

Inherent Threats Posed by Sanctuaries

We have briefly discussed the problems posed for durability by those sanctuaries that appear to be a threat to outsiders, but particularly to combatants who see themselves engaged in a life-and-death struggle between good and evil. The difficulty in maintaining a neutral stance in highly ideological conflicts is nothing new. In such settings some potential threats emanating from even the most calculatedly neutral sanctuaries are obvious and arise from the denial of benefits to both sides because of the existence of the neutral zone—access to an easier route, to supplies, to labor, or to intelligence. Other threats are one sided and can be dealt with by action on the part of those organizing the sanctuary or through agreements with local combatants. In China during the period of the 1937–41 Japanese invasion, missionary compounds were sometimes asked to ensure that there would be no Chinese troops within one kilometer in exchange for Japanese forces respecting their freedom from attack (Quale 1957, 242). The dilemma for maintaining a sanctuary in the midst of a protracted intra-societal conflict is whether the denial of those factors that once offered advantage to one side or disadvantage to the other and their replacement by a strict impartiality will so anger the previously advantaged as to engender retaliation or whether the new impartiality will make up for loss of the old relationship.

More subtly, there can be occasions when the very existence of a neutral sanctuary can pose at least a symbolic threat to one or both sides during a protracted intra-society conflict. In some situations the withdrawal of a community into a peace zone or other form of sanctuary represents a form of rejection of the adversaries that in itself becomes a criticism and undermining of their aspirations in the struggle. Indeed, it calls into question the very legitimacy of the struggle being waged. Often such struggles are characterized as being between government and a set of rebels, or between freedom fighters and the forces of tyranny. The existence of an uncommitted community indicates to observers in the rest of the world that claims of "representativeness" put forward by the adversaries need to be treated with some skepticism. This is especially so if numerous peace communities come into existence in an effort to provide security from combatants claiming to fight on the people's behalf. The greater the number of communities saying through their actions what amounts to "a plague on both your houses," the greater the threat to the credibility of the adversaries.

Patronage

A third factor likely to play a major part in determining whether intra-societal sanctuaries remain inviolable is the degree of outside protective influence that can be exercised by foreign actors in behalf of the individuals or communities that are seeking safety and security. This factor emerged as critical in the case of the Christian missionary sanctuaries in early twentieth-century China, where the protection afforded missionary compounds arose directly from their connections with their own governments and the willingness of those governments to intervene—with force if necessary—in behalf of their citizens and the missionaries' clients and converts. The relationship was an indirect but usually effective one, often running from local missions to governments "back home," thence to the national government in Peking, and onward to local Chinese officials who bore the brunt of both foreign and court displeasure for violations of agreements regarding the kinds of protection the missions could offer.

While the case of the missions in China can be viewed as an extreme example of outside protection increasing the inviolability of sanctuaries, the pattern of such influence seems to repeat itself in many types of sanctuary, with differences of degree but not of principle. Many domestic sanctuaries manage to establish links with outside organizations that, in turn, are willing to use leverage on influential institutions to help sustain those sanctuaries and their protective functions. In the case of the Chinese missions the links were to national governments (the United States and Britain, particularly) and were strong and effective because those establishing and organizing the sanctuaries were citizens of those governments. In other cases the links were between the sanctuaries and bodies in other countries, such as humanitarian or peace organizations, or to grassroots communities. For the Chinese missions the relationships between their government patrons and national or local authorities in China charged with maintaining the missions' security were official and often based on formal government-to-government agreements. For other sanctuaries the relationship between them and their nongovernmental patrons was informal and personal and between those patrons and their own government private and unofficial. The nature and extent of leverage open to the China missions' patrons were of a different magnitude from that available to present day NGOs, churches, relief groups, and humanitarian organizations acting as patrons for contemporary peace communities and other forms of sanctuary. Here we are comparing the full range of government sanctions, up to and including military force, with influence frequently based simply on publicity and protest, revelation and embarrassment. However, the latter activities can work to help protect and maintain a sanctuary to the degree that government ministers and officials—or even the government's adversaries—care about reputation, image, credibility, and international support.

To summarize this argument, the effectiveness of outside patronage in helping to maintain the existence and inviolability of sanctuaries involves at least two key dimensions. The first is the strength of the ties between those establishing and supervising the sanctuary— the local organizers—and external patrons who have an interest in supporting them. In the case of the missionaries in early twentieth-century China, the links were strong because those organizing and supervising the sanctuaries were citizens of the protecting countries and members of influential churches within those countries. The second dimension involves the degree of influence those patrons have on parties that might threaten the survival of the sanctuary and its ability to offer protection and safety—usually the national government but in some circumstances insurgent or separatist organizations engaged in a protracted conflict with that government. Both factors will play a role in the degree of influence likely to be wielded on behalf of the sanctuary and the likely effectiveness of the patron's efforts. These relationships are summarized in a simple model on which the situation of particular sanctuaries can be plotted (see Figure 10–2).

FIGURE 10–2. EFFECTIVENESS OF OUTSIDE PATRONAGE

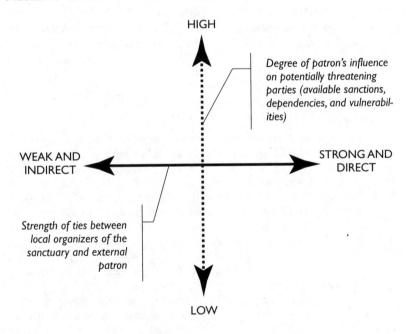

HIGH

Degree of patron's influence on potentially threatening parties (available sanctions, dependencies, and vulnerabilities)

WEAK AND INDIRECT

STRONG AND DIRECT

Strength of ties between local organizers of the sanctuary and external patron

LOW

Conclusion

It seems likely that this list of suggested influences on the inviolability and durability of sanctuaries is as near to a theory of sanctuary as we can come at the present moment. All that we might be able to say, given our current knowledge and the disparate evidence that we have found so far, is that the likelihood of a sanctuary surviving and being able to provide some form of safety, security, and protection to those dwelling within can be increased by paying close attention to the following factors: strong internal cohesion and leadership plus efforts to expand the functions of the sanctuary beyond protection; declared neutrality and impartial behavior; presence of credible sanctions for violation; absence of perceivable threat to outside interests; a framework of accepted rules and norms regarding rights and obligations; a low level of benefits for violation; strong patron interest in the preservation of sanctuary and leverage on all potential violators; and clear markers on the limits of the sanctuary.

Any deeper understanding of the reasons for sanctuaries "working" will require much more systematic study than that to date, together with an increasing number of careful case studies to tease out the nuances of survival and the details of what has succeeded in a variety of environments. This chapter and the others in this volume make a start at understanding what factors are likely to increase the inviolability and the durability of intra-societal sanctuaries. But this is still only a start.

Notes

[1] This focus on the issue of jurisdiction might lose one lesson that the history of some of the Greek sanctuaries teaches; namely, that *remoteness* could increase the inviolability of some sanctuaries even though they remain within the jurisdictional boundaries of a society (in the Greek case, of a city-state). This would be because of the physical difficulties of approaching the sanctuary but also because of the fact that its remoteness can mean that those within can only be directly involved in continuing political events with much difficulty. In other words, their nuisance value might be reduced by distance, in much the same way that the influence of "dangerous" political adversaries usually declines once they go into exile (across a boundary and into the sanctuary provided by another country).

[2] This is not always violence directly associated with the major protracted conflict in the society. In Peru, as Jennifer Langdon and Mery Rodriguez emphasize, the northern *rondas* were established to protect against the crime of cattle rustling, while in the Philippines the pioneering peace zone in Naga City grew out of a desire to protect against the depredations of out-of-control local militia rather than the armed clashes between the NPA and the AFP. And in El Salvador the LZP was formed partly to address the criminal violence of gang members repatriated from the United States.

[3] There may be many problems involved in such changes of function. Zosima Lee has noted that several of the early Filipino peace zones were embraced by the Ramos government in the mid-1990s and declared SDAs (others were not, which led to questions about favoritism or criteria for

selection); provided with funds for projects; and given planning, allocation, and development functions for which some were ill prepared (Lee 2000).

[4] This is especially true for El Salvador's LZP, which was formed in part to address the gang-related crime in the region but has rapidly expanded its operations to provide positive peace for both former gang members and ordinary campesinos.

[5] Indeed, as Avruch and José point out, the national background that encouraged the formation of some of the early Filipino peace zones was the nonviolent, nationwide EDSA revolution, which overthrew the Marcos dictatorship and then sought a general peace. Hence, this particular process seems to have involved a national-level peace process contributing to the growth of local-level peace initiatives rather than the other way around.

[6] For example, the OLS experience benefited from similar work undertaken during El Salvador's civil war to immunize children (see Shankar 1998, 32–33), leading the United Nations to replicate the initiative with OLS. In contrast, the peacebuilding work done in the LZP in El Salvador is currently being expanded by the FSSCA in its Meso-American Peace Project, which seeks to harness indigenous peacemaking methods throughout Latin America to build a broader culture of peace (FSSCA 2004).

[7] Much of the literature on LZPs having an impact at the national level seems aspirational rather than empirical. Positive effects at the national level may result from the establishment of LZPs, but there is also evidence to support alternative arguments that there is no direct connection at all or even that the setting up of separate LZPs and the opting out of the local communities actually impede the search for a more general peace. We need much greater clarity on what effects are supposed to take place and what factors chiefly affect whether or not these effects will indeed occur.

[8] Colombian peace communities faced somewhat different problems during the administration of President Pastrana, who launched two serious peace initiatives with the main guerrilla organizations during his presidency (even though the violence continued without a cease fire) compared with those they have had to deal with during President Uribe's policies of democratic security, military campaigns against the rebels and peace talks only with the paramilitaries.

[9] Even during general truces local violence may not die down completely. One should never underestimate the influence of factors such as lack of discipline, lack of centralized control, or factional disapproval of the negotiations themselves, which can lead to efforts to wreck them, pursuit of personal revenge, or simply the continuation of coercion and violence as a way of making a living.

[10] The experience of the negotiations between President Pastrana's government in Colombia and the FARC guerrillas, especially with regard to FARC's continuing assaults, kidnappings, and attacks launched from its own safe zone in Meta, should provide a warning against a too easy assumption that things always "ease up" while negotiations are in train.

[11] In Colombia armed actors—especially paramilitaries—have had as their prime objective driving original inhabitants off their land and replacing them with others able and willing to grow coca and other highly profitable crops.

[12] The dangers of having the "wrong people" within a sanctuary are well illustrated by the dilemmas for LZPs in places such as Colombia or the Philippines where there may be relatives—even distant relatives—of known members of the opposing parties living in the village. Often the mere fact of being a cousin of X, the known guerrilla, or of Y, the accused paramilitary, is enough for violence to be visited upon such individuals, who are taken to be supporters and sympathizers of one side or the other.

[13] Michael Walzer emphasizes that the fundamental obligation is one of impartiality. "It is not only fighting on one side that is prohibited, but every sort of official discrimination" (1977, 235).

[14] Bauslaugh notes that the range of accepted and acceptable neutral activity has historically been subject to politically influenced variation. "Greater restriction on neutral activity and insistence on formal abstention follow when the relative power of the collective belligerent forces is superior to that of the neutrals, but greater freedom, especially of trade, and stricter respect for territorial integrity, property and the life of the neutrals results when the collective power of the neutrals is greater than that of the belligerents" (Bauslaugh 1991, xxii). It seems unlikely, however, that this principle will apply to intra-societal sanctuaries of any type as they are unlikely ever to be in a position to outmatch the power—at least, the power to coerce through threats of violence—of local combatants.

[15] In comparing the practice of neutrality in classical Greece with the rules of twentieth century "legal" neutrality as set out in the 1899 and 1907 Hague Conventions, Bauslaugh outlines five common principles that might serve as guidelines for intra-societal peace zones or communities: (1) neutral territory is inviolable and cannot be traversed or used by belligerents for military purposes, so neutrals have an obligation to prevent such passage or use; (2) belligerents are not to recruit combatants on neutral territory and neutrals have an obligation to prevent this; (3) neutrals can allow the passage of individuals bound for belligerent states, the export of goods (even military) to belligerent states, and the conduct of business by belligerents within their territory, but whatever is allowed to one belligerent must be allowed to the other; (4) defense of neutrality, even by force, cannot be regarded as an act of hostility; and (5) individuals cannot take advantage of their neutrality to commit hostile acts against a belligerent without liability to severe punishment (Bauslaugh 1991, 246–47).

[16] In later times the code of Theodosius stipulated that sanctuary seekers in churches had to fulfill the supplication "decently" and obey the local clerics—on pain of expulsion.

[17] The quid pro quo for the host state's protection in the territorial sanctuary is that those seeking the safety and security from attack will themselves refrain from any provocative behaviors while in sanctuary. (This will depend on the host state's ability to prevent such behavior and its willingness not to encourage it.) Lischer notes: "The duties of the receiving state include disarming and demobilizing any non-civilian exiles who wish to integrate into the refugee camp, preventing the flow of arms to refugee areas, protecting the refugees from attack and intimidation and separating those who do not qualify for international protection—for example, war criminals—from

the refugees. In the optimal case, the receiving state provides physical and legal protection to the refugees while humanitarian organizations provide material assistance" (2005, 28).

[18] Lischer contrasts situational refugees with persecuted refugees who seek sanctuary because they and their clan, tribe, or community are the direct and deliberate targets of violence. Her other category consists of what she calls state-in-exile refugees—groups that "contain political and military leaders who, in some cases, organize the refugee crisis as a strategy to avoid defeat in a civil war" and "refuse to return home unless they can do so in victory" (2005, 10). These last refugee groups "present a greater threat to the sending state than other types of group, thus increasing the chance of preventive, cross border attacks against the refugees" (2005, 25).

[19] In February 2005 President Uribe announced publicly that "peace communities have the right to exist in Colombia . . . but they cannot . . . obstruct justice, reject government troops, prohibit the trade of legal products or limit the freedom of citizens living there" (AP report, March 20, 2005).

Works Cited

Bauslaugh, Robert A. 1991. *The concept of neutrality in classical Greece.* Berkeley and Los Angeles: University of California Press.

FSSCA. 2004. What is the Meso-American Peace Project? Available on the fssca.net website.

Lee, Zosimo E. 2000. Peace zones as special development areas: A preliminary assessment. In *Building peace: Essays on psychology and the culture of peace,* ed. A. B. I. Bernardo and C. D. Ortigas. Manila: De La Salle University Press.

Lischer, Sarah Kenyon. 2005. *Dangerous sanctuaries: Refugee camps, civil war, and the dilemmas of humanitarian aid.* Cornell studies in security affairs. Ithaca, NY: Cornell University Press.

Mitchell, Christopher. 1981. *The structure of international conflict.* New York: St. Martin's Press.

Quale, G. Robina. 1957. The mission compound in modern China; The role of the United States Protestant mission as an asylum in the civil and international strife of China, 1900–1941. Ph.D. diss., University of Michigan.

Sales, Peter M. 2004. Reinventing the past or redefining the future? An assessment of sanctuaries of peace in the Southern Philippines. Paper presented at the Oceanic Conference on International Studies. July 14–16. Australian National University, Canberra, Australia.

Shankar, Ram Anand. 1998. Analyzing health initiatives as bridges toward peace during complex humanitarian initiatives and the roles of actors and economic aid in making these bridges sustainable. Halifax, Nova Scotia: Dalhousie University.

Walzer, Michael. 1977. *Just and unjust wars: A moral argument with historical illustrations.* New York: Basic Books.

CONTRIBUTORS

Kevin Avruch is professor of conflict resolution and anthropology, associate director of the Institute for Conflict Analysis and Resolution, and a senior fellow in the Peace Operations Policy Program in the School of Public Policy at George Mason University. He has published widely on culture and conflict resolution, ethno-religious and nationalist movements, negotiation and third-party processes, human rights and political violence. In 1996–97 he was a senior fellow in the Jennings Randolph Program for International Peace at the United States Institute of Peace.

Landon E. Hancock is currently an assistant professor of political science at Kent State University's Center for Applied Conflict Management. He began working with the Local Zones of Peace project while completing his Ph.D. in conflict analysis and resolution at George Mason University. He was visiting faculty at the University of Baltimore's Center for Negotiations and Conflict Management and has taught courses for both the Institute for Conflict Analysis and Resolution and American University on conflict resolution, peacebuilding, and conflict research. His work has appeared in *International Studies Perspectives* and *Civil Wars,* and in 2003 he was a summer fellow at the Solomon Asch Center for the Study of Ethnopolitical Conflict at the University of Pennsylvania.

Pushpa Iyer is a doctoral candidate at the Institute for Conflict Analysis and Resolution at George Mason University. Her research interests are in identity conflicts, civil wars, and peace processes. Her doctoral thesis is on identifying the internal factors that brought two non-state armed groups—the LTTE (Sri Lanka) and the MILF (Mindanao, Philippines)—to the negotiating table. Iyer is active in championing the cause and the rights of minority and vulnerable communities—Muslims, Christians, Adivasis (Tribals), and Dalits—in the state of Gujarat, India.

Roberto S. Jose is currently in the master's degree program at the Institute for Conflict Analysis and Resolution. As a college activist in the late 1980s he witnessed the humanity, courage, creativity, and determination of the pioneering communities that declared the peace zones in the Philippines. As soon as he graduated, he worked for the Gaston Z. Ortigas Peace Institute, the secretariat office for what was then a burgeoning Philippine peace movement. As a twenty-something peace advocate, it was enough for him to be part of the movement and to know that, on various occasions, the Philippines' peace

223

process worked. Now in his late thirties, he revisits his own experiences and reviews the evolution of the peace zones since the late 1980s, asking the questions that led him to this collaborative project: What has worked? Why? What lessons can we ultimately draw from the Philippines' peace zone experience?

Jennifer Langdon teaches in the Criminal Justice Program of Towson University and is currently a Ph.D. candidate at the Institute for Conflict Analysis and Resolution at George Mason University. Her research interests focus broadly on the concept of conflict resolution as a form of justice making, with a specific interest in the uses of conflict resolution in criminal justice processes.

Christopher Mitchell is emeritus professor of conflict analysis at George Mason University having taught there for eighteen years and acting as Director of the Institute for Conflict Analysis and Resolution between 1991 and 1994. In England he held teaching posts at University College, London; the University of Southampton; and The City University, London. He has published widely on conflict and its resolution, his latest book being *Gestures of Conciliation* (Palgrave/Macmillan, 2001). Since 1999 he has been a member of the Institute's local Zones of Peace research group, taking a special interest in grassroots peace processes in Colombia.

Nancy Morrison holds degrees in clinical psychology and English literature and is currently completing a doctorate in conflict analysis and resolution. Her academic area of interest is in world religions and diplomacy. She has presented papers on grievance arts and revolution in Beijing, on conflict and social perceptions of the monstrous in Budapest, on religion and conflict in Dublin, and other papers in Boston, Omaha, and the Washington, D.C. area. Her publications include articles on her experiences in Isfahan during the 1979 revolution, her more recent experiences in southern Sudan, as well as on critical thinking. Between 2001 and 2003 she worked in southern Sudan to establish a full-time medical clinic, conducted community-level women's leadership development workshops, and implemented a soap-making micro-industry development project.

Krista Rigalo is currently a doctoral candidate at the Institute for Conflict Analysis and Resolution. Prior to her doctoral studies, she worked for eleven years in various conflict and post-conflict situations, most notably in the Great Lakes region of Africa. In eastern Congo she co-founded a network of local NGOs involved in peacemaking and peacebuilding in that turbulent region. Seconded to the UN High Commissioner for Refugees on Swaziland, she assisted Great Lakes refugees to form peer mediation structures within the UNHCR-sponsored camps, while in Angola she worked with faith-based organizations in peacebuilding and humanitarian aid organizations. An accomplished trainer, she authored a "train the trainers" manual in conflict transformation currently used by faith-based groups in Angola. Rigalo holds a bachelor's degree in communication arts and master's degrees in agricultural education and conflict transformation. She currently works at the US Peace Corps as country desk officer for Malawi, Madagascar, and Mozambique.

Catalina Rojas recently completed her doctorate at the Institute for Conflict Analysis and Resolution. Originally from Colombia, she has over ten years' experience working with and for peace organizations, most recently Women Waging Peace. In addition, she has taught in a variety of universities in Colombia. Her current areas of interest include Central American peace processes, civil society and women's peace initiatives, and the political economy of post-conflict reconstruction. Her work has been published in a number of countries, including Colombia, Venezuela, Spain, and the United States.

Mery Rodriguez was born and raised in Bogotá, Colombia. She holds a bachelor's degree in social communications from the Javeriana University in Colombia. She has worked as a human rights activist and social issues researcher and has taught as a professor at the Catholic University of Colombia. She has served four years at the Institute for Conflict Analysis and Resolution, earning her master's degree in conflict analysis and resolution. She is currently working on a Ph.D., also from ICAR. She specializes in local peacebuilding initiatives, particularly in Colombia, Peru, and Latin America in general. Currently her work focuses on zones of peace and laboratories of peace, and she is part of ICAR's Zones of Peace project.

INDEX

Also from Kumarian Press...

Peacebuilding and Conflict Resolution:

Peace Operations Seen from Below: UN Missions and Local People
Beatrice Pouligny

Reducing Poverty, Building Peace
Coralie Bryant and Christina Kappaz

War and Intervention: Issues for Contemporary Peace Operations
Michael Bhatia

New and Forthcoming:

Invisible Governance: International Secretariats in Global Politics
John Mathiason

Humanitarian Alert: NGO Information and Its Impact on US Foreign Policy
Abby Stoddard

A World Turned Upside Down: Social Ecological Approaches to Children in War Zones
Edited by Neil Boothby, Alison Strang, and Michael Wessells

Complex Political Victims
Erica Bouris

Visit Kumarian Press at **www.kpbooks.com** or
call **toll-free 800.289.2664** for a complete catalog.

 Kumarian Press, located in Bloomfield, Connecticut, is a forward-looking, scholarly press that promotes active international engagement and an awareness of global connectedness.